T0305322

Agricultural Finance

Agricultural Finance

From Crops to Land, Water and Infrastructure

Hélyette Geman

WILEY

This edition first published 2015
© 2015 Hélyette Geman

Registered office

John Wiley & Sons Ltd, The Atrium, Southern Gate, Chichester, West Sussex, PO19 8SQ, United Kingdom

Library of Congress Cataloging-in-Publication Data

Geman, Hélyette.
  Agricultural finance : from crops to land, water and infrastructure/Hélyette Geman.
    pages cm. – (The Wiley finance series)
  Includes bibliographical references and index.
  ISBN 978-1-118-82738-3 (hardback)
  1. Commodity exchanges.   2. Agricultural prices.   3. Agricultural industries. 4. Investments.   I. Title.
  HG6046.G457 2015
   338.1'3–dc23
                              2014036004

A catalogue record for this book is available from the British Library.

ISBN 978-1-118-82738-3 (hbk)   ISBN 978-1-118-82737-6 (ebk)
ISBN 978-1-118-82736-9 (ebk)   ISBN 978-1-118-82735-2 (ebk)

Cover Design: Wiley
Cover Image top: ©istock.com/jenjen42
Cover Image bottom: ©istock.com/77studio

Set in 10/12pt Times by Laserwords Private Limited, Chennai, India
Printed in Great Britain by TJ International Ltd, Padstow, Cornwall, UK

To Arnaud, Laure and Nathanaël
To the memory of my sister

Table of Contents

Acknowledgments   xiii
About the Author   xv
Preamble   xvii

1 Physical and Financial Agricultural Markets   **1**

  1.1 Agriculture and the Beginning of Human Sedentarization   1
    1.1.1 Some recent numbers   2
    1.1.2 The growing role of Africa   2
  1.2 The Outlook of Agricultural Commodities Markets   3
    1.2.1 Recent mergers and acquisitions   3
    1.2.2 'Trading places': from the ABCD to the NOW   4
    1.2.3 The physical markets   9
    1.2.4 The global flows of commodities   10
    1.2.5 Back to the future: a new age for barter   11
    1.2.6 The sources of information in agricultural commodity markets   12
  1.3 History of Commodity Futures and Spot Markets   12
    1.3.1 The actors in financial markets   12
    1.3.2 The actors in agricultural commodity exchanges   13
    1.3.3 The growth of Futures markets exchanges and the recent mergers   14
    1.3.4 Futures markets and price volatility   15
    1.3.5 The role of indexes in the creation of efficient commodity spot markets   16
    1.3.6 Commodities and numéraire   17
  1.4 Shipping and Freight   17
    1.4.1 International trade   18
    1.4.2 Price formation in freight markets   18

2 Agricultural Commodity Spot Markets   **25**

  2.1 Introduction   25
  2.2 Price Formation in Agricultural Commodity Markets   25
  2.3 Volatility in Agricultural Markets   27
    2.3.1 Volatility of the price level versus return in agricultural
        commodity markets   32

2.3.2 Which factors drive volatility?   36
2.3.3 Conclusion   38

**3 Futures Exchanges – Future and Forward Prices – Theory of
    Storage – The Forward Curve**   **39**

3.1 Major Commodity Exchanges   39
3.2 Forward Contracts   41
3.3 Futures Contracts   43
     3.3.1 Definition   43
     3.3.2 Exchange of Futures for physicals (EFP)   44
3.4 Relationship between Forward and Futures Prices   45
3.5 Example of a Future Spread   47
3.6 Inventory and Theory of Storage   47
     3.6.1 Spot and Futures prices volatilities   49
     3.6.2 Development of the theory of storage: inventory
            and prices   51
3.7 The Benefits of Forward Curves   52
     3.7.1 Trading strategies around forward curves   52
     3.7.2 Example of a seasonality-based Futures spread   53
     3.7.3 From linear to convex payoffs   54
3.8 Stochastic Modeling of the Forward Curve   55

**4 Plain Vanilla Options on Commodity Spot and Forward Prices. The
    Bachelier–Black–Scholes Formula, the Merton Formula, the Black Formula** **59**

4.1 Introduction   59
4.2 Classical Strategies involving European Calls and Puts   62
     4.2.1 Straddle   62
     4.2.2 Strangle   62
     4.2.3 Call spread or vertical call spread   63
     4.2.4 Butterfly spread   64
4.3 Put–Call Parity for a Non-dividend Paying Stock   64
4.4 Valuation of European Calls: the Bachelier–Black–Scholes
     Formula and the Greeks   66
     4.4.1 Consequences of the Black–Scholes formula   70
     4.4.2 The Greeks   71
4.5 The Merton (1973) Formula for Dividend-paying Stocks   75
4.6 Options on Commodity Spot Prices   77
4.7 Options on Commodity Futures: the Black (1976) Formula   78
4.8 Monte-Carlo Simulations for Option Pricing   79
     4.8.1 The founding result   79
     4.8.2 Monte-Carlo methods for plain vanilla options on non-dividend
            paying stocks   80
     4.8.3 Monte-Carlo methods for plain vanilla options on the spot commodity 82
4.9 Implied Volatility, Smile, and Skew in Equity Option Markets   83
4.10 Volatility Smile in Agricultural Commodity Markets   86
     4.10.1 Where is the liquidity in agricultural commodity option markets? 86
     4.10.2 Extracting the implied volatility from options on commodity Futures 86

5 **Commodity Swaps, Swaptions, Accumulators, Forward-Start,
   and Asian Options**   **89**

   5.1 Swaps and Swaptions   89
   5.2 Accumulators   92
   5.3 Forward-Start Options (or Calendar Spread Options on the Spot Price) 93
   5.4 Asian Options as Key Instruments in Commodity Markets   95
        5.4.1 Approximation of the arithmetic average by a geometric average 96
        5.4.2 Approximation of the distribution of the arithmetic average
               by a log-normal distribution   97
        5.4.3 Monte-Carlo simulations for Asian options valuation   98
        5.4.4 Exact results (Geman and Yor, 1993)   100
   5.5 Trading the Shape of the Forward Curve through Floating-strike Asian Options 102

6 **Exchange, Spread, and Quanto Options in Commodity Markets**   **103**

   6.1 Exchange Options   103
   6.2 Commodity Spread Options and Their Importance in Commodity Markets 105
   6.3 Commodity Quanto Options   109

7 **Grain Cereals: Corn, Wheat, Soybean, Rice, and Sorghum**   **113**

   7.1 Introduction   113
   7.2 Corn   113
   7.3 Wheat   118
        7.3.1 Wheat trading   119
        7.3.2 Global wheat   119
        7.3.3 The wheat supply chain   120
   7.4 Soybeans   123
   7.5 Rice   126
   7.6 Sorghum   129

8 **Sugar, Cocoa, Coffee, and Tea**   **133**

   8.1 Sugar   133
        8.1.1   Links of sugar with other commodities   134
        8.1.2   Sugar trading   135
        8.1.3   The European Union   136
        8.1.4   Special relations of the EU with other countries   136
        8.1.5   The United States   136
        8.1.6   Special relations of the USA with other countries   137
        8.1.7   Brazil   137
        8.1.8   China   138
        8.1.9   India   138
        8.1.10 Thailand   139
        8.1.11 Australia   139
        8.1.12 Guatemala and Cuba   139
        8.1.13 Sugar cane in Mauritius   140
   8.2 Cocoa   140
   8.3 Coffee   146
   8.4 Tea   149

9 Cotton, Timber and Wood, Pulp and Paper, Wool   **153**

9.1 Cotton   153
9.2 Lumber and Wood   156
9.3 Pulp and Paper   158
    9.3.1 Pulp NBSK and BHKP indexes   159
    9.3.2 Pulp US NBSK index   160
    9.3.3 Pulp BHKP China   160
    9.3.4 Pulp NBSK China   161
    9.3.5 When bank notes go plastic   161
9.4 Wool and Cashmere   162
    9.4.1 Cashmere   163
    9.4.2 From the Kashmir Goat to high quality yarns   164

10 Orange Juice, Livestock, Dairy, and Fishery   **165**

10.1 Orange Juice   165
10.2 Livestock   166
    10.2.1 Livestock markets   167
    10.2.2 Cattle   168
    10.2.3 Hogs   169
    10.2.4 Pork bellies   169
    10.2.5 The US live cattle contract specifications   170
    10.2.6 Australia   171
    10.2.7 The USA   171
10.3 Dairy   172
10.4 Fish Markets   173
10.5 Poultry and Eggs   174

11 Rubber, Palm Oil, and Biofuels   **177**

11.1 Rubber   177
11.2 Palm Oil   180
    11.2.1 The oil palm and palm oil   181
    11.2.2 Markets   182
11.3 Ethanol, Biofuels, and Biomass   183

12 Land, Water, and Fertilizers   **187**

12.1 Land Types, Yields, and Erosion   187
    12.1.1 Yield-at-risk   187
    12.1.2 Land competition   188
    12.1.3 Farmland in the USA   188
12.2 Fertilizers   189
    12.2.1 Fertilizer markets   191
    12.2.2 Fertilizer Index, corn, and wheat price trajectories over
           the period 1991 to 2011   193
    12.2.3 Fertilizer producing companies and share price returns
           over the period 2004 to 2011   193

        12.2.4 A factor model for the share returns of fertilizer firms   198
    12.3 Water and its crucial Role in the World Economy   207
        12.3.1 The case of Australia, China, and Saudi Arabia   208
        12.3.2 The case of Brazil   208
        12.3.3 Competition for electricity, water, and land   209
    12.4 Projections for the Future of Agriculture   209
        12.4.1 Farm insurance   210
        12.4.2 Estimating long-term agricultural supply   210
        12.4.3 Market concentration   211
        12.4.4 Spare capacity   211
    12.5 Subsidies and Export Bans   211
        12.5.1 Subsidies   212
        12.5.2 Export bans   212
    12.6 Market-oriented Farming   212
        12.6.1 Open wheat market takes root in Canada   213
        12.6.2 Kansas City wheat Futures trading coming to an end after
                157 years   213
        12.6.3 China food needs   214

13 **Infrastructure and Farming Management in the Digital Age**   **217**
    13.1 Introduction   217
    13.2 Agricultural Infrastructure   218
        13.2.1 Total factor productivity   218
        13.2.2 Climate change   219
        13.2.3 Irrigation and increased productivity   219
        13.2.4 Trends in irrigation   219
        13.2.5 Storage   220
        13.2.6 Grain elevators   220
        13.2.7 Soybean crushers   220
        13.2.8 The Brave New World of Monsanto   221
        13.2.9 Infrastructure in sub-Saharan Africa   221
        13.2.10 Gabon: after black gold, green gold?   221
        13.2.11 Agricultural Transformation Agenda (ATA) in Nigeria   222
        13.2.12 Digital age on the farm: prescriptive planting   222
        13.2.13 Sugar biofactory for ethanol in Brazil   224
        13.2.14 After ethanol, railway, and natural gas   224
        13.2.15 From iron ore mining to cattle farming in Australia   225
        13.2.16 Robots for cow milking   225
        13.2.17 Containers for agricultural commodities   226
        13.2.18 Singapore as a hub for refrigeration containers   226
        13.2.19 The trip of the banana   226
        13.2.20 Energy, water, and infrastructure for DAP and agriculture
                 in Saudi Arabia   227
    13.3 Country Risk: the Example of Ukraine in 2014   227
    13.4 Analyzing the Risks Involved in an International Wheat Tender Offer   228
    13.5 Weather Risk and Weather Derivatives   229

14 Investing in Agricultural Commodities, Land, and Physical Assets   233

   14.1 Purchase of Commodity Futures   233
   14.2 Purchase of Commodity Options and Structured Products   235
   14.3 Commodity Index Investing   236
      14.3.1 Some prominent commodity indexes   236
      14.3.2 How commodity indices are constructed   238
      14.3.3 Commodity-linked bonds   239
   14.4 Investing in Commodity-related Equities   239
   14.5 Investing in Land   240
      14.5.1 The US case   241
      14.5.2 The world case   241
   14.6 Acquisition of Infrastructure and Physical Assets   242
      14.6.1 Valuation of a transformation plant using a real
            options approach   242
      14.6.2 DCF approach to the valuation of a transformation plant   243
      14.6.3 Valuation of a silo (or an aquifer, or any storage facility)   245
   14.7 Conclusion   247

Glossary   248

References   252

Index   257

Acknowledgments

First, I would like to extend my very warm thanks to my PhD students Bo Liu for his remarkably intelligent and merciless proofreading of the book – all remaining typos or repetitions are my sole responsibility – and Pedro Vergel and Tara Velez for their talent in building a number of price trajectories and forward curves. I would also like to thank Hugo Forget and Patrick Slama for their help in editing.

Second, I want to express my gratitude to my friends Hilary Till, from Premia Capital Management, and George Martin, from Wood Creek Capital Management, for the great discussions and reports exchanges we had over the years, some of them being reflected in this book.

Lastly, I am grateful to Javier Blas, editor at the Financial Times and other journalists at the FT, the Wall Street Journal, the Economist, the Business Times (Singapore), and other newspapers for their prompt and beautiful coverage of a number of new developments in the world of agricultural commodities; they allowed me to corroborate my own findings. I tried to trace and pay tribute to the first publication, sometimes a World Bank, USDA or another official organization valuable report.

On a side note, I wish to mention that I chose the article 'he' throughout the book for ease of use and did not intend to place the male gender above any other gender.

About the Author

Hélyette Geman is Director of the Commodity Finance Centre at Birkbeck, University of London and Research Professor at Johns Hopkins University. She is a graduate of Ecole Normale Supérieure in Mathematics and holds a Master's degree in Theoretical Physics as well as a PhD both in Probability from the University Pierre et Marie Curie and in Finance from the University Panthéon-Sorbonne.

Professor Geman has been a scientific advisor to major financial institutions, energy and mining and commodity companies for the last 21 years, covering the spectrum of interest rates, electricity, crude oil and natural gas, metals, and agriculturals, including fertilizers and land. She was for four years Head of Research at Caisse des Dépôts in Paris and has been a scientific advisor for Louis Dreyfus, EDF Trading, BHP Billiton, Bunge, Total, and many other commodity companies. Professor Geman has published more than 125 papers in top international finance journals. In 1994 she received the First Prize of the Merrill Lynch Awards for her work on exotic derivatives pricing and in 1995 the first AFIR (Actuarial Approach for Insurance Risk) prize for her work on catastrophic risk. She became in 1993 a Member of Honour of the French Society of Actuaries and was in 2000 the first President of the Bachelier Finance Society.

Professor Geman was named in the Hall of Fame of Energy Risk in 2004, and in 2008 she received the Alma Studiorum Prize of the University of Bologna for her contribution to the CGMY model, a pure jump Lévy process widely used in finance.

Her books include *Insurance and Weather Derivatives* published in 1999 by RISK books, and *Commodities and Commodity Derivatives: Energy, Metals and Agriculturals* published by Wiley Finance in 2005, which has become the reference on the subject.

In 2010 Professor Geman became a scientific advisor to the European Union on the subject of agricultural commodities. She has been since 2007 a member of the board of the UBS–Bloomberg Commodity Index and counts among her former PhD students Nassim Taleb, author of *The Black Swan*.

Hélyette Geman is presently on the Board of a green energy company and an active participant in a 'precision farming' project involving 12,500 farmers in East Africa.

Preamble

Agriculture has always been at the center of human life. It is today the intersection of challenging issues between growth of the world population, soil erosion, and arable land scarcity on the one hand and trade finance after the 2008 crisis, competition for land with the mining industry, new towns and cities in developing countries, competition for water with other industries such as shale gas fracking or oil sands, or between neighboring countries on the other. Small farmers try to stay competitive in the presence of big investors who can afford better machinery and infrastructure. Governments struggle to find the proper way to provide small farms with the right form of subsidies, be they fertilizers, seeds or minimal prices. International institutions like the World Bank face another type of choice: letting weak economies struggle to feed their population, or helping them and destroying the incentive of self-sufficiency. The same difficult dilemma holds for infrastructure such as water sanitation and distribution.

In this complex picture, commodity trading houses – some of which have existed for more than 160 years – continue to be active in their role of 'origination' with local farmers around the world while financial players or 'speculators' provide liquidity to producers and agrifood companies needing to hedge their price exposure. In contrast, we have seen over the last decade the arrival (and partial departure) of new players in 'agricultural finance.' The well-rehearsed speech on financial speculators driving food prices to very high levels has been defeated by a number of respected academic studies. As we shall depict throughout the book, *weather risk* and *country risk* are the two main drivers of price spikes – obviously, these may be made worse by actions that regulators ought to monitor properly. At the same time, confusion between high prices and high volatility – both undesirable, but the former being toxic for the many populations – keeps the picture blurry for the public at large. In some developing countries, agricultural prices pushed higher by governments trying to secure farmers' votes are harmful to the country and to a proper formation of prices in general. In developed countries, the lackadaisical attitude of regulators about the ownership of physical assets, such as power plants, large metal warehouses or grain storage facilities by financial players who were shareholders of the relevant exchanges as well as 'primary actors' on these exchanges, proved its damaging effects.

After eight to ten years of significant synchronicity of commodity price moves with equity markets, commodities are decorrelating from these; commodity correlations with equities computed for example on 90-day rolling windows were in the second quarter of 2014 at their lowest since the financial crisis – agricultural commodities, because of their unique specificities, were mildly part of this 'financialization.' Regarding the global space of commodities, we are back to the situation that prevailed before 2004, with price dynamics specific to each subclass – metals, energy, and agriculturals – and to each commodity within a class in its own right: in 2013, corn and silver prices collapsed by 40%; gold, coffee, and soy oil decreased by more than 20%; cocoa prices rose by 20%; and palm oil and cotton rose by 10%. In 2014, fundamentals, namely supply/demand, weather risk, and country risk for agricultural commodities, are returning as the main factors of price levels, and drought in Brazil was the main reason for the recent extraordinary rise in coffee prices. Not only has 'financialization' greatly receded in all commodity classes – including because of the departure of a number of financial players – but commodity index investing, at least in its previous form(s), is less popular and has to reflect the importance of fundamentals.

On the front of agricultural commodities, China has recognized that, in contrast to the view it had a few years ago, the farming, processing, and safety skills required all along the food supply chain were too demanding and has decided 'to buy rather than produce.' China owns one-tenth of world arable land but its food consumption is twice as large compared to available land. After metals and coal, China has turned aggressively to the problem of agricultural commodities, signing loans for crops *barter* agreements with Ukraine and acting through its gigantic state-owned company COFCO to buy originating and processing companies around the world to properly feed its population. The Chinese sovereign fund has in parallel identified agriculture as a strategic sector and is massively investing in agricultural production worldwide.

Raw materials, be they phosphate rock transformed into fertilizer or soybean crushed into soy oil, remain the center of value. And land is the ultimate source of all of them – a gigantic receptacle of substitutability between mining, crops, and farmland and a reservoir of optionalities/convexities and 'anti-fragility.' The ownership of land should ultimately remain in the hands of the *nation*, and not be acquired from poorer countries by wealthier ones wishing to solve their problem of farmland *scarcity* by means of ephemeral paper money.

The importance of scarcity, one of my recurrent concerns when analyzing agricultural commodities, was highlighted by the flamboyant economist John Law (1671–1729), author of *The Scarcity Theory of Value*. Analyzing the famous 'water/diamond' paradox, namely that useless diamonds are more highly valued than the more useful water, Law regarded the relative scarcity of goods as the origin of the value of a good in society and any changes in this value were due to variations of *demand and supply*, the central theme I will also modestly emphasize.

At the end of this preamble, I would like to recognize that agricultural finance is not only a technical subject. It also raises a whole host of moral and ethical issues, which are not discussed in this book. Malthus would be horrified to hear the projections of the World Bank on a population exceeding 9.6 billion on the planet by 2050. At the same time, the rate of increase of the number of obese people (often because of poverty and low quality food) is sadly growing faster than the rate of decline of skinny and underfed human beings – both being terrible news. Some struggle with 'food safety' while others suffer from 'food insecurity.' Food waste and food needs are not even brought together at the level of a city, let alone at the level of a country or beyond. Besides land erosion, the move of young people to better-paid jobs in cities contributes to the decline of cultivated land in regions where agricultural production is so necessary. At the same time, agricultural price subsidies by governments are wrong, in my view, as they take place at the very beginning of the production chain and distort world prices: there is always a poorer country that won't receive the same subsidies and will be disadvantaged. Directly subsidizing poor people is a better solution.

I will conclude on a scientific note and observe that *time and space**, the first state variables in all sciences, are particularly crucial in the agricultural commodities universe: *time* is the harvest or the news on the harvest – not necessarily calendar time. *Space* is transportation, infrastructure, and the shipping of spices and raw materials to distant destinations – all large sources of risks that were already depicted centuries ago in Shakespeare's *Merchant of Venice*.

---

* 'Time and Space in Mathematical Finance' Henry McKean, *First World Congress of the Bachelier Finance Society*, June 2000 – Collège de France, Paris.

1

Physical and Financial
Agricultural Markets

'You should buy land, they don't make it anymore.'

Mark Twain

1.1 AGRICULTURE AND THE BEGINNING OF HUMAN SEDENTARIZATION

Commodities have been produced and exchanged throughout history and trade is an integral part of human civilization. In fact, one can argue that the rise of the latter has its origin in organized commodity production and distribution. As nomadic men settled on land to cultivate crops and graze their cattle, an agriculture-based economy came to existence, while some became carpenters, ironsmiths, goldsmiths, and shipbuilders. Goods were provided by the producers of diverse crops and livestock products in exchange for services. Farmers would bring their excess crops to a central location where they were carefully weighed – interestingly, the existence of weights can be traced back to several millennia before our era. The crops were then stored in a public building, which was the first form of a warehouse.

It was the emergence of barter and soon-emerged bazaars and markets that today still defines the centers of towns and villages. Trading merchants and artisans were organized into 'guilds' as early as the fourth century CE. From the first century CE, gold coins, wine, wheat, and linen were traveling east from the Roman Empire; ivory, silk, and precious stones were sent from India. As civilizations spread over the world, vessels started carrying goods, spices, and silks across the oceans. Indian literature from the beginning of our era mentions the existence in Southern India of separate markets for different commodities, such as grains, spices, cloth, and jewelry, located in particular in towns along the coast. Guilds and merchant groups were formed to represent the population.

The name of these merchant guilds in the northern part of Europe was the 'Hanseatic League,' which was part of Bruges in Belgium. Bruges was the main commercial city in the world during the 13th century, at the intersection of many trade roads, with wool coming from Scotland to feed the weaving industry in the city. In 1277, the first merchant fleet came to Bruges from the Italian port of Genoa, linking the city trade to the Mediterranean sea. This opened Bruges to the trade of spices and also to large capital flows brought by foreign merchants. The 'Bourse' opened in 1309 and is considered to be the first stock exchange in the world, showing that financial trading followed the trading of raw materials, and not the other way around. Even though Bruges fell behind Antwerp after 1500 as the economic capital of the region, Zeebrugge – the port of Bruges today – is an important location since the underwater natural gas interconnector from Bacton in the UK ends in Europe, and Zeebrugge is, at the time of writing, the main natural gas index in continental Western Europe.

Similarly, global trading and financial centers such as London, New York, Rotterdam, and Hong Kong owe their position in the present world economic map to their age-old trading culture. With the creation of the World Trade Organization (WTO) in the mid-1990s, commodity markets have experienced a new dramatic growth, both in physical goods and through derivatives platforms. Many types of different players came along to offer financial products infinitely more complex than the simple Futures contracts traded on the Chicago Board of Trade since 1848.

Looking back at the last two centuries, the world has witnessed a dramatic increase in wealth and prosperity in both the developed and developing countries. Poverty has reduced significantly not only in the developing countries of Asia and South America, but also in Africa. Shipping has continued to play its crucial role, while modern multi-purpose warehouses and elevators came to existence together with the advent of sophisticated commodity securitization. Looking back at the last 50 years, the boom of the 1970s in commodities was followed by 20 years of stagnant prices – in fact largely decreasing if adjusted for inflation for all commodities and agricultural ones in particular, with subsequent damage for the commodity-producing developing countries. The years 2001 to 2005 for energy and metals, and 2006 and 2007 for agricultural commodities, saw gigantic rises in all commodity prices. The financial crisis sent all prices down (except for gold) during the second half of 2008. Since 2009, commodity prices have rebounded but *volatility* became even more diverse across commodities.

The spectrum of *scarcity* is one of the key drivers of this volatility, in a world where the population could exceed 9 billion by 2050.

1.1.1 Some recent numbers

Between the beginning of 2014 and the political changes in Crimea, wheat prices went up by 27%. In an unrelated manner, coffee prices went up by 72% because of a severe drought in Brazil, cocoa by 8%, orange juice by 11%, sugar by 6%, and milk by 42% (because of a rising milk demand from Asian countries) – making breakfast quite expensive for the fortunate citizens of the world who can afford all or part of these items!

In the USA, meat prices have gone up as well, because of tight cattle supplies after years of drought in states such as Texas and California.

1.1.2 The growing role of Africa

Some economic experts compare Africa today to China 10 or 20 years ago. What is certain is the fact that Africa's GDP and exports are notably higher. More importantly, agricultural commodities represent an increasing fraction of these exports, which is great news since crude oil in Nigeria and some other African countries arguably represents the *resource curse.*

- Nestlé, which already owned 36 production units in Africa, opened three new ones in Angola, Mozambique, and Democratic Republic of Congo.
- Coca-Cola plans to inject $12 billion in its African bottling sites by 2020.
- Between 2007 and 2011 Ghana doubled the quantity of cocoa processed in the country, bringing it to 25% of local production – a number still far from the 94% fraction of cocoa that is processed in Indonesia and exported in the semi-transformed form of cocoa butter, generating extra revenues and jobs for the country.

- In 2011, out of a total amount of $581.8 billion of exports, coffee, tea, and cocoa represented $15 billion; vegetables and fruit $11.5 billion; and fertilizers in a raw or processed form $80.3 billion.

1.2 THE OUTLOOK OF AGRICULTURAL COMMODITIES MARKETS

1.2.1 Recent mergers and acquisitions

- In 2010, Wilmar acquired the Australian sugar company Sucrogen.
- In 2010, a bid by BHP Billiton to acquire Potash Corp. for $39 billion was stopped by the Canadian government.
- In 2011, Gavilon bought the US grain handler DeBruce Companies.
- Also in 2011, Cargill acquired the grain business part of the Australian company AWB for $677 million.
- In 2012, Glencore acquired the Toronto-listed agriproducts company Viterra for $6.1 billion.
- In 2012, the giant food company Sara Lee spun off its coffee and tea business and renamed itself Hillshire. In 2013, it bought Van's Natural Foods, which makes gluten-free products.
- In 2013, Marubeni from Japan purchased the agriculture business of the US firm Gavilon for $2.7 billion.
- An attempt by Archer Daniel to buy Australia's giant Grain Corp. in 2013 was rejected by Australian regulators – in that deal, ADM was in particular trying to have direct access to China and emerging markets. ADM is keeping its existing stake in Grain Corp.
- In 2013, China's agrifood company Shuanghui bought Smithfields Foods, the huge US-based pork and meat company, for $4.7 billion, plus $2.4 billion in its debt buyout.
- Cofco (China National Cereals, Oil and Foodstuffs Corp.) bought in February 2014 a majority stake in the Dutch grains trader Nidera for $1.3 billion and is in talks to possibly build a joint venture with Nobel Group from Singapore.
- In 2014, Wilmar invested $200 million in a sugar joint venture with the Indian group Shree Renuka.
- In March 2014, JP Morgan was supposed to sell its physical commodities business (including a large inventory position) for $3.5 billion to the Geneva-based trading house Mercuria. According to a UK consultancy group, commodity trading income for the bank had fallen from a peak of more than $14 billion in 2008 to $5.5 billion in 2012, while trading houses benefited from not facing the same rules on capital as banks.
- In March 2014, the sugar and cocoa trading house Sucres et Denrées (Sucden) said it was buying the commodity merchant Coffee America, mentioning its synergies with Sucden's cocoa business. Both companies are privately owned.
- At the time of writing, Cargill is awaiting an anti-trust approval to form a three-way joint venture in US flour milling with the agricultural companies CHS and ConAgra, in order to optimize silo and processing capacity.
- In 2014, the Chinese company Bright Food bought Tnuva, the leader of food production and distribution in Israel, for $1.8 billion. In 2010, it had bought Synlait, the milk producer from New Zealand, and in 2012 had acquired 60% of Weetabix, the British cereals maker.
- In September 2014, Noble Group formed an agri-business joint venture named Noble Agri, with a 51% stake for Cofco and some minority co-investors such as Hopu Investment, a Chinese private equity firm, Temasek, IFC and Standard Chartered Private Equity.

The 2014 merger activity in the food industry

In May 2014, the American agrifood company Mondelez International merged its coffee activity with DEMB, a deal which will allow coffee numbers two and three to control more than 16% of the world market and try to get closer to Nestlé, the number one. The merger between the two coffee giants is likely to be funded by at least $10 billion in debt financing. Under the planned merger, Mondelez will give its coffee brands in exchange for $5 billion in cash and a 49% stake in the new company, which will be called Jacobs Douwe Egberts and be based in the Netherlands. The loans will be partly used to refinance existing debt on the balance sheet of Master Blenders.

The debt package will be one of the largest leverage financial deals since the financial crisis. The new company will represent a coffee giant with annual sales of $7 billion, which will challenge Nestlé, the market leader.

In July 2012, the famous American agrifood company Sara Lee, founded in Illinois in 1939, split into Hillshire Brands, which covers its North American operations and Master Blenders, in charge of the international bakery business. The latter is owned today by the investment group JAB Holdings, which bought it for about $10 billion in 2013.

Mondelez, which is well known for its snack brands, e.g., Ritz crackers, was spun off from Kraft in 2012.

The merged company will include the world's second and third largest coffee groups, with brands such as Jacobs Carte Noire, Gevalia and Millicano, and have a large share of this profitable market in more than 20 countries.

It will also combine DEMB Senseo capsules with the Mondelez Tassimo brand, putting them in a position to overtake Nestlé's Nespresso capsule coffee in a world coffee market of $80 billion.

Besides DEMB in 2013, JAB Holdings bought in 2012 the Caribou Coffee chain for $340 million and the Peet's Coffee & Tea chain for $1 billion, trying to invest in many ways in the high-margin coffee business.

After the transaction, Mondelez should generate 85% of its revenues from snacks, up from 75%.

The company Hillshire Brands (former Sara Lee, as stated above) bought in May 2014 Pinnacle Foods for $6.6 billion including debt, adding Pinnacle's Duncan Hines cake mixes, Log Cabin syrups, and the famous Wishbone salad dressings to its meat-centered range of products, in a context of higher prices for beef and pork prices partly due to the drought that has thinned US herds. Under the terms of the deal announced on May 12, Pinnacle investors will receive $18 in cash and half a Hillshire share for each Pinnacle share they own, representing an 18% premium to Pinnacle's May 11 closing price.

The private equity fund Blackstone had paid $2.2 billion in 2007 for Pinnacle, which went into an initial public offering (IPO) in March 2013.

At the time of writing, the bidding war for Hillshire Brands between Tyson Foods, the US food maker, which offered $8.55 billion, and Pilgrim's Pride, is still ongoing.

1.2.2 'Trading places': from the ABCD to the NOW

Transporting billion of tonnes of commodities and raw materials across the world requires a gigantic and expensive infrastructure comprising trucks, merchandise trains, barges, vessels, silos, crushers, elevators in ports, and a large expertise in the risk management of commodity prices, shipping rates, bunker fuel costs, currencies, and shipping insurance.

Credit is managed by trade finance banks, which secure the transactions or provide credit letters or collateralized trades. A central risk platform in big trading houses has to aggregate all exposures and positions, both physical and financial.

To address the needs of the world population, in terms of increased quantity and quality of food, the trading houses are massively investing in elevators and harbor infrastructures on the American continent, in Asia, and in the Black Sea.

All the companies described below are aware of the value of physical stocks against which logistics, crushing, and production are optimized. Moreover, in their origination activities with farmers, they are aware very early on of any weather event, plant disease or unusual vessel queues in narrow harbors like Sydney – all key elements to monitor and trade the volatility of these indispensable commodities.

Cargill

Cargill was founded in 1865 by William Wallace as an Iowa grain elevator and has since expanded into 65 countries. The company is now the world's largest trader of agricultural commodities and has the biggest market share in sugar, corn, and wheat. It increased its size with the purchase in 1998 of its arch-rival Continental, the grain trading giant.

Its 500 vessels travel between the continents with their cargoes of wheat, cocoa, and peanuts. From its office in Geneva, Cargill manages the delivery of more than 30 million tonnes of cereals and oilseeds per year, and activities ranging from grain silos in Canada to chicken farms in China.

In 2003 Cargill built the fund Black River Asset Management, an independent company that manages today $5.9 billion invested in commodities, farmland, and agribusiness across 13 offices in the world.

Cargill is 80% held by the descendants of the Wallace family, the rest by employees. Its profits amounted to $2.3 billion in 2013 (down from a record of $3.95 billion in 2008) for revenues of $137 billion and 142,000 staff members in 67 countries.

Archer Daniels Midland (ADM)

ADM came into existence in 1902 when George Archer and John Daniels began a linseed crushing business. Today it owns 10.8% of Wilmar International and 80% of the grain trading house Alfred Toepfer. ADM owns 270 plants where thousands of tonnes of oilseeds, wheat, and cocoa are crushed every day. It is one of the largest producers of corn-based ethanol and biodiesel, and is a major corn trader. ADM is listed on the New York Stock Exchange and has offices in Rolle, between Geneva and Lausanne.

In 2013, it bid $2.9 billion for the Australian GrainCorp, which it already owned at 20%. The deal has stirred concern among some politicians and growers. Australia's Foreign Investment decided at the end of November 2013 that the deal was not in Australia's national interest, given GrainCorp's ownership of 280 storage sites in Australia and seven of the 10 grain port terminals in New South Wales, Queensland, and Victoria.

ADM has a subsidiary called ADM Investor Services, which manages the risks of the company and offers investment and brokerage services to outside customers.

Its profits were $2 billion in 2012 (down from a record number of 2.15 billion in 2007) for revenues of $80.6 billion and 30,000 employees in 75 countries.

In 2013, the revenues of Arch Daniels were $89 billion; its market capitalization is about $26 billion.

Louis Dreyfus Commodities (LDC)

LDC came to existence in 1851, when Leopold Louis-Dreyfus, the 18-year-old son of a farmer from Alsace, first purchased wheat from local farmers and transported it for sale in Basel, eight miles away. More than 160 years later, the company has operations in the following global regions: North America; north Latin America, south Latin America; Europe and the Black Sea; Asia; and the Middle East and Africa. It covers most traded agricultural commodities such as grains, oilseeds, rice, cotton, coffee, fertilizers, and dairy. LDC specializes in 'origination,' an activity of developing customized, long-term transactions with market counterparties such as producers, large industrials, and storage companies.

LDC is the 'D' of what is known in the industry as the ABCD, with Archer Daniels, Bunge and Cargill, groups that dominate agricultural flows.

In 2011, LDC started Edesia Asset Management whose hedge fund, dedicated to agricultural commodities, collected $2 billion.

In September 2012, Louis Dreyfus Commodities tapped the capital markets for the first time in its 160-year history, raising $350 million in a perpetual bond, in order to develop its activities along the supply chain. The bond issue illustrates the new needs for funding created by high commodity prices, acquisition of new logistics and infrastructure, and European banks' scale back of their lending activities. LDC said that the bond issue strengthened its balance sheet without diluting the existing family shareholders

The bond pays a coupon of 8.25% and is listed on the Singapore Exchange. Buyers of the bonds, which were three times oversubscribed, were mostly Asian and Swiss investors. LDC has the option to buy back the bond after five years.

With net profits of $735 million in 2011, LDC is probably the world's largest trader of cotton and rice, as well as a leading trader in grains, sugar, coffee, and orange juice. LDC recently stated that they planned to spend $5 billion over the next five years to keep up with the consolidation in global agribusiness.

The Louis-Dreyfus family owns 80% of the company and 500 employees own the rest.

The net profits amounted to $1.1 billion in 2012, its best year, for revenues of $57 billion and 20,000 employees in 75 countries. The revenues of LDC in 2013 were of the same order.

Bunge

Bunge was founded in Amsterdam in 1818 by Gottlieb Bunge, with the purpose of being an import/export grain company. In 1859, Gottlieb's grandson Edouard relocated the company to Antwerp, where it became one of the world's leading commodity traders; Edouard's brother took the Bunge name to Argentina. In 1905, Bunge expanded into Brazil and entered food chain production with a wheat milling business. Bunge grew in the following 100 years together with Brazil's agricultural economy.

In 1918, a century after its founding, Bunge began trading commodities in North America, the world's largest agricultural market. In 1923, it acquired a Brazilian cottonseed processor and from that moment, balanced its growth between North and South America.

In 1935, Bunge built a major grain-handling facility in Minnesota and became a grain originator in the USA. In 1938, it entered the Brazilian fertilizer market and became both a supplier and customer to farmers. In 1945, Bunge dispatched its first shipment of Brazilian soybeans to become today the largest exporter of agricultural products from Brazil – and created a Brazilian company called Fertimport to manage raw materials shipments.

In 1961, Bunge opened an export grain-handling elevator in Louisiana in order to connect its US grain business to the world markets; it then built its first US soybean processing plant.

During the 1970s and 1980s, Bunge grew along the food production chain by building grain origination, soy processing, and food products businesses in North and South America. In 1979, it became the world's largest corn miller by acquiring the Lauhoff Grain Company. At the same time, it joined the US food aid program meant to combat hunger in the world.

In 1997, Bunge started a major expansion in South America by acquiring IAP, a Brazilian fertilizer manufacturer, and Ceval, the largest soy processor in Brazil. Other acquisitions made Bunge the largest fertilizer producer and soy processor in South America. In 1998 the company built a big soybean crushing and refining plant in the US.

Bunge went public in 2001 in an IPO listed on the New York Stock Exchange.

As of 2004, it moved into Eastern Europe by opening a new port in Turkey; purchased the first soybean refining plant in the port city of Rizhao in China; and acquired Petrobras' fertilizer operations in Argentina.

In the last few years, Bunge bought a number of sugarcane mills in Brazil where it operates a large sugar and bioenergy business producing sugar and ethanol.

Its net profits in 2012 were $64 million, with revenues of $61 billion and 36,000 employees in 40 countries.

Noble Group

Noble was founded by Richard Elman in Hong Kong in 1987, but the company quickly branched out beyond Asia. It acquired in the early 2000s assets and customers from the Lausanne-based trading house Andre & Cie, which was the fifth largest commodity house after ABCD but went under because of its high leverage and the non-monitored activities of a soybean trader. The company is viewed today as a mini-Glencore because it has diversified across energy, metals, and agricultural trading.

Listed in Singapore in 1997, the founder's family is the largest shareholder; China's sovereign wealth fund, China Investment Corporation, is the second.

Noble's net income was $0.47 billion in 2012, with a record of $0.60 billion in 2010. Its revenues in 2013 were $98 billion.

Wilmar

Wilmar was founded in 1991 in Singapore by the Kuok family, which in 1949 had already started a trading business in Malaysia. It is the world's biggest producer of palm oil, farming palm and processing its oil. Palm oil is a key ingredient in processed food.

Wilmar has positioned itself as the leading trader and supplier of vegetable oil to China, covering a quarter of the market. It controls 60% of the retail market of vegetable oil in China.

It was listed in Singapore in 2006. ADM acquired a 17% stake, making it the largest shareholder after the Kuok family.

The company also moved into soybeans, on the assumption that China's middle class would raise demand for meat, hence soybean meal for cattle and pigs. The strategy paid off until an aggressive expansion of China's state-owned processors caused overcapacity in the sector.

Wilmar is now pushing into palm oil and edible oils in Africa where a greater spending power is finally emerging.

It is also diversifying into sugar, a commodity long dominated by Cargill, ED&F Man, Sucres & Denrées, and Louis Dreyfus. Wilmar acquired the Australian company Sucrogen in 2010.

In 2014, the company entered India, the world's second largest sugar producer, with a $200 million investment in a joint venture with the Indian group Shree Renuka, which has 100,000 hectares of sugar cane in Brazil, itself the world's largest sugar exporter.

Sugar now accounts for 7% of the group profits, while oilseeds have halved from 26% in 2009 to 13% in 2013 and consumer-oriented plantations for 15%.

Palm oil refining continues to account for 48% of pre-tax profits, but Wilmar is now facing tough competition from refining capacity in Indonesia.

The group is expanding into higher-margin areas such as oleo chemicals and specialty fats.

Its pre-tax profits amounted to $1.32 billion in 2013, with a record of $1.88 billion in 2009; its market capitalization went down to $17 billion in 2013.

With Noble and Olam, Wilmar constitutes the NOW, the Asian counterpart to ABCD. NOW is in search of the same profits with the same strategies as ABCD.

Vitol

Vitol was founded in 1966 in Rotterdam by two Dutch businessmen, Henk Victor and Jacques Detiger. It trades gas, coal, power, and emission credits, and has expanded into sugar and grains. The company has been profitable from the start and belongs to its 330 employees.

Its net income was $1.05 billion in 2012, with a record year of $2.28 billion in 2009.

Glencore

Glencore, the largest commodity trader specializing in metals and minerals and based in Zug, Switzerland, diversified into agriculturals trading by buying in 2012 the trading group Viterra, based in Canada, for C$6 billion.

Glencore floated its shares in London in 2011. The total revenues of Glencore were $240 billion in 2013 for the various types of commodities traded.

Cofco (China National Cereals, Oil and Foodstuffs Corp.)

China's food giant Cofco Corp. announced in February 2014 that it was buying a 51% stake in the Dutch grains trader Nidera. By doing so, China's largest state-owned grain trader will have a greater control of world prices as well as better access to major grain regions such as Latin America and Russia. The deal will also put China in direct competition with global agricultural trading houses such as the ABCD.

Cofco was targeting Nidera for its operations platform in Brazil, Argentina and Central America, and Europe as well as a very large global network of customers.

Cofco units include Mengniu Dairy Co., beverage and wine producer China Foods Ltd, and China Agri-Industries Ltd, which processes and trades commodities such as oilseeds and rice.

So far, Cofco had only been making small deals overseas, such as a $136 million acquisition of the Australian sugar producer Tully Sugar in 2011.

Cofco currently trades about 20 million tonnes of grains annually – this can be compared to 55 million tonnes for Marubeni after it acquired Gavilon.

Cofco is in talks with Noble Group to establish a joint venture in sugar, soybeans, and wheat. It has the budget to assemble a formidable international presence. Cofco also wants to raise its processing capacity in corn grinding and oilseed crushing from 50 million tonnes in 2012 to 77 million tonnes in 2015.

Cofco revenues rose 13% last year to $31.7 billion, but profits fell 20% to $585 million, numbers that are comparable to $136.7 billion and $2.31 billion for Cargill.

Nidera

Nidera was founded in the 1920s and took its name from the countries where it was trading: Netherlands, the (East) Indies, Deutschland (Germany), England, Russia, and Argentina.

Nidera trades a variety of agricultural commodities, including grains and soybeans, and employs 3800 people in 20 countries

The total firm value of Nidera was estimated by experts to be $4 billion at the time of the deal with Cofco (Merco Press, March 20, 2014).

Sucden

The company was founded by the French businessman Maurice Varsano in 1952. It is private and headquartered in Paris.

A market leader in global sugar activities, Sucres & Denrées is involved in sugar sourcing, logistics, risk management, trading, processing, and distribution. The group originates and ships annually more than 8 million tonnes of sugar (bulk/bagged/container) while also selling over 1 million tonnes in domestic markets. Logistical and industrial activities have been developed in Russia, Brazil, Mexico, India, United States, and several African and Latin American destinations.

Over the years, Sucden has expanded into products such as cocoa, ethanol, ocean freight, coffee, as well as Futures and options trading on major exchanges.

It has 4000 staff across 30 locations worldwide. The revenues in 2013 were $5.5 billion, the profits $83 million.

US food companies' dollar revenues in 2013

Krafts	18.2 billion
General Mills	18.1 billion
ConAgra	17.4 billion
Kellogg	14.8 billion
Campbell	8.4 billion
Hillshire/Pinnacle Foods	4 + 2.6 billion
McCorming	4.1 billion

1.2.3 The physical markets

Markets take place mainly in three forms:

1. Small regional markets with limited storage capacity that are only able to serve small areas; the commodity changes hands immediately after the transaction is concluded.
2. Auction markets that bring together many players in a centralized and open platform where they interact through ex-ante transparent prices – as happens in the world of art.
3. The warehouses of exchanges where the physical commodity is delivered to the buyer of a Futures contract who did not close his/her position prior to maturity.

In June 2013, the World Bank's Food Price Index remained 12% below the recent all-time peak of August 2012, but was only 2% lower than in June 2012. The picture was different across subclasses: the food index was down 2%, grains up 5%, fats and oils down 4%, fertilizers down 15%. Among the grains, corn/maize was up 12% over the year June 2012–June 2013, rice was down 10% (5% for the Thai price), wheat up by 13%, sugar down by 16%, soybean oil by 12%.

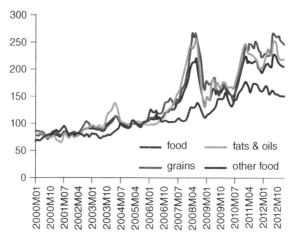

Figure 1.1
Source: World Bank DECPG. The World Bank Global Food Price Index weighs spot prices in nominal US dollars of a variety of food commodities around the world; base 100 in 2005 in the above chart

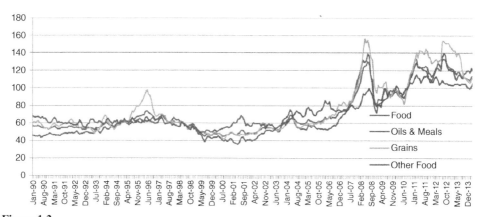

Figure 1.2
Source: World Bank

Current wheat prices reflect expectations that world production will rebound in the agricultural year 2013–2014 (*Food Price Watch*, July 2013). Good harvests are expected from major producers – with the exception of the USA – such as Europe, the Black Sea, Australia, and China. China's wheat is benefiting from higher subsidized inputs such as seeds, fertilizers, and fuel.

Corn production is expected to reach a record high in the new agricultural year, with substantial increases expected in China, Brazil, Argentina, Europe, and the USA. (See Figures 1.1 and 1.2.)

1.2.4 The global flows of commodities

According to the German grain trader Toepfer International, about 300 million tonnes of grains are traded globally each year, about 15% of the total world production.

In 2011–2012, the commodity flows were as follows:

- Europe imported 35 million tonnes of soybeans, exported 41 million tonnes of wheat and 15 million tonnes of corn.
- Africa imported 40 million tonnes of wheat, 13 million tonnes of corn and 7 million tonnes of soybeans.
- North America exported 48 million tonnes of soybeans, 43 million tonnes of wheat and 38 million tonnes of corn
- South America exported 85 million tonnes of soybeans, 4 million tonnes of corn and imported 9 million tonnes of wheat.
- Asia imported 89 million tonnes of soybeans, 39 million tonnes of corn and 10 million tonnes of wheat.
- The US Department of Agriculture foresees that world trade in coarse grains used to feed livestock will rise 25% to 179 million tonnes in the next decade.
- The Food and Agriculture Association (FAO) forecasted a wheat production at 704 million tonnes and a world total cereal production of 2515 million tonnes, resulting in an increase of 572 million tonnes by the end of the 2014 crop season, and a stock-to-use ratio approaching 24%, the highest since 2002–2003.

In May 2014, the WTO raised its forecast for growth in global trade to 4.7% for 2014, up from a previous estimate of 4.5% but still below the 5.3% 20-year average, a number that the WTO estimates for 2015.

Over the years 2012 and 2013, growth averaged only 2.2%, a number remarkably lower.

The WTO sees improved prospects for the USA and Europe, but highlights geopolitical risks as threats to global recovery, because of territorial disputes in the Middle East, Asia, and Eastern Europe that could disrupt trade flows if they escalate.

In 2013, the European Union became the first exporter of agricultural products, with 120.1 billion euros of exports and an increase of 5.3% (it was 12% in 2012 versus 2011), ahead of the USA which generated 115 billion euros, down by 1.7% compared to 2012.

1.2.5 Back to the future: a new age for barter

- In October 2012, Ukraine signed a loan-for-crops contract with the Export-Import Bank of China, according to which Kiev got $3 billion in credit lines.
- In exchange, China will get 3 million tonnes of corn every year, to be supplied at the-then market price.
- According to estimates of the US Department of Agriculture (USDA), China will have bought overseas about 8.3 million tonnes of corn between 2011 and 2013, as much as it imported over the previous 15 years combined.
- Under Beijing's policy of 'self-sufficiency,' corn imports alone will grow almost half to 152 million tonnes.
- In the past, China used to buy corn from the USA and Brazil through international trading houses such as Cargill and Louis Dreyfus.
- China became the world's fifth largest importer of corn, importing in 2012 5.3 million tonnes of corn, versus 100,000 tonnes from 1997 to 2009. Corn is a key feed-meal to fatten cows, sheep, and pigs as consumption of meat in China continues to grow.
- The Ukraine/China deal is likely to raise concerns among other big importers of agricommodities in Asia, like Japan and South Korea.

- Ukraine said the Chinese loans would be used for the purchase of Chinese agricultural technologies, herbicides, and pesticides.
- It is worth noting that Beijing has used its financial power over the period 2007 to 2012 to secure supplies of commodities (particularly crude oil), offering Russia, Brazil, Ecuador, and others multi-billion dollar loans repaid with raw materials rather than money.
- Venezuela doubled in May 2012 its line of credit with China, reaching a debt of $32 billion. It has been shipping 100,000 barrels a day of crude oil, or 5% of its production, to repay a $4 billion loan from the China Development Bank.

1.2.6 The sources of information in agricultural commodity markets

- International agencies and NGOs
- Food and Agriculture Association of the United Nations
- World Food Program of the UN
- UN Commission on Trade and Development (UNCTAD)
- International Fund for Agricultural Development
- World Trade Organization
- World Bank: World Bank Observer, World Bank Economic Review
- International Monetary Fund
- OECD
- US Department of Agriculture
- Business publications such as *Fertilizer Week*, CRU publications.

On the industry side, a number of websites are available: American Farmers Bureau; US Grains Council; Grain Growers of Canada; US Meat Export Association.

1.3 HISTORY OF COMMODITY FUTURES AND SPOT MARKETS

1.3.1 The actors in financial markets

We need to keep in mind that in any market, be it stocks, bonds, currencies or commodities, there are at all times four types of players:

- *Hedgers*, who buy or sell Futures contracts in order to eliminate the uncertainty brought to their revenues by the random evolution of the prices of one or several assets that are central in their economic activity. On the exchange, these actors declare themselves as 'commercials.' For instance, a farmer would sell corn Futures contracts in January in order to eliminate from that moment the randomness in the selling price of his crops harvested in September. An agrifood company that has a production cycle of processed coffee in four months would buy coffee Futures today.
- *Arbitragers*, whose activity is solely to observe the prices and identify anomalies between prices of Futures of different maturities or between a Futures contract and the underlying commodity prices. The existence of these arbitragers ensures that anomalies do not last very long and makes the assumption of 'No arbitrage' discussed in Chapters 3 and 4 roughly legitimate. We can note that, obviously, these arbitragers are not numerous since this activity requires a large confidence in one's ability to know the 'fair price' of an asset at all times.

- *Speculators* are all the other market participants, those who did not have a hedging need or identified a price anomaly. Consequently, they take risk in their trading activity in order to make profits. According to this definition, we certainly recognize the existence of speculation in commodity Futures and spot markets, as the hedgers need counterparties to build the long and short positions that will lock the selling (or buying) price of a commodity ahead of time. Hence, we will state, as did many famous economists over time, that speculators are *liquidity providers*.
- *Market makers* act on behalf of both hedgers and speculators and facilitate their trading activities in the exchange of fixed commissions.

Given the sensitivity of issues related to food, agricultural commodities trading has regularly been accused of being responsible for high prices and/or high price volatility, sometimes by governments facing a difficult situation in the country. The charges are particularly leveled against financial players and Futures markets. It is important, however, to keep in mind some numbers: in August 2013, the dollar value of the total open interest in all agricultural commodity Futures was about 9.6% of one year's worth of global production (because of the gigantic number of small farms around the world feeding the local population) and 3% of a single year's transactions in all physical markets.

1.3.2 The actors in agricultural commodity exchanges

We will follow Dana (The World Bank Report, 2008) to recognize four categories of actors on these exchanges:

1. Producers, consumers, and processors

   Most producers, consumers, and processors trade on the exchange through trading houses and brokerage firms.

   They use the exchange instruments for the purpose of hedging commodity price risk, which is a major component of their physical trading. Consumers and processors are more active than producers because market access is not always available for producers who are often located in developing countries.

2. Trading companies

   A number of international, multi-commodity houses such as Bunge, Archer Daniels, Dreyfus, and others use the exchange to manage the physical and financial exposure of their trading activities in grains and soft commodities around the world.

3. Brokerage houses

   These are financial institutions, also called commissioned houses, that act as market intermediaries and make profits based on fixed commissions. Most brokerage houses are active on more than one exchange and hold relationships with market participants such as producers, consumers, processors, funds, and investors. International banks with commodity lending portfolios and credit finance activities may also have a commodity brokerage division designed to mitigate the risk of lending and earn profits from market-making activities.

4. Managed funds and institutional investors

   Pension and university endowment funds (e.g., Harvard and Yale) and insurance companies have been investing in commodities for a long time as a way to mitigate inflation risk. Since the beginning of the 2000s, a massive number of financial players such as hedge funds have been attracted to commodities by the combined properties of diversification and the large returns that did not prevail in the 1990s.

1.3.3 The growth of Futures markets exchanges and the recent mergers

Governance rules

Futures markets are an essential element of risk management in physical markets. They must provide an infrastructure ensuring a market clearing price at all times. Warehousing and delivery systems linked to Futures exchanges also represent an important element of efficient price formation, which helps the convergence of Futures to spot (physical) prices. While industrial metals warehouses are needed close to consumption areas, agricultural commodities require a location next to production areas since they must immediately go to proper storage, and shortly after to delivery. The exchange must enforce trusted procedures to assess product quality and enforce effective supervision of the delivery process such as minimum *loading-out rates* by the warehouses, a necessary condition for the convergence of spot and Futures markets at maturity, generated by the commitment to deliver attached to a Futures contract and the reason for the *price discovery* benefit of Futures markets.

The difference between the spot and Futures price around the last trading dates is called the *premium* and is due to the costs of delivery and storage created by supply bottlenecks and delivery queues. This premium is paid by the buyer of the Futures contract. It was an average of 10% in the Chicago Board of Trade (CBOT) corn Futures contract in 2011 and this number should be an upper bound for Futures markets to keep their fundamental 'raison d'être.'

The necessary *infrastructure* has to be organized by the exchange near the production areas in the case of agricultural commodities (in contrast to consumption places for metals); the mandated warehouses regularly monitored and the delivery rules clearly specified. Until recently, the delivery rules of the London Metal Exchange left open a large window for delivery and the exchange was itself getting part of the storage fees charged by the warehouses to the buyers of Futures contracts.

Some history

The Chicago Board of Trade came to existence in 1848, was relocated in 1885 in a skyscraper building now listed as a National Historic Landmark, and features in its atrium a three-story art deco statue of Ceres, holding a sheaf of wheat in her left hand and a bag of corn in her right hand (Ceres was the Roman goddess of agriculture, grains, crops, and fertility). With this statue, the exchange wanted to make sure that members on the trading floor would keep Ceres in mind as well as the integrity crucial to the continuation of Futures markets.

In 2007, the CBOT merged with its rival the Chicago Mercantile Exchange; in 2008, the NYMEX merged into the combined CME Group.

At the beginning of 2013, the Hong Kong Futures Exchange bought the London Metal Exchange for $2 billion. ICE (Intercontinental Exchange), an ambitious trading center based in Atlanta, USA, with a primary specialty in energy and commodity contracts and an existence of less than 15 years, had acquired in December 2012 NYSE Euronext for $8.2 billion; it bought in November 2013 the Singapore Mercantile Exchange for $150 million, securing for itself an introduction in a part of the world that is becoming the main battlefield for derivatives trading. SMX is a small commodity exchange launched in 2010 with $75 million in capital from Financial Technologies, which also owns India's MCX commodities exchange. It offers Futures markets for metals, currencies, energy, and agricultural commodities but has suffered from low volumes since the start.

The move puts ICE ahead of rivals CME Group and Deutsche Börse to capture business in Asia, where China's needs for raw materials are creating greater use of hedging strategies. It allows ICE to position itself with respect to its rivals in the region – including the Singapore Exchange (SGX) whose derivatives are the fastest growing activity – and become the first non-Asian exchange to own a clearing house in the region, hence offer clearing in Asia directly as opposed to having energy and commodity derivatives cleared in London. SGX reacted positively to the news and observed that the deal pushed Singapore as the pre-eminent Asian place for commodities trading.

According to the Futures Industry Association, Asia accounted in 2013 for 15 to 20% of global exchange-traded derivatives volume, with the rest roughly equally split between North America and Europe. Deutsche Börse and CME Group are also considering building derivatives clearing houses in Asia.

The security of the margining system

The proper amount of initial margin and maintenance margin that an exchange must request from market participants placing orders is crucial since this deposit will be the intermediary collateral before the margin call is paid after a large market move.

The system that is used by most exchanges, including the CME, the Shanghai Exchange, and the Singapore Exchange, is called SPAN (Standard Portfolio Analysis). Indeed, the exchange holds a gigantic portfolio of short and long positions since it is at all times the counterparty for buyers and sellers. The SPAN rules, which have existed for more than 30 years, were from the start quite conservative and there has been no problem so far (see Carr, Geman, Madan and Yor, 1999).

Our view is that the initial and maintenance margins per contract should increase (see Carr *et al.*, 2001) with the size of the position when it goes above a level defined specifically for each commodity from the careful analysis of numbers of trading volume and open interest over a long period (e.g., 20 years), as well as scenarios chosen outside the familiar models.

1.3.4 Futures markets and price volatility

Among the first papers on the subject, Boyle (1922) argues, on the basis of more than 100,000 pieces of data, that the establishment of the CBOT Futures market was responsible for the corn price volatility decrease between 1841 and 1921. Looking at Europe, the Berlin Produce Exchange was a very influential food market on the continent until grain consumers in the German Reich suffered an increase in both level and volatility of prices after a disastrous harvest took place in 1891 in Germany and Russia. This resulted in a public agitation against speculative activity on the Bourse and an Imperial Commission was established to investigate the efforts of stock exchanges. From January 1, 1897, the Berlin Produce Exchange was forced to incorporate representatives of agricultural and milling interests in its executive committees. The publication of Futures and spot prices was prohibited – a major mistake as price transparency is the most desirable property regulators could wish for at all times – and trading grains was banned. Berlin went to the status of a small provincial market. At the same time, wheat prices and price volatility spiked... In April 1900, the Berlin Futures market was reopened.

Returning to the USA, the Onions Futures Act in the fall of 1958 marked the only time in the history of the country that Futures trading in a commodity was banned. It is well known that it is essentially impossible to store onion crops from one year to the next, hence an increase in price volatility at the approach of harvest is expected – in full agreement with the intuition and the Theory of Storage discussed in Chapter 2. The ban of the onion Futures triggered a spike in spot price volatility in the following six months, and higher price volatility in the following five years. No exchange trades onions today since this commodity is usually consumed where it is produced.

All these points are discussed in the paper by Jacks (2007), who investigates the relationship between Futures markets, speculation, and commodity price volatility. The fundamental result the author exhibits is that, in fact, Futures markets are systematically associated with lower levels of commodity price volatility.

Geman (2011) argues that scarcity in the spot commodity markets is not only the key driver of the spot price volatility, but is also an important factor to explain the shape of the forward curve. She notes that the very high prices of food commodities observed in the recent years were triggered by weather events in the major producing countries for wheat and corn and suggests that regulators should primarily be worried by the systemic risk created by the ownership of large amounts of the underlying physical commodity by major financial players.

At the time of writing, the bank JP Morgan was about to sell to the Swiss hedge fund Mercuria, for roughly $2 billion, its large physical commodities business built from the addition of the Bear Sterns commodity unit in 2008, parts of UBS Commodities in 2009, and assets from RBS Sempra Commodities in 2010 for a cost of more than $2 billion – which allowed the commodities revenues of the bank to double between 2006 and 2009. Using special exemptions granted by the Federal Reserve and approved by the US Congress, a number of banks had bought after 2009 large amounts of infrastructure to store commodities and deliver them to consumers – from pipelines and refineries in Oklahoma and Texas; to fleets of double-hulled tankers at sea around the globe; to companies controlling operations at major ports like Oakland and Seattle. JP Morgan acquired Henry Bath & Son Ltd, a network of metals warehouses. In 2010, Goldman Sachs bought Metro International Trade Services, a company that owns 27 industrial aluminum warehouses in the Detroit area.

1.3.5 The role of indexes in the creation of efficient commodity spot markets

The existence of large players in agricultural commodities and shipping renders the risk of spot prices manipulation significant. In the Futures markets, this is not feasible, in principle, since Futures prices are posted at all times by the exchange – hence, the benefits of liquid and transparent indexes, preferably quoted by a third party not involved in trading activities, such as either a statistical company that accumulates data or an entity like the World Bank, which publishes for instance the World Fertilizer Index.

Benchmark-based pricing mechanisms, which apply a discount or premium to a liquid reference price, rely on the liquidity of a reference contract, which is typically the front-month Future contract.

Liquid indexes reduce 'moral hazard':

- They allow the elimination of opacity.
- They are neutral to all parties.
- They make difficult manipulations of the spot price.
- Hence, they represent a necessary condition of the existence and development of liquid derivative instruments since they will be the reference price in the numerous cases of financial settlement.

1.3.6 Commodities and numéraire

Most commodities are still today denominated in US dollars; exceptions do exist – for instance, salmon contracts traded in Oslo are expressed in euros and Norwegian kroner. Hence, hedging against commodity prices involves also hedging the dollar component versus one's domestic currency.

After the catastrophic 16% fall of the Argentinian peso in 2013, soybean growers have been packing their dollar-denominated crops instead of sending them to the markets and getting pesos with little value. By the end of January 2014, only 6% of their most recent crop was sent to crushing plants and exporters, according to Macquarie's experts. The number was much lower than the 11% at the same time in 2013 and 25% in 2012. With Argentina's inflation rate of nearly 30%, USDA does not expect farmers to liquidate soybean piles as these are viewed as a protection against further devaluation of the Argentinian peso. In a parallel manner, USDA estimates that soybean inventories will reach a record 9 million tonnes this year, almost twice as much as the year before. Argentina accounts for about one-tenth of the world's soybean exports and almost half of soy meal trade.

In peso terms, soybean prices went up 20% during the first six weeks of 2014, compared to 1.6% for the CBOT soybean Futures.

It is one of the many examples where the tangible commodity has more value than the local currency.

1.4 SHIPPING AND FREIGHT

Ships and vessels have developed alongside humankind evolution. The first cargoes were transported by sea more than 5000 years ago. Moving silks and other precious merchandise across the oceans was already quite active in the 15th century, as evidenced in Shakespeare's *Merchant of Venice*. And the shipping of gold bullion to Wellington's army in Spain and Portugal was decisive in ensuring his victory. Today, freight has become an integral part of modern trade, with the transport of commodities by sea becoming cheaper and more reliable over time. For instance, the costs of shipping dry bulk like grains or iron ore have increased by only 70% (in nominal terms) over the last 50 years, a very small number compared to other industrial services and inflation numbers. This is due in particular to important technological innovations that occurred in the maritime sector and made it possible to move commodities across the world at a very competitive price.

Shipping markets are recognized today as a key component of the commodity asset class, playing a role in final prices of energy, agriculturals, and metals. The last 14 years have been the stage of major transformations for commodity markets, with the remarkable growth of the BRICs, government interventions in commodity-producing countries such as Canada, Australia, and China, and the necessity to feed the growing world population to cite the most visible explanations. For those who own vessels readily available for various destinations, 'locational arbitrage' may be achieved when the locational spread is greater than the cost of shipping. As for the originators and merchant houses who sell the commodity under a CIF (Cost of Insurance and Freight) label, transportation is such an important component of the revenues/profits that a whole department of the firm is dedicated to the shipping activity and its risk-management.

1.4.1 International trade

The first sea trade network that can be traced was developed 5000 years ago between Meso-potamia, Bahrain, and western India. The Mesopotamians exchanged their oil and dates for copper and ivory (see Stopford (2009)). The maritime code developed by the Mesopotamians was remarkably similar to the one prevailing today: ships were hired at a fixed tariff, pro-portional to the capacity of the vessel, and freight costs were paid in advance. The so-called Baltic Exchange was established as early as the mid-18th century, prior to the Chicago Board of Trade (1848) or London Metal Exchange (1877). It was primitively known as the Virginia and Baltic Coffeehouse, located in London's financial district, and was registered as a limited liability company with shares in 1900 (see Barty-King (1994) for an interesting history of the Baltic Exchange). Today, the exchange is owned by its members and operated by a board of directors. It is the world's single independent source of maritime information.

The year 1985 saw the creation of the Baltic Freight Index (BFI) as a benchmark for the world freight market, against which derivatives contracts would be financially settled. The original BFI was defined as a weighted average of spot rates covering 13 voyage routes related to a variety of dry-bulk vessels with cargoes ranging from 14,000 to 120,000 metric tonnes. Each major route incorporated in the BFI referred to a vessel size, a certain cargo, and a route description. The weights were assigned according to the importance of the route in the dry-bulk sector. For instance, the routes from the US Gulf of Mexico to Rotterdam and Japan were the most important ones, followed by the US Pacific Coast to south Japan.

The Baltic Capesize Index (BCI) is calculated on the shipping costs observed on 10 available routes for a Capesize dry bulker. Each route is weighted according to its importance relative to the nine others. The Baltic Panamax Index (BPI) is computed on the four available routes for a Panamax dry bulker, each route having the same weight (25%). Supramax vessels have six trip charter routes and three voyage charter routes but the Baltic Supramax Index (BSI) is only based on the six trip charter routes: two routes (S_2 and S_3) each account for 25% of the index and the other four each have a weight of 12.5%. Lastly, the Baltic Handysize Index consists of six routes, out of which two (HS_2 and HS_3) have each a weight of 25% and the four others 12.5%.

The Baltic Dry Index (BDI), the flagship today for dry bulk shipping costs, is computed as an arithmetic average of the Baltic Capesize, Panamax, Supramax, and Handysize indexes. Over the years 2009 and 2010, the conversion factor of the BDI rate into dollars has been 1/0.113473601; hence, on a day when the BDI value was 2269, for instance, the average char-ter price was \$12,672/day (to be adjusted to the size and voyage of a specific vessel).

We will mostly focus on dry bulk vessels and won't discuss the fascinating topics of oil or LNG tankers. However, we can note that in case of excess supply in the oil tanker market, oil tankers can be cleaned, dried, and used to transport cereals.

The expansion of international trade has been facilitated by large agreements within the WTO, the development of trade finance with new countries, the gigantic input of countries like Brazil and China, the explosion of cross-border trade across the world, and the deployment of a global world of activities of commodity producers and merchants.

1.4.2 Price formation in freight markets

The major types of dry bulk vessels are the categories of Capesize, Panamax, and Handymax, themselves defining indexes attached to each category; Supramax vessels are smaller in num-ber at this point, but increasing for bunker costs efficiency as the harbors and canals become

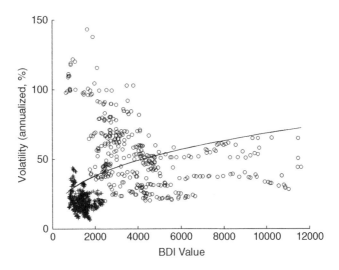

Figure 1.3

wider and deeper. It was said before that in order to represent the market as a whole, the Baltic Dry Index (BDI) is defined as the arithmetic average of these indexes; in all cases, the price of bunker fuels accounts for roughly 20% of the shipping rate.

The major actors in the spot and forward freight markets are the large shipping companies, and unsurprisingly old commodity houses like Cargill or Louis Dreyfus and banks such as Rabobank or Morgan Stanley, which have been involved in the trading of commodities for a long time.

The importance of Asia in shipping and international trade is illustrated by the 'Shipping Times' pages (Figure 1.4) of the Singaporean newspaper *The Business Times* where a large number of voyages, vessels, and cargo services are proposed, illustrating the existence of a shipping spot market in such shipping hubs as Singapore, London or Baltimore.

The supply of cargo ships is generally both tight and inelastic – it takes two to three years to build a new ship, and ships are too expensive to take out of circulation the way airlines park unneeded jets in the Arizona desert.

Hence, marginal increases in demand can push the index high quickly, and marginal demand decreases can cause a rapid drop in the index, as displayed in the price trajectories and volatility.

It should be noted at this point that grains and other agricultural commodities are not the only components of dry bulk activity. Metals and coal represent the other ones, although larger in terms of weight. Hence, it is useful to follow the dry bulk market as a whole when importing or exporting agricultural commodities. Looking at the BDI trajectory, very low prices are observed in the period starting mid-2010: this corresponds to the moment when a large fleet of new vessels that China decided to build to transport imports of coal, copper, and grains came to completion, creating a large increase in supply at a time when the growth of the world economy was slowing down. A decade ago, some analysts used to propose alternatively the BDI or copper prices as early indicators of the world economic health; the excess supply presently prevailing in the dry bulk market surely takes away any predictive power in its current value.

For an extensive description of the shipping markets, the reader is referred to the book by Alizadeh and Nomikos (2009); a tentative modeling of the BDI trajectory for trading or hedging purposes can be found in the paper by Geman and Smith (2012).

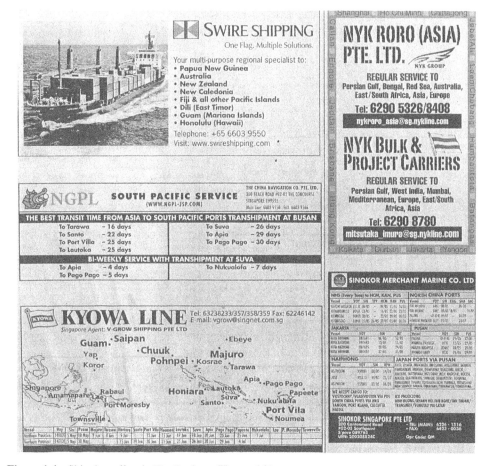

Figure 1.4   Shipping offers in The Business Times of Singapore

The inelasticity of supply to demand makes the BDI behavior and volatility similar to those of electricity, the sole commodity that is not yet economically storable (except for hydro). We observe similar – though not identical – spikes. A simple mean reverting model is not quite appropriate either; nor is a so-called jump mean – reverting diffusion, as the force of mean reversion necessary to bring prices down from high peaks makes small ordinary moves quasi impossible. The jump-reversion model of Geman and Roncoroni (2006) for electricity can do a reasonable job to fit the BDI over the period 2002 to 2013.

As stated above, copper prices on the one hand and the BDI on the other were proposed by experts as early indicators of the world economy. In the graph in Figure 1.7, we can see that the two trajectories moved in the same direction during the years 2003 to 2010 (which include the financial crisis). They strongly decoupled as of 2010, which was the moment when a large number of vessels built in China came on line, following the Chinese decision not to rely on anyone to import into the country the commodities it needed. As usual, the force of supply and demand comes first in any commodity market.

Figure 1.5   Baltic Capesize Index 2001 to 2013

Forward freight agreements

At the moment, the only liquid derivatives traded on freight rates are Forward Freight Agreements (FFAs).

An FFA is a contract where the long position secures the cost of freight for a specific cargo route over a defined future period.

It is based on a defined voyage or time charter or a specific index and is financially settled, like a forward rate agreement. The only difference is the fact that the underlying here is a freight index, instead of an interest rate index.

Since the settlement is based on a *shipping market index*, this one is very important and has to be assessed by an independent entity, as discussed earlier in this chapter. In practice, it is provided by the Baltic Exchange or the information provider Platt's, and is typically defined as the average of the last seven days in the expiration month or the monthly average, again to avoid manipulation or any undesirable phenomenon that may take place in the freight market on an isolated day.

In order for the indexes to be reliable, unbiased, and accurate reflections of the global spot market, the Baltic Exchange appoints panel companies that are assigned the task of reporting freight rates to the exchange on a daily basis. These panelists have to be members of the exchange, and represent broking firms (rather than shipowners or charterers) that are able to

Figure 1.6   The BDI Index over the period 2000 to 2013

estimate how much it cost to move various cargoes of raw materials on various routes: for instance, 100,000 tonnes of iron ore from San Francisco to Hong Kong or 1 million tonnes of rice from Bangkok to Tokyo. Once the panelists have submitted their figures, the London-based Baltic Exchange is responsible for calculating the final index figures, which are published at 1 pm for the dry cargo. The BDI and the other major freight rates can be accessed from the Baltic Exchange or major news services such as Thomson-Reuters or Bloomberg.

Since the index on which a transaction of goods is concluded may be CIF (cost of insurance and freight paid by the seller) or FOB (this cost is paid by the buyer), one can lock in arbitrage opportunities ahead of time if it happens that the implied forward freight contained in the forward prices of the CIF and FOB indexes be different from the value of the FFA related to the same period and points of observation. The CIF and FOB prices of coal between Rotterdam and Richards Bay are widely scrutinized; in agricultural commodities, some residual inefficiencies may be identified and a successful arbitrage implemented.

Trading activity
Baltic Exchange (London) used to offer Futures contracts, but now only offers forwards. Imarex (Oslo) provides daily quotes on maritime shipping. LCH-Clearnet (London) is a central place for spot and forward trades in shipping.

Figure 1.7   The BDI and copper price trajectory decoupling as of the end of 2010

New York, Baltimore, Singapore, and Hong Kong are other major centers of shipping trading.

The daily values quoted as the Baltic Forward Agreements (BFAs) are estimated mid-prices of bids and offers for the dry (and wet) market based on submission from brokers at 5.30 pm London time for the dry routes BFA Capesize, BFA Panamax, BFA Supramax, and BFA Handysize. Futures on the BDI were introduced, and then discontinued, by the International Maritime Exchange (IMAREX) in Norway, an exchange dedicated to shipping derivatives. IMAREX relies on the Baltic Exchange to provide it with independent assessments in order to clear its transactions. The settlement prices of FFAs are produced on the last working day of the month and computed as an average over a seven- or 10-day period of daily values. Moreover, the volume and open interest related to FFAs written on the BDI (and other dry indexes) are published on a weekly basis.

The expansion of commodity markets during the 2000s and the double-digit growth of the developing countries and BRICs have contributed to an amazing boom in maritime transport and shipbuilding. All records were shattered in the dry bulk market, with an unprecedented interest in bulk carriers. Moreover, the concomitant rise in bunker prices persuaded operators to reduce speeds, which in turn required the addition of more vessels to maintain the schedules. Interestingly, the congestion of major harbors plays such a key role in the supply/demand balance for shipping that options written on congestion indexes have been traded for a number of years among the major actors; most send 'spies' to watch round the clock the length of the queue of vessels in Sydney Harbor or at the Suez Canal gates.

The sporadic building of strategic commodity inventories by some countries or large firms should be added to the list of unobservable sources for vessel demand changes. The supply of cargo ships, on the other hand, is inelastic under market conditions that can only be changed in the short term by changing vessel speeds, a costly solution in terms of bunker fuels. In the longer term, more permanent changes can take place by building new ships and/or scrapping older ones. Currently, it takes one to three years to build and deliver new ships, influencing essentially the longer-term supply for freight services.

The volume of international seaborne trade has vastly increased in the years 1975 to 2005 (see Alizadeh and Nomikos (2009)) and it continues to grow with the world population's food needs.

Shipping rates exhibit large swings and volatility related to the cycles in the world economy, commodities consumption, and transport. Moreover, bunker prices are quite volatile since they are related to crude oil prices. Lastly, other risks influencing prices include fluctuations in scrap vessel prices, piracy, accidents, weather patterns (which create increased demand for energy-producing fossil fuels) as well as the bottleneck problems in some ports mentioned earlier.

Lastly, let's mention that shipping was crucial in the development of the Silk Road; over 4,000 miles for the trade of Chinese silk as of 206BC. Besides its economic role, the Silk Road permitted the growth of cultural trade among the various civilizations on the way – China, India, Persia, Europe and Arabia in particular (see Shah and Rath, 2009).

2
Agricultural Commodity Spot Markets

'Investing in agriculture today will be like investing in the oil sector in 2001–2002.'
Marc Faber, Gloom, and Doom Report – May 2011

2.1 INTRODUCTION

We first provide a brief description of the current world agricultural situation – what is grown in which location.

Table 2.1 describes the major agricultural crops grown in terms of acreage (acreage harvested, in hectares), all figures from the Food and Agricultural Organization (2010). Wheat, corn, rice, and soybeans are the most important crops worldwide for human beings.

For these major four crops, the USA is a prominent producer, and even more dominant as an exporter. China and India are also major producers, but with large populations most of their production is for domestic consumption. Brazil and Argentina join the USA as the dominant exporters of both corn and soybeans. Most rice is produced in and exported from Asia, as discussed in Chapter 7.

2.2 PRICE FORMATION IN AGRICULTURAL COMMODITY MARKETS

As for other commodities, the major elements driving spot prices are

- supply
- demand
- inventory

with the additional consideration of perishability for the inventory.

However, in contrast to metals where demand (through income growth) is the crucial element, supply factors are more important drivers of price formation and changes in the case of agricultural commodities.

Quality and type also play a major role:

- Robusta versus Arabica coffee
- Kansas City wheat versus Chicago wheat
- Hence, the inevitable presence of basis risk, namely a price difference between the grade of the commodity underlying a Future contract and the one this contract was supposed to hedge. This 'basis risk' has to be monitored during the lifetime of the Future contract.

Table 2.1 Acreage of the world's major crops in 2010

Crop	World acreage
Wheat	217 million hectares
Corn	162
Rice	153.6
Soybeans	102.4
Barley	48
Sorghum	40.5
Millet	35.1
Cotton	32.1
Rapeseed	31.7
Groundnuts	24.1
Sugarcane	23.8
Sunflower	23.1
Oil palm	15.0
Coffee	10.2
Cocoa	8.9

Supply is composed of three components:

• Current year production
• 'Carry-in' from the previous year
• Imports from other regions or countries.

Demand essentially covers two categories:

• Domestic use
• Exports.

'Carry-over' is defined as the remaining supply from the previous year plus current year production plus imports minus demand. It is this carry-over that links Futures prices in different years.

Stocks-to-use ratio

• is defined as current year ending stocks divided by current use
• is a very important indicator in technical analysis as it expresses how short supplies may be
• has a high impact on price volatility.

Unlike the case of metals and fossil fuels, there are no 'underground reserves' for agricultural products. Each year, a given crop is planted, grown and harvested, and some is consumed. What is not consumed is stored in inventory, linking one year to the next. The ratio of this inventory to yearly consumption (the so-called 'stocks-to-use' ratio) is therefore a closely followed value in agricultural commodities since inventories serve as an important buffer, absorbing both short-term shocks in demand and, more importantly for agricultural products, protecting against (negative) shocks in supply, often caused by adverse weather.

The stocks-to-use ratio provides some information about short-term scarcity or abundance. But, with stocks-to-use ratios of typically between 10% and 30% of annual consumption, inventory values provide only short-term information[1] since an inventory of 10% of consumption could be exhausted in a single bad year – global corn production fell 11% in 1993 from the previous year, and dropped a disastrous 21% in 1983 mainly due to extreme drought in the USA.

According to the International Cereals Council, world production of cereals should decrease by 2% to 1935 million tonnes between the agricultural years 2013–2014 and 2014–2015, because of an expected lower harvest of corn in the USA where cold weather delayed sowing, with a negative impact on corn and wheat. The stocks at the end of the agricultural year should remain stable at 390 million tonnes. On the other hand, demand for cereals should keep rising and reach 2325 million tonnes.

2.3 VOLATILITY IN AGRICULTURAL MARKETS

Price volatility means the dispersion of prices around the mean. In a period of high volatility, the price level experiences harsh swings. In a period of low volatility the price level changes very moderately. Conventional wisdom associates a period of high volatility (like the one that started in 2007) with harming consumers and producers. On the consumer side, the price transmission from the agricultural commodities to the food prices is relatively moderate in developed countries. Indeed, bread producers tend to increase the price only when the price of commodities is high for a relatively long period of time. Consequently, the volatility borne by the consumer during a period of high agricultural commodity volatility is very modest. In contrast, in developing countries, poor households devote most of their budget to food and are very sensitive to spikes in food prices. High prices are crucial and create concerns amid citizens and governments. In 2007 and early 2008, food riots broke out in some African countries. According to Zezza *et al.* (2008), 200 million households are very vulnerable to commodity price peaks around the world.

The graph in Figure 2.1 (from the World Bank) shows that grains represent the agricultural commodity with the highest spikes over the period 1990 to Jan 2014, with dramatic consequences for poor and populated countries around the world.

The graph in Figure 2.2 shows that meat prices have exhibited a steady rise with a low volatility since 2000; grain prices started increasing many years later.

On the production side, volatility is associated with more risk. Farmers postpone their investments in tractors or fertilizers as long as the volatility is high because they are not able to forecast future revenues. Shrinking investment of farmers harms in turn the entire agricultural sector, especially the machinery and equipment sector and the agribusiness sector in general. We can note that fertilizers belong to the group of storable commodities, both in the primitive form and across the various stages of the supply chain.

Table 2.2 presents the key characteristics of the volatility of corn and wheat.

---

[1] Short term means providing information only about the next few months up to 18 months, hence for planting and trading purposes. Long term means two to five years, hence strategic decisions on types of products to grow.

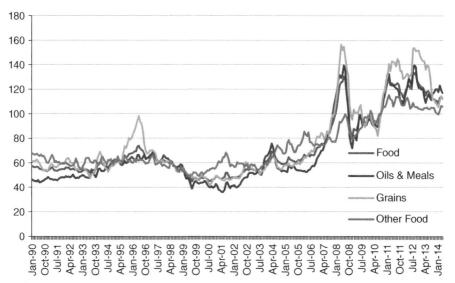

Figure 2.1

Figure 2.2

In the case of corn and wheat, the periods 2006–08 and 2009–11 stand out for exhibiting the highest volatility. As observed from the table, both volatility distributions display positive skewness and excess kurtosis, rejecting normality and making tests relying on normality inapplicable.

In the case of log volatility, standard sample skewness and kurtosis are reduced, making normality a more acceptable assumption – a property that will allow us to use the Bai and Perron (2003) technique for the detection of breaks.

Table 2.2   Average annualized volatilities (%) and descriptive statistics

Annualized volatilities (%)				Descriptive statistics over the period 1991 to 2011		
Years	Corn	Wheat				
1991–93	16.7016	21.631			Corn	Wheat
1994–96	19.6542	22.5276		Mean	24.2401	27.7671
1997–99	22.1859	23.9612		St. dev.	10.527	10.255
2000–02	21.6461	24.2922		Skewness	1.0803	1.2581
2003–05	23.0489	27.4608		Kurtosis	4.8239	4.9259
2006–08	33.6159	36.6865		X squared	86.02121	107.8262
2009–11	32.828	37.8102				
All years	24.2401	27.7671				

Given the spectacular changes in prices and volatilities of corn and wheat between the periods 1991–1993 and 2006–2008 for instance (see Table 2.2), we decided to look for breaks in the trajectories of these four quantities over the period 1991–2011. In this order, the Bai and Perron (2003) algorithm was used, with a number of breakpoints increasing from one to five. A focus was then made on a single break, the one that explained the dramatic changes between the periods 1991–1993 and 2006–2008 and is identified by the largest reduction of the BIC (Bayes Information Criterion). The results are presented in Table 2.2 for corn and wheat and Figure 2.6 for the World Fertilizer Index.

We use the same algorithm to investigate one to five structural breaks in the volatility time series, in order to test the assumption of changes in the mean of volatility and log volatility time series. The results of the tests do not differ substantially in the break dates; we will refer to the set of results derived from log volatility since the latter provides us with a time series that is closer to normality (as shown by Jarque Bera tests).

For all commodities, it is important to look at price levels; for agricultural commodities it is even more so, given the social and political consequences of high prices. Consequently, we focus on the price series of corn and wheat and the way they relate to volatility. We repeat the same analysis of structural breaks for the prices and log prices of corn, wheat, and Fertilizer Index. As before, we are interested in changes in the mean price and use the log prices series to use the Bai and Perron algorithm.

We find that a major structural break in the corn price trajectory occurred in October 2006 with a confidence interval ranging from July to November 2006; and in April 2006 with a confidence interval ranging from January to November 2006 for the log volatility.

The results for wheat price and volatility are presented in Figure 2.4. For wheat prices, we find a structural break in September 2006 with a confidence interval ranging from July to October 2006; and in April 2006 with a confidence interval ranging from December 2005 to August 2006 for wheat volatility. The focus on a single break was mentioned above. In the

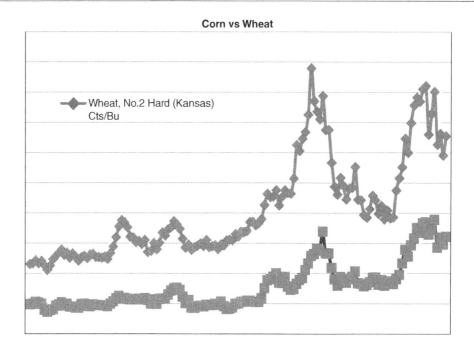

Figure 2.3   Corn and wheat prices from Jan 2000 to July 2011

case of corn log prices, the first break reduces the BIC value from 177.7 to –83.7, while the second and third breaks only reduce it to –114.9 and –140.2, respectively. In the case of wheat log price, the first break reduces the BIC from 181.5 to –82.5, while the second and third breaks achieve a reduction to –119.3 and –160.5, respectively.

Figure 2.5 includes the results for the World Fertilizer Index log prices, where the index is the one provided by the World Bank. Its volatility is described in Table 2.3.

We observe a rise in fertilizer volatility as of 2004 and a spike in 2007–2008. Accordingly, the Bai and Perron algorithm exhibits a structural break for the Fertilizer Index log price in April 2007, with a confidence interval ranging from February to May 2007. Fertilizer log prices present a reduction from 414 to 9.9 for the first break, with further breaks only reducing the BIC to –97.6 and –96.4.

The above results exhibit the remarkable synchronicity of the breaks in corn and wheat price trajectories during the period September–October 2006, the time of the first recent food crisis; this is in agreement with the substitutability between these two commodities, which are central in the production of bread, cereals, feedstock, and similar human and animal food. The fact that the break in the Fertilizer Index price trajectory took place some months later probably reflects the delayed price increase of fertilizers decided by producing companies facing a rising demand from farmers worldwide in a search for better productivity

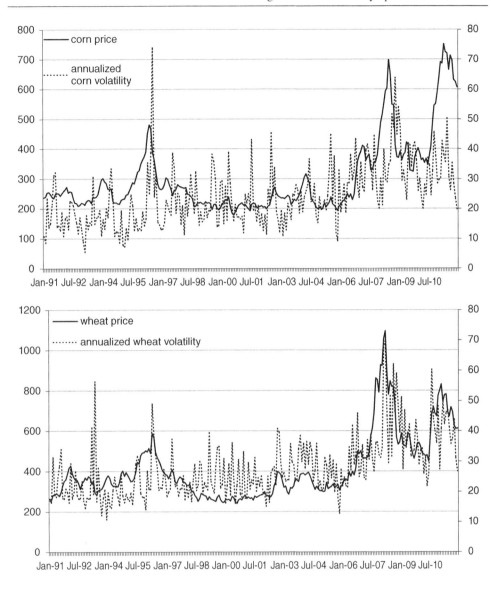

Figure 2.4 Top: corn price and annualized corn volatility; bottom: wheat price and annualized wheat volatility, from January 1991 to December 2011

in the next harvest. It is important to keep in mind that during the period 1990–2005, prices of the agricultural commodities and fertilizers, if adjusted for inflation, were strictly declining; hence, an upward adjustment had to take place at some point to reward the producers. The related effects between corn, wheat, and Fertilizer Index price movements are further displayed in Figure 2.6.

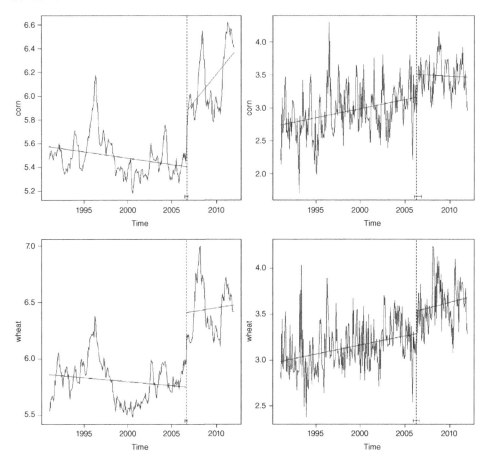

Figure 2.5   Top: monthly average corn log price and log volatility; bottom: monthly average wheat log price and log volatility, from January 1991 to December 2011

Table 2.3   World Fertilizer Index volatility

Year:	1995	1996	1997	1998	1999	2000	2001	2002	2003
Volatility:	12.63	10.12	6.82	5.36	4.63	13.22	9.84	6.02	9.58
Year:	**2004**	**2005**	**2006**	**2007**	**2008**	**2009**	**2010**	**2011**	
Volatility:	15.28	11.76	11.47	14.98	48.97	21.26	9.67	16.16	

2.3.1 Volatility of the price level versus return in agricultural commodity markets

The literature on commodities has reproduced the tools used in the financial world, by measuring the volatility of the price return – see Piot-Lepetit and M'Barek (2011) for a review. This is due to the fact that volatility in finance is defined as the standard deviation of returns, in portfolio theory as well as in the celebrated Black–Scholes–Merton formula.

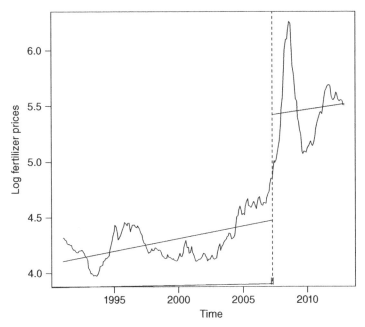

Figure 2.6 Monthly average Fertilizer Index log prices with one structural break, from January 1991 to December 2012

Return is indeed the quantity that matters for corporation shareholders and potential buyers of long positions in stocks, either directly or through call options. On the other hand, returns to prices take positive and negative values, hence they may be represented by normal distributions (in particular over long holding periods) and normality is a useful/necessary assumption in a number of econometric models.

Commodities are an asset class quite different from stocks and policymakers as well as econo-mists should be interested in the *volatility of the price level* instead of the return, computed either as the standard deviation of prices or as the coefficient of variation of prices.

Moreover, a way to focus on price dispersion over the year – which again matters in the hedging decisions, storage logistics, and calendar spread trading strategies – is to consider the inter-year coefficient of variation defined by

$$CV = \frac{\sqrt{\sum_{i=1}^{12}(P_i - \bar{P})^2 \Big/ 12}}{\bar{P}}$$

Geman and Ott (2013) compute this coefficient of variation for corn and wheat over the period 1978 to 2011, as displayed in Figure 2.8.

For all three major grains – wheat, corn, and soybeans (Figures 2.8 and 2.9) – volatility was relatively low until the mid-1990s; afterwards began a period of higher volatility. For all three, a different regime started around 2006 and exhibited the highest volatility since 1978. There are also idiosyncrasies. Indeed, for corn and soybeans, the lowest period of volatility had begun around 1990 until 1995, whereas from 1995 to 2006, a moderately high volatility

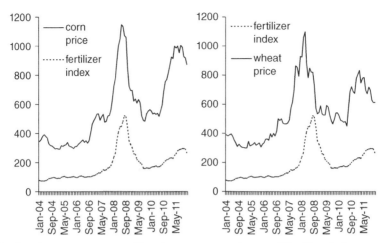

Figure 2.7 Quasi-contemporaneous effects between corn, wheat, and Fertilizer Index returns, January 2004 to December 2011

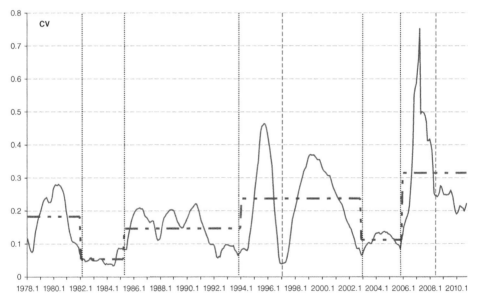

Figure 2.8 Wheat intra-year coefficient of variation (spot proxied by first nearby, soft red winter, CBOT) above and corn below

has prevailed. The volatility from 1978 to 1989 is the average of the volatility observed during the sample for corn and soybean. In contrast, the breakdown of the volatility of wheat is different. Wheat experienced two short periods of low volatility in the beginning of the 1980s and the 2000s. The relatively high period of volatility of wheat had started from 1995 until 2003, before the spike of 2006–2007.

Besides the inter-year coefficient of variation, we argue that the two other indicators to follow are the changes in the coefficient of variation of prices computed on an annual basis, as well as the standard deviation of price levels, as displayed in Figure 2.10.

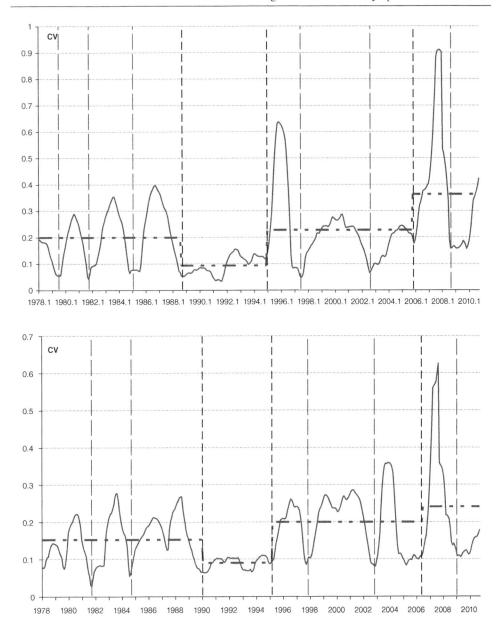

Figure 2.9   Soybean inter-year coefficient of variation

Figure 2.10 indicates that as early as 2004, large and erratic movements in corn prices (the graphs for wheat are very similar) should have been a warning factor for the large crises that took place repeatedly as of the agricultural year 2006–2007. Food commodities, crucial for the existence of human beings, are not financial instruments and require appropriate tools and risk indicators in particular.

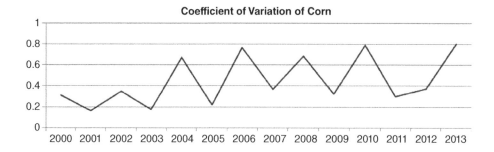

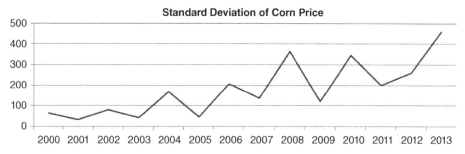

Figure 2.10

2.3.2 Which factors drive volatility?

To shed some light on the factors driving the intra-year volatility of the three commodities considered, a regression estimate is conducted. Hereafter the different variables included are discussed.

The micro-factors

- Storage

   The spot market and the storage market combine to determine an equilibrium price. Consequently, price volatility is determined by the interaction between supply, consumption, and storage. The level of the stock drives most of the storable commodity price volatility according to the theory of storage (Williams and Wright, 1991). Indeed, empty stockpile cannot act as a buffer to serve the market in case of a low harvest year. On the contrary, high stocks allow mitigating supply or demand shocks; the stock can then dampen price swings. As a result, the stocks-to-use (demand) ratio heralds all information regarding the clearing of the spot and stock market.

- Trade restriction

   A thin market on an international scale is often blamed by market experts to drive up volatility. Any trade restriction might harm the match of world supply and world demand and so provoke large price swings. The degree of market internationalization can be measured by the ratio of total world export divided by total world production (in volume). The degree of competition in a given market can also impinge on commodity price movements. Trade restrictions of a given country have a real effect only in case of strong market power. Consequently, the normalized Herfindahl Index may be used. An index close to zero means that the market is very competitive, and an index close to 1 means a monopolistic market (the index is defined as the sum of the squares of the market shares – in percentage – of all players).

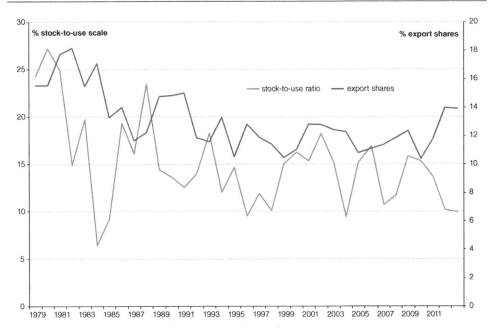

Figure 2.11 The stocks-to-use ratio and export shares of corn

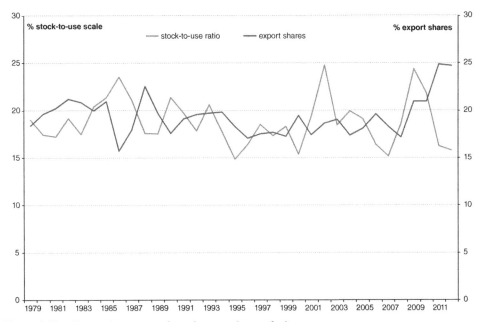

Figure 2.12 The stocks-to-use ratio and export shares of wheat

The macro-factors

The overall macroeconomic environment and shocks might significantly impact the volatility of commodity prices. Indeed, the business cycle and the global growth of the economy might be of major importance (GDP, industrial production index, CPI inflation). Geman and Ott (2013) argue that micro-factors, such as inventory levels and export bans, play the most important role in explaining commodity price volatility even when the usual macro-variables are included such as GDP, industrial production, and CPI inflation.

The empirical results

The coefficient of variation of wheat, corn, and soybeans was calculated as explained above.

For wheat and corn, most of the volatility is driven by the level of stock relative to the demand. Indeed, it can be seen in Figures 2.11 and 2.12 that since 2003, the stocks-to-use ratios have often been very low for wheat and corn. This low level of stock is the main impediment to stable prices. Free trade lowers also significantly the volatility as depicted in the bar graphs. Conversely, trade restrictions (e.g., export bans, high tariffs) drive up volatility in all three grains relatively equally. Trade restrictions in recent years in agricultural commodities worsened price volatility (Heady and Fan, 2008). This can be observed for wheat in 2007 and 2010 (see Figure 2.8). The occasional influence of macro-factors can be quite important for corn and especially soybean (e.g., year 2009). To conclude, the factor explaining the upsurge of volatility since the mid-2000s is the stocks-to-use ratio of wheat and especially of corn, the latter having been historically low since the beginning of the 2000s. For wheat, trade restrictions added to the volatility especially in 2007 and 2010 (Russian export ban). Finally, speculation activity lowers volatility, contrary to popular/populist belief.

2.3.3 Conclusion

Policy makers should pay attention to realized (or historical) volatility as the *coefficient of variation* of deseasonalized price levels. Unit root tests with structural breaks show that agricultural commodity prices are mean-reverting over cycles, and each period begins with a break. By analyzing the evolution of the CVs over time using rolling windows, it is shown that wheat, corn, and to a lesser extent soybeans experienced a period of high volatility (actually the highest since 1978), which started around 2006. As regards the factors explaining this rise of volatility, the stocks-to-use ratio of wheat and especially of corn was historically low from the beginning of the 2000s. For wheat, trade restriction added up the volatility. Finally, speculation activity lowers volatility contrary a popular belief and weather events and export bans represent the true danger.

The author's findings agree with those exhibited by Will *et al.* (2012): 'Is Financial Speculation with Agricultural Commodities Harmful or Helpful? A Literature Review of Current Empirical Research'.

As summarized in the abstract, the four authors survey 35 empirical studies published between 2010 and 2012 that analyze the influence of financial speculation on agricultural commodities. They conclude that, 'according to the current state of research, there is little supporting evidence that the recent increase in financial speculation has caused either a) the price level or b) the price volatility in agricultural markets to rise. Rather, fundamental factors are responsible for this.' Most papers are not in favor of erecting market barriers by regulation. 'Those who are interested in fighting global hunger should take care of fundamental factors and take appropriate measures to keep supply in step with demand, which is likely to rise in the near future.'

The author modestly converges with these findings, and strongly objects in particular to (populist) subsidies given by governments of wealthy countries to their farming groups, since there will always be a poorer country hurt by these subsidies.

3

Futures Exchanges – Future and Forward Prices – Theory of Storage – The Forward Curve

'I know of no pursuit in which more real and important services can be rendered to any country than by improving its agriculture and its breed of useful animals.'
George Washington

3.1 MAJOR COMMODITY EXCHANGES

Agricultural commodity prices have been experiencing unprecedented price moves in the period 2006 to 2014 – in a non-uniform way across commodities, however – and there is no sign of change at the time of writing, with disruptions in supply created by weather or political events. The markets have evolved in a parallel way, with a dramatic growth in volumes and variety of traded contracts, number of operating exchanges (ICE, Mumbai Exchange, Qatar, and Kuala Lumpur), and categories of participants; the prices have reflected the specifities of each commodity in its own right.

The same volatile market conditions across the spectrum of the three commodity classes – energy, metals, and agricultural – are unlikely to drastically change in the near future, with land becoming rare and water insufficient, disruptions occurring because of electricity shortages, geopolitical and social issues in a number of countries producing commodities, and the world population growth. A number of banks have closed their commodities desks at the time of writing, but private equity funds have joined commodity houses in the acquisition of physical assets such as gas storage facilities, soybean crushers or grain elevators that provide sure transformation revenues.

Looking back, one should keep in mind that the history of commodities has been filled with booms, busts, seasonal volatility, weather events, and geopolitical tensions. The physical constraints of delivery and storage make spot commodity trading difficult or impossible for ordinary investors, and transactions on commodity Futures exchanges can only be performed through a broker who is a member of the exchange. Today, instruments like ETFs (exchange-traded funds) are available to individual investors as well as trackers on a number of commodity indexes.

After the long period of nearly 20 years of stagnation in commodity prices, the years 2001 to 2008 experienced a spectacular growth in commodity trading, structured products, new index funds, as well as a greater activity in the shipping spot market and forward freight agreements, since more goods had to be transported to satisfy various needs across the planet. Amid these changes, Futures exchanges have kept their usefulness and financial stability across the last 160 years, exhibiting by their 'survival' the soundness of their operating rules. Table 3.1 lists a number of examples of commodity exchanges.

In a deal spanning Wall Street, Atlanta, and the financial centers in Europe, NYSE Euronext, which owns the 220-year-old New York Stock Exchange (and five exchanges in Europe),

Table 3.1   Some examples of commodity exchanges

NYMEX (New York, 1872)	Crude oil (WTI), natural gas, heating oil, propane, unleaded gasoline
IPE (1980) bought by ICE (2005)	Crude oil (Brent), natural gas
Nordpool, EEX, APX, Powernext, GMX, OMEL . . .	Electricity
LME (London, 1877) bought by Hong Kong Exchange (HKEX) COMEX, SHFE	Aluminum, copper, nickel, tin, lead, silver
London Bullion Exchange, CBOT, Mumbai, Dubai	Gold and silver
CBOT (Chicago, 1850), bought by CME	Corn, soybean, wheat, rice
CME (Chicago, 1898) now CME Group	Pork bellies, beef, lumber
Dubai Exchange, Kuala Lumpur, Bovespa IMEX (Qatar)	Middle East crude oil, gold, wheat, rubber, meat Liquid natural gas (LNG)

agreed in December 2012 to an $8.2 billion deal to sell itself to the Intercontinental Exchange. The combined company will have its headquarters in ICE's home of Atlanta and in New York.

The takeover underscores the continuing attraction of London's booming business in the trading of derivatives.

NYSE Euronext owns the London International Financial Futures and Options Exchange (LIFFE), itself modeled on the CBOT. NYSE Euronext is the product of a large-scale merger: in 2007, the NYSE, looking to ramp up its international profile and extend its electronic trading business, merged with Euronext, a collection of electronic stock trading hubs spread over Europe. NYSE Euronext currently operates exchanges in New York, London, Paris, Brussels, Amsterdam, and Lisbon.

ICE, an ambitious upstart trading center with a specialty in energy contracts and commodities, has tried for years to increase its exposure to derivatives in London and had tried an unsuccessful bid on the London Metal Exchange. The 136-year-old LME was finally bought in 2012 for $2 billion by the Hong Kong Stock Exchange.

ICE had also teamed up with NYSE Euronext's main rival, the NASDAQ OMX Group, in an $11 billion hostile takeover bid for NYSE Euronext but this one was finally blocked by the US Justice Department.

Some liquidity numbers on the exchanges
By the end of March 2014, the total open interest in the major commodity Futures was the following:

- $30 billion for the CBOT corn, where the 'total open interest' is the sum of the amount of open interest (pairs of positions held by a buyer/seller) in each contract multiplied by the price of this contract.
- $42 billion for CBOT soybeans; $13.7 billion for soybean meal; and $7.5 billion for soybean oil (these numbers show that soybean in its various forms is greatly traded).
- $12.7 billion for CBT wheat; $5.6 billion for KBT wheat; $2.6 billion for MGE wheat.
- $16.1 billion for raw sugar on the NYBOT/ICE.
- $8.3 billion for raw cotton on the NYBOT/ICE.
- $11.9 billion for coffee on the NYBOT/ICE.
- $21 billion for the CME Live Cattle.

3.2 FORWARD CONTRACTS

A forward contract written on a commodity (corn, for instance) is an agreement signed at date 0 between two parties A and B, according to which party A has the obligation to deliver at a fixed future date T a given quantity of the commodity, and B the obligation to take physical delivery of the commodity and pay A an amount $f(0, T)$ agreed upon at time 0 between the parties. T is called the maturity of the forward contract.

Note that later on, a new type of forward contracts came to existence, with a financial settlement based upon the value $S(T)$ of the underlying commodity at date T, feasible only in the case of the existence of a liquid, third-party estimated *index* for S.

Comments
1. In the above definition, party A is called the seller of the forward contract and will have to deliver the merchandise at maturity T; party B is called the buyer and will have to 'buy at date T,' i.e., take delivery and pay the amount $f(0, T)$ specified at date 0.
2. The value $f(0, T)$ is called the *forward price* at date 0, even though there is neither payment made at date 0 nor any exchange of cash flow. In the case where the forward contract is cleared by an exchange, it will require some collateral to be paid by both parties at date 0.
3. In the case of a plain OTC (over the counter) forward contract not cleared by an exchange, there is counterparty risk for both sides since the party who is losing money at date T may just disappear.
4. The forward contract may be customized to the needs of one party as long as the other agrees.
5. By no arbitrage between the spot and the forward markets, the following holds at maturity

$$f(T, T) = S(T)$$

A forward contract reaching maturity gives rise to immediate delivery and payment, hence is equivalent to a spot transaction.

6. What is more problematic is the *convergence* of the forward price $f(t, T)$ when t approaches T. If a continuity argument in t was valid, obviously $f(t, T)$ should converge to T. But there is no reason why we should expect this to hold for all commodities at all times. It is not true for electricity because the non-storability may create dramatic spikes in spot prices during weather events, these spikes being much milder in the forward market for obvious reasons. But for other commodities such as grains, where full information on spot prices is not always available, the convergence of the forward to spot may be quite abrupt at maturity T. Some market participants may be caught off guard if they wrongly believe this continuity has to hold, as it happened in the years 2012 and 2013 in the metals markets for metal consumers. Obviously, this convergence is highly desirable for the hedgers using forward and Future contracts.
7. Let's consider a farmer producing on average every year a quantity Q of corn. The harvest takes place in September but the farmer wants to order new machinery ahead of time making the harvest more efficient. He has (at least) two choices:
   – Do nothing in January, wait until September and sell his crops in the spot market, generating revenues equal to $Q.S(T)$. If the spot price at date T is very high, he will have plenty of dollars to buy his equipment and more. But if the harvest is plentiful and the spot price very low, he may not be able to afford a new machine. Hence, he might have been better off by hedging his revenues against the randomness of corn prices in September.

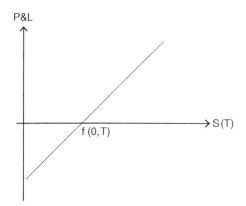

Figure 3.1   P&L at maturity T of a long forward position entered at date 0

- Sell at date 0 = Jan 2 a forward contract written on the quantity Q of corn, with maturity T = September 30 and a forward price $f(0, T)$ corresponding to his estimate of the fair value of his corn at date T, and such that a so-called speculator is willing to be the counterparty, namely the buyer.

We observe that in absence of a credit risk event on the part of the buyer of the forward contract, the farmer has locked in at date 0 a value of $f(0, T)$ dollars for his crops; this amount is received when the corn is delivered but the price was defined ahead of time at date 0, hence the name of forward price for $f(0, T)$. This activity of eliminating the randomness of asset prices involved in a given economic activity is called *hedging*. The benefit for the farmer of entering the forward contract at date 0 resides in the gained peace of mind that allows him to focus on better seeds or water-saving irrigation devices.

8. Regarding the speculator who had entered a long position at date 0, his profit or loss will be revealed at date T. At that time, he will pay $f(0, T)$, get delivery of the corn, and turn around and sell it in the spot market at the price $S(T)$, since he has no interest in holding corn and does not have a storage facility for it. Hence, the physical commodity comes and goes and his financial profit or loss is defined by the cash flows that took place at date T from the execution of the forward contract and the sale of corn in the spot market.
   Hence

$$\text{P\&L (long forward)} = S(T) - f(0, T)$$

This quantity is random prior to T – hence the risk involved in a speculative position – and is revealed at date T when $S(T)$ is observed. It will be positive if spot prices have risen between date 0 and date T, making the 'bet' of the speculator a correct one *ex post*. Moreover, the P&L being a linear function of $S(T)$, the underlying asset price at date T, the forward contract is called a *linear* instrument. (See Figure 3.1.)

Moreover, we see that except for trying to liquidate their position if some kind of secondary market existed, there is nothing for both parties to do to manage the forward contract, held long or short, during the period $(0, T)$ – for practical purposes, the purchase or sale of other forward contracts could nullify the position (if no credit risk exists in any of them). Hence, the main action was the 'right' choice of the number $f(0, T)$ at date 0. This is a key difference with options, where the price at date 0 matters but also the delta hedging of the position during the lifetime of the option. Since forward and Futures represent the main derivatives in the commodity markets (as it was the case 150 years ago), we will spend a large amount of time in this chapter and others discussing forward prices and all properties around them.

9. At date 0, the farmer may choose to also/alternatively enter a forward contract maturing 12 or 15 months down the road, if he has the storage facility for his harvested corn and is able to get a better price from the buyer. Hence, we see that many forward contracts may be signed at date 0 for different maturities T – and different prices. The collection of these prices $\{f(0, T)$ for $T = 1$ month, 2 months…1 year$\}$ is called the term structure of corn forward prices at date 0. Its graph is called the *forward curve*.

10. Economists (see for instance Hicks (1931) and Lucas (1992)) have proposed in the case of interest rates the *rational expectations hypothesis*, namely the hypothesis that the forward rate is a non-biased estimator of the spot rate observed at a future date, namely

$$f(t, T, h) = \text{Expec}\{R(T, h)/\text{Info at date } t\}$$

where $f(t, T, h)$ denotes the forward rate observed at date t for the period starting at date T with length h, $R(T, h)$ is the spot rate at date T for the time to maturity h, and the expectation is conditional on the observation available at date t. The relationship was tested in many economics papers and proven not to hold exactly, but up to a difference called a risk premium.

In the case of commodities, the same question naturally arises: can we state that the forward price observed today is an unbiased estimator of the spot price in the future? I.e.,

$$f(t, T) = \text{Expec}\{S(T)/\text{Info at date } t\}$$

Again, the equality does not hold exactly and the difference between the left-hand side and right-hand side is called the risk premium. It is positive when inventories are very low and buyers are prepared to pay a higher forward price than the price forecast. Hence, the rational expectations hypothesis expresses a valid economic intuition, but cannot be viewed as a strict equality. Let's note that the equality does hold if the expectation is computed under a probability measure that is adjusted for the commodity risk premium (and possibly the stochastic nature of interest rates; those interested in the corresponding technicalities may read, for instance, Geman (1989) or Geman (2006)). In all cases, the current forward curve contains the market expectations of future spot prices and deserves to be properly paid attention to.

3.3 FUTURES CONTRACTS

3.3.1 Definition

A Future contract is a forward contract traded on an exchange such as the CBOT, standardized in terms of traded maturities, quantity of the commodity underlying the Future contract, and giving rise to physical delivery by the seller at maturity. If the settlement is specified as financial, there must be a liquid reliable index to represent the underlying at date T (e.g., uranium Futures). Unlike an option, a Futures contains an obligation to buy (or sell).

1. For both the buyer and the seller, the counterparty is the Clearing House of the Exchange.
2. In order to avoid any credit event with the counterparty, the clearing house requires all exchange participants to pay a margin deposit at the start. This one can be paid in cash or Treasury bills; recently, some exchanges have started accepting gold.
3. *Margin calls* have to be paid/received every day: if a trader holds a long Future contract with maturity T, the value of his position has changed between date t and $t + 1$ day by

    $$F(t + 1 \text{ day}, T) - F(t, T)$$

    If this quantity is negative, a margin call equal to the loss has to be added to the account of the trader with the exchange, otherwise the position is closed and the margin deposit is used to offset the loss.
4. The value of the Future contract at all date t has to be posted by the exchange, and for all traded maturities. This brings *price transparency*, not only in the Futures markets, but also for future spot prices since the Futures price does express some forecast (up to a risk premium) on which the buyer and seller agree to settle.

    This transparency also explains why the *first nearby*, e.g., the Future with the shortest maturity, is chosen as a proxy for the spot price in the case of non-existence of a liquid index for the underlying commodity.
5. The Exchange must also provide information on
    – Daily traded volume.
    – *Open interest*, namely the number of contracts 'open' for a maturity T with a buyer and a seller at each end – important information to decide on the size of the order one may want to place, be it an order to sell or a buy order. The open interest is obviously one measure of the market depth.
    – Number of long and short positions held by 'hedgers,' so-called commercials.
    – Number of long and short positions held by non-commercials (obviously, across categories, there is always a buyer for a seller).
    – Amount of *inventory* held by the exchange (in fact its affiliated warehouses) in the given commodity.
6. The exchange must specify the type (Arabica versus Robusta for coffee) and grade of the commodity underlying the Future contract, as well as the grades acceptable for delivery at date T – in which case the seller will choose the least expensive one, exercising her *cheapest to deliver* option, meaning that she will choose the least expensive type accessible to her.
7. Termination of a Futures position: a Futures position can be closed by
    – Taking delivery of the goods according to rules specified by the exchange, each exchange *defining its warehousing and delivery rules.*
    – Entering a Futures position offsetting the existing one.
    – Contracting an *EFP.*

3.3.2 Exchange of Futures for physicals (EFP)

An EFP is an off-exchange (or 'ex pit') transaction in which a Future contract is exchanged for an actual physical good; in other words, an existing Futures position is swapped for a corresponding position in the underlying physical. The information is then transmitted to the exchange but EFPs are not part of the Futures market mechanism. The transaction is considered through a broker or directly between the parties.

EFP transactions take place for hundreds of thousands of contracts because both parties may benefit from them, for instance closing out a hedge position they do not need any more.

Without an EFP, the sale or purchase of a physical product and the separate entry into a Futures contract may result in 'price slippage' due to market volatility or fluctuating trading volume in the spot and/or Futures markets.

3.4 RELATIONSHIP BETWEEN FORWARD AND FUTURES PRICES

1. It is clear that at maturity T

$$F(T, T) = f(T, T) = S(T)$$

since a purchase in the spot, forward or Future markets would lead to immediate delivery, hence at the same price.

For the sake of comprehension, we will discuss in another paragraph the type of convergence that may take place when approaching expiry.

2. Now, a key question is obviously to compare the forward and Future prices at a date t such that $0 \leq t < T$.

A. Since counterparty risk is obviously a trait differentiating forward and Futures contracts, we will leave it aside in a first stage and consider a world with no credit risk. In this case, we have the remarkable following result.

Theorem

i. If we assume non-stochastic interest rates over the period $(0, T)$, then the forward and Future prices for the same underlying S and maturity T are equal:

$$F(0, T) = f(0, T)$$

ii. In the case of stochastic interest rates, the same remarkable result holds if the correlation between interest rates and the underlying S is zero.

Remarks

We can first observe that the first part of the theorem is fairly counterintuitive since forward contracts involve no intermediary cash flows and Futures involve daily margin calls.

Regarding the second part of the theorem, we note that agricultural commodity prices exhibit little correlation with interest rates and, in contrast to stocks, bonds or even crude oil, we may reasonably argue that we are in the (pleasant) situation where forward and Future prices are equal in the absence of credit risk. This will be our assumption in the rest of the book.

B. Incorporating counterparty risk.

If we turn now to the case where one of the two parties does not have a perfect risk profile – the real case in practice – the forward and Future prices won't be equal any more since only the former involves counterparty risk. In order to have an intuition of the result, we can take an example: a large company ABCD needs to buy corn, delivery eight months down the road. The firm ABCD has the choice between buying its corn on the CBOT at the price $F(0, 8$ months$)$ or buying it from a small farmer at the price $f(0, 8$ months$)$.

It is clear that in the latter case, ABCD will demand a lower price, arguing that a weather event may prevent the farmer from fulfilling delivery at maturity, with no backing solution.

Hence,

$$f(0, 8 \text{ months}) < F(0, 8 \text{ months})$$

In general, the inequality

$$f(t, T) < F(t, T)$$

will hold (or the other) whenever the buyer has a better (lower) risk profile and can *impose* his price on the seller.

For the rest of the book, we will consider the forward and Future prices to be equal, including for the construction of forward curves. Whenever counterparty risk comes into play, the reader will make the adjustment described in this section 2.B.

C. Comments
1.   We note accordingly that

$$f(T, T) - f(0, T) = F(T, T) - F(0, T) = S(T) - f(0, T) = \text{P\&L of a long forward}$$
$$\text{or Future position}$$

In the case of a forward contract, this P&L is paid or received in a single payment at maturity T.

For a Future contract, the same P&L is paid daily, along the formula

$$F(T, T) - F(0, T) = \{F(T, T) - F(T - 1\text{day}, T)\} + \{F(T - 1 \text{ day}, T) - F(T - 2\text{days}, T)\}$$
$$+ \dots + \{F(\text{day } 1, T) - F(0, T)\}$$

2. A direct consequence is the fact that the *forward curve* will be built using the visible prices of Futures contracts continuously posted by the exchange. Note that the contract with the shortest maturity is called the *prompt* month or first nearby.
3. As shown by the P&L of a long forward displayed earlier, the possible loss for the seller of a Future contract is unbounded.

Profit and loss (P&L) of a long Future position

This P&L of a long Future is fully revealed at date T and *marked to market* every day. Ignoring the impact of these daily margin calls – which is more than psychological in the case of a big market move since the fund may go under in the case of non-payment – it is the same linear function as the one displayed in the case of a forward position.

3.5 EXAMPLE OF A FUTURE SPREAD

Soybean (S), soybean meal (SM), and soy oil (SO) Futures have been traded for decades on the CBOT and the relationship between them is commonly referred to as the *crush spread*.

This crush spread used to be calculated in a 1:1:1 relationship. A long spread refers to buying the meal and oil and selling the beans, and owners of soybean crushing mills try to identify the periods when the spread is abnormally large to sell it and lock in their margin profits.

As of 1992, the CBOT changed the soy meal contracts specifications from 44% protein to 48% protein. As of that moment, the crush spread has been traded with 10 soybean, 9 soy oil, and 11 soy meal contracts.

In order to allow soybean refiners to lock in the margin generated by the transformation of soybean into soybean meal and soybean oil in a single trade, the CME introduced in 2009 a specific Future spread contract on the CME Globex, which can be traded in parallel to the individual Futures where the liquidity is obviously much greater.

Soybean crush Future contract specs

contract size	50,000 bushels
Price unit	Cents per bushel
Spread legs	To short the crush, long 10 soybeans – short 11 soybean meal – short 9 soybean oil
Contract months	January (F), March (H), May (K), July (N), August (Q), September (U), October (V), December (Z)
Settlement	Physical
Ticker symbol	SOM

Obviously, if a cross-commodity Future spread is not directly available, traders will get long and short on the exchange, making sure that there is consistency across the traded maturities not to add undesired risks to the position.

3.6 INVENTORY AND THEORY OF STORAGE

The role of inventory in explaining the shape of the forward curve in commodity markets is central in the theory of storage developed by Kaldor (1939) and Working (1949) and has since been documented in a vast body of literature, including the reference paper by Fama and French (1987). The adjusted spread of the forward curve relative to the first nearby was first defined by Working (1949), and its relationship to inventory later tested by Telser (1958) and Brennan (1958) in the context of several agricultural commodities. The Kaldor–Working hypothesis[1] states that the convenience yield depends inversely upon the level of inventories.

---

[1] Brennan (1958) is the first to call this hypothesis in reference to Kaldor (1939) and Working (1948, 1949).

Brennan (1959) found strong evidence for an inverse relationship between inventory level and convenience yield for gold, silver and copper, heating oil, lumber and plywood. The strength of this inverse dependency seems to increase with the consumption preference of the corresponding commodity.

The models considering the level of inventories in order to understand the behavior of commodity prices vary from equilibrium structural models to reduced-form models. Deaton and Laroque (1992) analyzed the link between the current price and the expectation of Futures prices at a given inventory level, looking at annual price data on 12 agricultural commodities, and they showed that the conditional variance of prices increases with the current price. Furthermore, Sorensen (2002) argued that the convenience yield can be understood as an inventory-dependent endogenous variable. Sorensen also points out that in a competitive rational expectations model of storage, when storage becomes low because of relative scarcity of the commodity available, convenience yields should be high.

Since low inventory should correspond to higher spot prices, which are in turn determined by higher convenience yields, one way to confirm (indirectly) the Kaldor–Working hypothesis is to evidence a significant positive linkage between spot prices and convenience yield.

In the economic literature on commodities, two important sets of results can be recognized: (1) the conjecture of normal backwardation proposed by Keynes (namely that commodity forward curves are most of the time backwardated), an issue we won't address since it has not prevailed in full generality for a number of years, with instead shapes of backwardation alternating with contango; (2) the theory of storage underpinned by two main concepts, the inventory and the convenience yield. The theory of storage is a pillar of the economic theory related to commodity spot and forward prices and allows us to extend the famous carry relationship prevailing for currencies or equity indexes. Brennan (1958) advocates that at any point in time, various economic agents carry stocks into the next period for valid reasons. His view that 'a supplier of storage is anyone who holds title to stocks with a view to their future sale, either in their present or in a modified form' encompasses a wide range of commodity markets from agricultural to metals or energy markets.

Keynes (1930) was the first one to study the relationship between inventory and the shape of the forward curve and exhibit a positive correlation between backwardation (i.e., a negative spread of the forward curve) and low inventory. Let us note that the spread, in contrast to inventory, has the merit of being readily available for all commodities traded on an exchange (which is the case for nearly all of them today). In a seminal paper, Fama and French (1987) took as a given the property of the spread being an adequate proxy for inventory. This allows them to analyze 21 commodities including metals, for which good inventory data were often missing in their period of analysis (and still difficult to identify today). Other authors (see for instance Williams and Wright (1991)) proceeded in the same manner.

Geman and Nguyen (2005) reconstructed a world database of soybean inventory and established a quasi-perfect affine relationship between *scarcity* defined as inverse inventory and spot price volatility. Analyzing a 15-year database of US oil and natural gas prices and inventory, Geman and Ohana (2009) adjusted the spread of Working (1949) by a choice of maturities that filter out seasonality and test the relationship between this spread and inventory in the context of natural gas in the US market, which has experienced a large liquidity in Futures contracts of distant maturities or many years.

Commodities are stored for several reasons:

- As a buffer against uneven or seasonal supply – agricultural commodities have been stored in silos for thousands of years.
- As a reserve against uneven demand, the case of most energy commodities, which are typically used more in winter for heating.
- As a hedge against any other supply or logistical disruption, which would otherwise necessitate the expensive pause of an industrial process.
- In recent years, for investment purposes within physically-backed ETFs.
- For cash and carry strategies described later.

The theory of storage applies to any commodity that can be physically stored and makes two main predictions, both related to the quantity of the commodity held in inventory (also known as stocks). When there is a situation of scarcity, i.e., low inventory, spot prices will rise as purchasers bid whatever is necessary to secure supply.

The effect will be less pronounced in longer-term Futures, since market participants know that higher prices will, in the long term, stimulate increased supply and allow for a rebuilding of inventory. The effect of *spot price* > *Futures price* can be pronounced and is known as 'backwardation.'

Conversely, when supplies are ample, spot prices can become depressed respective to Futures prices. However, this effect, with *spot price* < *Futures price*, termed 'contango,' is usually less pronounced. At a certain point, the possibility of so-called 'cash and carry arbitrage' emerges, whereby a risk-free profit can be obtained by buying the commodity in the spot market, simultaneously selling a Futures contract at a higher price, and storing ('carrying') the commodity until the delivery date of the Futures contract. This possibility limits the degree of contango for storable commodities. This effect is asymmetrical – we cannot move a quantity of commodity from the future to the present, therefore there is no economic limit on the strength of backwardation imposed by storage. However, given sufficiently high spot prices, some consumers will cancel or postpone their demand, or possibly substitute their demand to another commodity. This economic argument provides some limit to the strength of backwardation. (See Figures 3.2 and 3.3 for examples of the shapes of backwardation and contango.)

3.6.1 Spot and Futures prices volatilities

In conditions of scarcity, not only will spot prices be elevated, but they will also experience elevated volatility. This is because in a tight market, any news about short-term supply, demand or inventory will have a large impact on the spot market. However, there should be little corresponding rise in the volatility of long-term Futures contracts, whose prices mainly respond to longer-term news.

In conditions of abundance, this effect will disappear, and there will be no pronounced difference between the volatility of spot and Futures prices.

We note that in general, the so-called 'Samuelson effect' states that commodity Futures become more volatile as they approach maturity, although unlike the theory of storage, it does not mention that such conditions mainly apply during scarcity. We might expect that spot price volatility will almost always exceed Futures price volatility, since long-term prices mainly respond to long-term news, whereas short-term prices should respond to both short *and* long-term news.

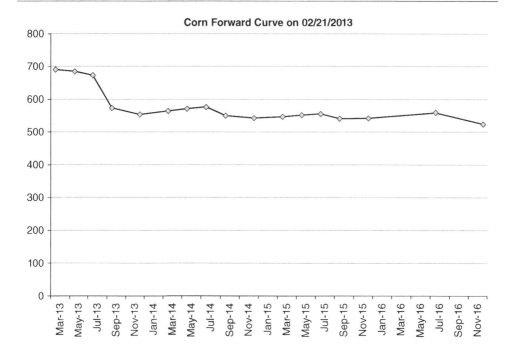

Figure 3.2   Example of a backwardated shape observed in corn in February 2013 (spot at $700)

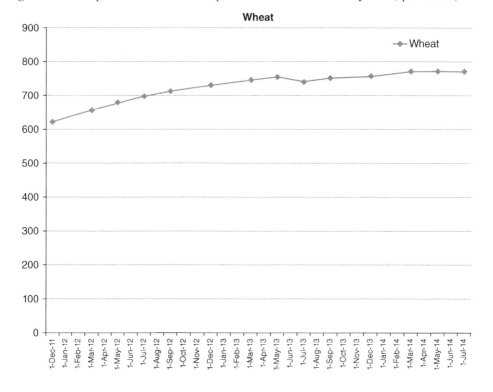

Figure 3.3   Example of a contango shape in wheat observed in December 2011 (spot around $615)

3.6.2 Development of the theory of storage: inventory and prices

We describe below the key steps of the theory of storage, which was established at the beginning for agricultural commodities.

We attribute the initial development of the theory of storage to Holbrook Working. In 1927, he was a researcher at the recently established 'Food Research Institute' of Stanford University. The institute decided to focus on wheat because of its great importance as a world staple food. Little was formally known about the large fluctuations in the prices of wheat Futures. Working theorized that the inventory levels of wheat, in particular the 'year-end carryover,' i.e., the inventory still existing at the end of one 'harvest year' just prior to the arrival of the new harvest, would be instrumental in understanding the behavior of wheat prices. Since reliable wheat inventory data, or indeed inventory data of any commodity, had not been collated and aggregated up to this date, Working and the Food Research Institute began to record new data and research previous years (Working, 1949). By 1933, Working had sufficient inventory data, and in two profoundly important but rarely cited papers (Working, 1948, 1953), he laid out in detail the concepts of the theory of storage, based on his empirical research on wheat. In the first paper, he described in detail the Futures markets in wheat and calculated price spreads between nearby and distant Futures. The US wheat harvest occurs mainly from June to August, with the harvesting peaking in July. During the months of June and July, before the harvest had been transported to market, shortages of wheat sometimes developed. By September, the harvest was complete and for a time there was abundance. Working plotted the July–September spread (comparing pre- and post-harvest prices), as observed in June, computed as F(June, September) – F(June, July) against the year-end inventory (as 'deviation from the normal'). A clear pattern emerged: in years of shortage, i.e., low inventory, the price of July Futures were much higher than September Futures, resulting in a negative spread. In years with no shortage, September Futures were slightly more expensive, by an amount roughly equivalent to the additional cost of storing wheat for two months. As well as this central result, Working also documented some other interesting features of Futures markets:

- Information affecting next year's harvest (i.e., long-term information) causes equal change in prices for July and September, resulting in no changes in the corresponding spread. Conversely, short-term information about this year's harvest affects short-term prices (July) more than long-term prices (September).
- The average weekly changes in price of July wheat (what we would now call weekly volatility) vary more and more as harvest approaches.
- In situations of scarcity, when July wheat rises in price over September, its volatility also rises greatly compared with situations of abundance (a feature exhibited for US crude oil and natural gas by Geman and Ohana (2009)).

In the second paper, Working (1953) continued developing the theory of storage. He noted that representing the spread as a percentage rather than a dollar amount, to facilitate comparison across long time periods, did not diminish the relationship. He also noticed the spread built up as harvest time approached, because a situation of impending scarcity or abundance only became clear towards the end of the crop year. Finally, he devoted some attention to years that deviated from the usual trend, showing that 'corners' and 'squeezes' had occurred in those years, whereby inventory was bought and withheld from the market by a single participant with the aim of distorting the market for profit, thus the market functioned as though that inventory did not exist.

Further development of the theory of storage was made by Kaldor (1939). Since Working's groundbreaking work was only published in the journal of his employer, the 'Wheat Studies of the Food Research Institute,' Kaldor was perhaps unaware of it but did not reference it. Kaldor noted that during backwardation, holding a physical position seems, at first glance, to be illogical, when it is clear from the Futures market that prices are expected to fall. Why not simply buy later at a lower price, or buy a long-dated Future rather than buy in the spot market? He coined the term 'convenience yield,' i.e., the convenience or benefit derived from holding the physical commodity rather than a paper Futures contract, which could be measured as a percentage yield (as proposed by Working), which the holder of the physical asset implicitly receives to offset the decline in price. Often the theory of storage is initially credited to Kaldor (Fama and French, 1987; Brennan, 1958; and others). We believe that much belated credit is mainly due to Working, partly because he 'got there first,' and partly because Working explicitly plots graphically the relationship between spread and inventory, whereas Kaldor only discusses the relationship in general qualitative terms.

Brennan (1958) contributed further to the development of the theory of storage. He took empirical data for a number of agricultural commodities (eggs, cheese, butter, wheat, and oats) over a period of years, and showed that the Working curve was observed in many markets. Whereas Working had framed the theory in terms of yearly observations, Brennan noted that it held at all times, using monthly observations. Further evidence to support the Working curve has been found over the years in a range of commodities, such as heating oil, copper, lumber (Pindyck, 1994), and soybeans (see Geman and Nguyen (2005)).

3.7 THE BENEFITS OF FORWARD CURVES

The list of benefits of forward curves for commodity producers, consumers, and traders is quite long, in particular since each point represents a forward price with the messages it contains as described in the previous sections. For a short summary, we can identify:

- Benchmark for valuation and marking to market
- Deal pricing
- P&L
- Internal consistency of the desk with other derivatives and physical commodity positions.

3.7.1 Trading strategies around forward curves

- The set $\{F(t, T), T > t\}$ is the forward curve prevailing at date t for a given commodity in a given location.
- It is the fundamental tool when trading commodities, as spot prices may be unobservable and options not always liquid.

- In the case of a steep contango, it allows one to exhibit an arbitrage trade by buying the spot commodity at date 0, selling a Future with maturity T and paying storage and cost of financing at maturity T while securing a sure profit at date 0 if the difference (Future – spot) is large.
- The shape of the forward curve is at any date t in a one-to-one mapping with the convenience yield, at least in a first approximation and in case of no seasonality.
- It reflects the seasonality for commodities such as natural gas or agriculturals and allows traders to build strategies based on calendar spreads, either static or dynamic.

3.7.2 Example of a seasonality-based Futures spread

Some opportunities in the commodity Futures markets have short option-like payoff profiles. One example is related to weather-fear premia strategies (see Till (2008)). In these trades, which can be found in the grain and tropical soft Futures markets, a Future price is systematically priced too high relative to where it eventually matures. This occurs before a time of unpredictable weather such as the Brazilian winter or summertime in the US Midwest and Northeast. In the case of the Brazilian winter, an extreme frost can damage Brazil's coffee trees (like in 2011). In the case of the US summertime, an exceptional heatwave can impair corn pollination prospects.

Over long periods of time, it has been profitable to be short these commodity markets during the time of maximum weather uncertainty. But during rare instances, these strategies can have very large losses, which create classic short options profiles.

If one includes short option-like strategies in a Futures portfolio, then the sizing of these trades needs to be reduced compared to the sizing of trades with long option-like profiles in order to preserve the program's overall long optionality and not be exposed to the large risk left open with final short option positions.

Bear calendar spreads in physically-settled commodity Futures markets typically have these short options profiles. In times of scarcity for a commodity, market participants will pay extremely high prices for the immediately deliverable contract, meaning that a rally will only substantially benefit the front-month price rather than later-month maturities. In extreme cases of scarcity, the front-month contract's price can become disconnected from the values of the rest of the commodity's Futures curve. If a trader is short the front-month contract and long a later-month maturity, then that trader is at risk of this scenario. In other words, a bear-calendar spread puts one at risk of extreme losses.

Miltersen and Schwartz (1998) noted how during 2006, wheat Futures traders at the Chicago Board of Trade had assumed there was 'free money' in establishing bear-calendar spreads prior to commodity-index roll dates. Unlike an equity index, one unique aspect of a commodity Futures index is that its precise rules need to specify on what dates each of its contracts have to be rolled before the maturity of each contract (see Chapter 14, the section on commodity indexes). These rules are known as 'roll rules.' The rules specify when a particular index constituent should be sold and a further-maturity contract should be bought. In advance of such a procedure, wheat speculators had historically sold the front-month while buying the next-month contract, establishing a bear-calendar spread. They would then unwind this position during index roll dates. Miltersen and Schwartz (1998) wrote that this strategy suffered during the fall of 2006 'when a [wheat] supply disruption in Australia caused sharp reversals in wheat spreads: certain calendar wheat spreads moved substantially against the speculative spreaders in a week.'

They reported that 'the use of bear calendars this way can be compared to an options writing strategy, which can offer consistent profits until one huge spike in volatility can wipe out months of profits and more.'

Remark
In the case of non-integrated markets for a given commodity, one can trade Futures *locational spreads*, using in both locations short-maturity Futures contracts accounting for the cost and time of transportation. Another possibility is to use the notion of distance between forward curves (as defined by Geman and Liu (2014) in the case of natural gas and LNG) to identify the *distance* between the forward curves beyond the maturities of heavy trading and enter profitable medium-term forward contracts. Obviously, all strategies of interest exhibited in the world of energy and metals should be reconsidered for agricultural commodities.

3.7.3 From linear to convex payoffs

A long position in a forward contract requires no payment at date 0 but may lead to a loss at maturity as represented by the dotted line in the graph in Figure 3.4 (which we saw previously) when the underlying S at maturity T has a value lower than $F(0, T)$; hence, the idea of introducing an instrument called a call option on S, with the same payoff profile, except that the loss is replaced by zero; in other words,

$$C(T) = \text{Max}(0, S(T) - k) \text{ , where } k = F(0, T)$$

This instrument gives its buyer the comfort of an outcome that is never bad at date T, while keeping the profits made in rising markets; hence, the success of call options. By no arbitrage, one has now to pay money at date 0 to purchase it. The identification of the 'fair' value of $C(0)$ is not straightforward and has been established in the models of Bachelier (1900) and Black–Scholes–Merton (1973). This important subject will be discussed in the next chapter.

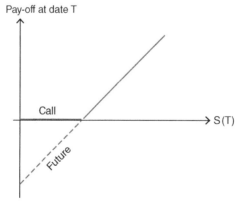

Figure 3.4 Dotted line showing the loss at maturity of a long position in a forward contract with no payment at date 0

3.8 STOCHASTIC MODELING OF THE FORWARD CURVE

For several centuries, commodity forward/Futures markets have been the main place of commodity trading – the Chicago Board of Trade was established in 1848 and the London Metal Exchange in 1877 – since they allow producers and manufacturers to manage commodity price risk. Market participants use all available maturities as long as they offer liquidity, and like in the world of interest rates, the term structure of forward prices $f(t, T)$ prevailing at date t for the different maturities T is a crucial object of analysis. Calendar-spread Futures represent a standard instrument when trading seasonal commodities.

These 'pairs' are used across the spectrum of seasonal commodities; the other standard trades are cross-commodities positions like spreads between copper and tin, platinum and palladium, sugar corn and ethanol, or crack-spreads between crude oil and gasoline or another oil refined product.

Forward curves are of great importance in commodity markets for multiple reasons. They provide information about the views of the market at future dates (the 'price discovery' property of Futures prices, which has long been discussed in the economic literature), anticipated trends, and information about future supply and demand. Forward prices are also essential for marking to market books of existing positions in Futures as well as for risk management activities such as Value at Risk calculations. Forward commodity prices influence storage, production, and other strategic decisions of oil companies and mining giants. Finally, Futures contracts provide the data to which the 'pricing measure' should be calibrated for the pricing of physical and financial options, as they are the liquid instruments. Note that we use in an equivalent manner the terminology 'forward' and 'Future.' We saw before that, in the absence of credit risk, one can prove (see for instance Geman (2006) for a simple proof) that forward and Future prices are equal, despite the presence of margin calls in the latter case, as long as interest rates are non-stochastic or non-correlated to the commodity price. We argue that the second assumption is quite acceptable in the space of agricultural commodities.

The Theory of Storage as introduced by Keynes (1936) and Working (1949) establishes that the preference for the ownership of the physical commodity instead of a forward contract written on it – thus ensuring a non-disruption of the production chain for a manufacturer in the case of a shock in the supply of copper for instance – can be represented by a quantity analogous to a dividend yield for a stock and called a convenience yield. Then, by no arbitrage arguments similar to those used in the FX markets, one can show that the forward price prevailing at date t for the maturity T is related to the spot price $S(t)$ through the carry relationship, where r denotes the cost of financing over the period (t, T) and y denotes the convenience yield net of storage costs:

$$f^T(t) = S(t)e^{(r-y)(T-t)}$$

When $(r - y)$ is negative, the forward curve is decreasing with T (backwardated); if $(r - y)$ is positive, forward prices increase with T and may offer some carry arbitrage opportunities if the contango is steep enough. For instance, the wheat forward curve depicted in Figure 3.5 and prevailing on September 15, 2011 – a year where interest rates were very low worldwide – shows that by buying the wheat spot using a loan, leasing part of a silo to store it, and selling a forward contract maturing in October 2012, one could generate a sure profit at maturity after receiving the forward price and repaying the loan with accrued interest and the lease rate.

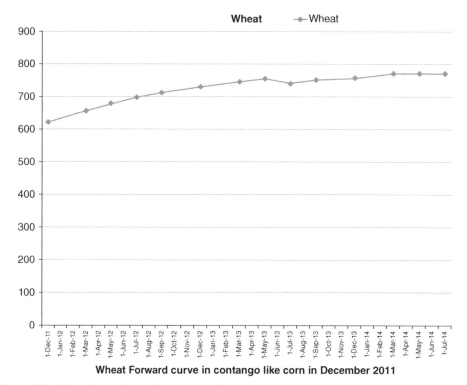

Figure 3.5   Wheat forward curve in contango like corn in December 2011

To offer an alternative to the classical approach consisting in deriving the whole forward curve evolution from the spot price dynamics ($S(t)$) – which may not be the most appropriate in some commodity markets, in particular those where the spot price is opaque or susceptible to manipulations and squeezes – Borovkova and Geman (2006), when analyzing the risk management of a book of forward contracts (long or short, with different maturities), propose an original model consisting in replacing the spot price as the first state variable by the average value $\bar{f}(t)$ of all liquid monthly forward contracts maturing up to date H, with H a multiple of 12 to properly incorporate the seasonality in the case of natural gas and agricultural commodities.

Now $\bar{f}(t)$, the 'backbone' of the forward curve – a key quantity indicating in which domain all forward contracts trade, which is also the one at stake in a swap contract ending at date H or an Asian option with maturity H, as we shall see in Chapter 5 – becomes the *numéraire* with respect to which all forward prices are written and the cost-of-carry relationship becomes

$$f^T(t) = \bar{f}(t)\exp[s(T) - (T - t)\gamma(t, T)]$$

where $s(T)$, $T = 1, 2 \ldots 12$ are the deterministic components of the relative cost of carry accounting for seasonality (if it exists), and obviously expressed as an absolute quantity (for instance, the month of January effect) and $\gamma(t, T)$ is the *rate of cost of carry* (including financing, convenience yield, and storage cost) relative to $\bar{f}$, assumed to be stochastic in t and deterministic in T (the latter assumption being possibly relaxed). The aggregation of $\gamma\,(t,\,T)$ and $s(t,\,T)$ accounts for the 'traditional' cost of carry relative to $\bar{f}$.

Note that the relationship between $\bar{f}$ and f^T holds by definition of $s(T)$ and $\gamma\,(t,\,T)$. Borovkova and Geman (2006) show the validity of the model using data relative to seasonal (natural gas) and non-seasonal (crude oil) commodities, and exhibit the property that the volatility of $\gamma\,(t,\,T)$ decreases in T, an interesting extension of the Samuelson effect. The average forward price $\bar{f}$ may also be obtained as the first component in a principal component analysis of the forward curve. It can be modeled by a diffusion, mean-reverting or not; the term structure of the $\gamma\,(t,\,T)$ can be driven by a uni- or multidimensional Brownian motion.

The use of $\bar{f}$ as the reference price when trading a book of forward contracts can arguably be quite relevant in the case of agricultural commodities for which the spot price is not observable or unreliable.

Geman and Sarfo (2012) used this model to analyze cocoa forward curves and exhibit a number of interesting properties, one of them being the quasi-absence of seasonality in cocoa prices; another, the benefits provided by cocoa-linked bonds issued to investors by cocoa-producing countries.

A granite statue representing Agriculture, greeting commodity traders at the entrance of the CBOT

4

Plain Vanilla Options on Commodity Spot and Forward Prices. The Bachelier–Black–Scholes Formula, the Merton Formula, the Black Formula

'The pricing formula will become a self-fulfilling prophecy.'
1973 – Robert Merton, Nobel Prize winner 1997

4.1 INTRODUCTION

Some technicalities in this chapter may be skipped. However, a few properties deserve to be emphasized in this Chapter because of their economic importance.

An option is a financial security granting its holder the right (but not the obligation) to buy (or sell) a given asset or commodity, called the underlying, at a predetermined price, called the 'strike' of the option, or at a given date, called the 'maturity' of the option. This unique exercise date can be chosen at any moment prior to maturity in the case of American options.

Hence, the characteristics of the option may be summarized as follows:

- Underlying asset: stock, stock index, currency, bond, commodity, etc. (denoted as S).
- Option type: call C or put P.
- Position type: buyer (long) or seller (short).
- Strike price: purchase or selling price guaranteed by the ownership of the option (denoted as k).
- Inception date: day on which the option is 'written' by the seller.
- Maturity date: or expiration date (denoted T in what follows); day on which the option may be exercised (European option) or last day of the exercise interval in the case of an American option.
- Option price: or premium, denoted $C(0)$ for the call and $P(0)$ for the put.

Indeed, two categories of options may be identified at the start: the European options, which may only be exercised at maturity, and the American options, which may be exercised on any business day during the lifetime of the option.

Another characteristic of the option, particularly important in the case of commodity markets, is the way the contract is settled: the buyer of the option may wish to take *physical delivery* of the underlying upon payment of the strike at maturity; in the case of commodities such as oil, where different grades exist, the exact type of the commodity will be specified in the option contract, as it is done for Futures contracts. Or the option contract may be financially settled, using for instance the last quoted price of the underlying asset at maturity. Index options – the index may be an equity index, a commodity index or an inflation index – are always financially settled, and according to our previous notation, the buyer of the call receives the cash flow max(0, $S_T - k$) where S_T is the value of the index at maturity. The notation 'max' classically represents the bigger of two quantities.

In this chapter, the founding results will first be established for stocks as underlyings, and then extended to commodities. The graphs and strategies displayed below hold, of course, for both. We can represent in simple graphs the payoff C_T and P_T of European call and European put options at maturity as a function of the underlying asset price S_T.

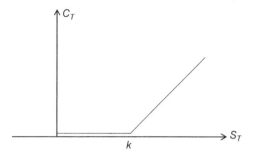

We have observed that a position in a forward contract requires no upfront payment but may lead to a very negative payoff at date T.

A call option bought at date 0 on the same underlying requires an upfront payment of C(0) but provides the holder with the 'comfort' of a non-negative payoff at date T:

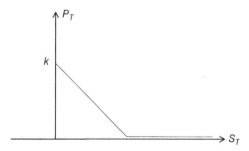

It is clear (and will be discussed in many ways further on) that the price at date 0 of the call (or put) is a positive number $C(0)$ (respect $P(0)$): by no arbitrage, in order to get a payout that is zero or strictly positive, a positive premium has to be paid at date 0.

Hence, the algebraic gain profile or P&L for the buyer of a call option between the dates 0 and T may be represented as follows:

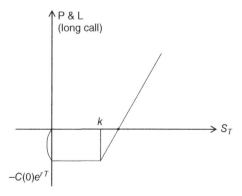

This graph is obtained from that of the call payoff by a downward translation of magnitude $C(0)e^{rT}$ since $C(0)$, the price paid by the buyer at date 0, must be augmented by accrued interest (represented by e^{rT} in continuous time) in order to be compared to the price S_T of the underlying asset at date T expressed in dollars of day T. Since there is a zero-sum game between the buyer and the seller, the P&L of the call seller is obtained by symmetry with respect to the horizontal axis.

We show below the P&L generated by a long position in a put bought at date 0:

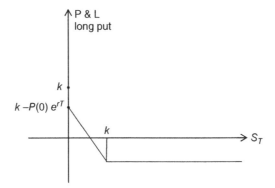

as well as the P&L of the short call and the short put:

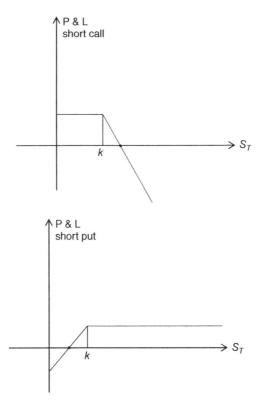

1. A market participant who anticipates an appreciation of the underlying asset will buy a call or sell a put; conversely, he will short the call or buy the put if he foresees a decline of S.
2. Out of the four P&L graphs, there is only one where the loss may be infinite: it is the short position in a call option. For practical purposes, this short position will always be hedged – using one of several possibilities that will be discussed in Section 4.4 – since no trader can leave open a position that may take the firm to bankruptcy.

4.2 CLASSICAL STRATEGIES INVOLVING EUROPEAN CALLS AND PUTS

Both because investors want to be able to bet on a more precise evolution of the underlying stock, or because hedgers who need to buy options try to spend as little money as possible, strategies involving combinations of long and short positions in calls and puts have become quite familiar now and some of them, with no goal of exhaustivity, are presented below.

4.2.1 Straddle

A long straddle consists in the simultaneous purchase of a call and put on the same underlying, with the same strike and maturity; the strike is most often chosen close to the current value of the underlying.

The investor has to pay both option premia but, in exchange, will benefit from the rise and the decline of the underlying:

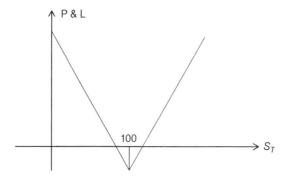

This strategy is appropriate if one anticipates a large move, upward or downward, of the underlying. It is a losing strategy in the case of 'flat markets,' the maximum loss being equal to the sum of the two option premia, with accrued interest. In the case of a short position in a straddle (i.e., anticipation of low volatility and small market moves), the loss may be massive in the case of big changes in the underlying price.

4.2.2 Strangle

A long strangle consists in the simultaneous purchase of a put with strike k_1 and a call with strike k_2, same maturity and $k_1 < k_2$:

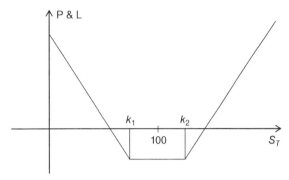

The investor buying a strangle anticipates a large move, upward or downward, of the underlying asset, either of them triggering a significant payoff of the call or put at maturity, at the cost of paying the premium of two options at date 0.

4.2.3 Call spread or vertical call spread

This consists in the purchase of a long call with strike k_1 and a short call with strike k_2, where $k_1 < k_2$, and same maturity. Since a call with a lower strike has a higher price at time 0, a long call spread has a positive premium equal to the difference between the two call prices and the P&L profile at maturity is the following:

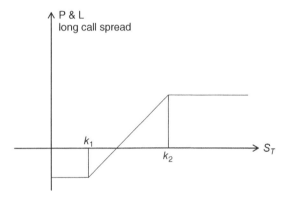

These instruments are very popular in the agri-insurance and reinsurance and weather derivatives market: the fact that the potential loss is bounded both for the buyer and the seller is a feature meant to encourage the existence of many sellers – in particular in markets where the fair value of the option is not easy to determine (see Section 4.4 for more details on market 'incompleteness') – as their loss at maturity is bounded, in contrast to just selling a call. It is easy to show that a vertical call spread is also a capped call, i.e., a call whose payoff at maturity is bounded by a constant A specified at inception of the contract; in our example $A = k_2 - k_1$. Finally, it is the difference between two calls, one with strike k_1, and the other with strike k_2 greater than k_1; hence, it has a positive value.

A *calendar spread* is the equivalent instrument, where the strike is replaced by maturity, i.e., the combination of a long call with maturity T_1 and a short call with maturity T_2, where $T_1 < T_2$, and the strike k is the same. Buyers and sellers of calendar spreads are taking views on a given *temporal* evolution of the underlying asset. This calendar spread is similar in use but not identical to the forward start option discussed in the next chapter.

4.2.4 Butterfly spread

This is a very popular strategy, resulting from the combination of a long call spread and a short one, involving in total three strikes k_1, k_2, and k_3, where $k_3 - k_2 = k_2 - k_1$. Equivalently, it consists in the purchase of two calls with strike k_2 and the sale of a call with strike k_1 and a call with strike k_2.

The P&L of a short butterfly spread at maturity has the following profile and expresses that the holder of such a position anticipates small moves of the underlying S during the lifetime of the option:

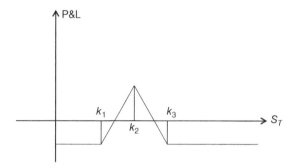

4.3 PUT–CALL PARITY FOR A NON-DIVIDEND PAYING STOCK

Before turning to the valuation at date 0 of the different European calls and puts involved in the above strategies, we are going to establish a result that requires *no assumption on the dynamics of the underlying asset price* as it is a static replication argument, which leads to the famous put–call parity. Its existence will reduce the problem of pricing calls and puts to the one of pricing calls. The main assumption, central in this book and in the theory of option pricing, was already discussed in the context of forwards and Futures and is the no-arbitrage assumption. In order to prove the put–call parity, we make the following assumptions (some of them will be relaxed later in the book):

A$_1$: No taxes, no transaction costs: 'frictionless markets.'

A$_2$: The underlying stock pays no dividend over the lifetime [0, T] of the option.

A$_3$: Interest rates are constant; r denotes the continuously compounded rate.

A$_4$: There are no arbitrage opportunities: with a zero initial wealth *and* taking no risk at date 0, the final wealth will be surely zero at date T.

Then, at date t, the European put P, which has the same strike k, maturity T, and same underlying S as the European call C has a price $P(t)$ related to $C(t)$ through the fundamental relationship

$$P(t) + S(t) = C(t) + ke^{-r(T-t)} \qquad (4.1)$$

where t is any date prior or equal to the maturity T.

Proof
Let us build the following position at date t: buy the stock S, buy the put P, and sell the call. The cash flows involved will be $-S(t)$, $-P(t)$, $+C(t)$. Since there are no dividend payments and the options are European, there is *no intermediate cash flow* until maturity T. At date T, the options expire and the stock is sold in order to liquidate the whole position.

This position over the interval (t, T) can be represented by Table 4.1.

Table 4.1 Position over the interval (t, T)

	t	T	
		$S(T) < k$	$S(T) \geq k$
buy the stock	$-S(t)$	$S(T)$	$S(T)$
buy the put	$-P(t)$	$k - S(T)$	0
sell the call	$+C(t)$	0	$-[S(T) - k]$
		k	k

At date T, the final payoffs of the call and the put depend on the stock being higher or lower than k. What is remarkable is that in all states of the world, the total value $V(T)$ of the position at date T is equal to k. Since it has the merit of having a terminal value independent of $S(T)$ – hence contains *no randomness* viewed from date t – the position is *riskless*[1].

Since it is riskless, involves no intermediary payment, and has a final value of k dollars at date T, building it at date t requires an initial outflow of $ke^{-r(T-t)}$ dollars, which is also the sum of the numbers in the first column:

$$-S(t) - P(t) + C(t) = -ke^{-r(T-t)}$$

and the put–call parity is established.

Note that the proof is exemplary in its simplicity, and does not require at any point the specification of the dynamics of S, such as continuous trajectories versus the possibility of jumps over the time interval $[t, T]$. Whenever it is feasible to use such arguments in order to prove a result or build a strategy, one should be happy to do so; unfortunately, this setting will be rare. Traders do try to identify such situations in practice as it does not involve any *dynamic trading*. The put–call parity expresses that a portfolio consisting of a stock and a European put can be *statically* replicated by a call and a position in the money-market account M. This money-market account is *the* riskless asset in the situation of constant interest rates (which will be our assumption in general) and grows at the continuously compounded rate r.

We also want to observe that, at date T, a portfolio P' comprising the commodity S and a put written on it has a final value equal to the sum of the components' market prices at date T:

$$S(T) + P(T) = S(T) + \max(0, k - S(T)) \tag{4.2}$$
$$= \max(S(T), k)$$

---

[1] For the author, *risk means randomness*, or equivalently a strictly positive variance for the value of a position at a future T. By definition, today is known since fully revealed, except in the case of opaque markets. Tomorrow is risky, except for a position carefully built today in order to eliminate all sources of randomness, in which case the position deserves the title of *riskless*; by no arbitrage, the return on a riskless position cannot be lower or greater than the risk-free rate.

If the stock (commodity) market goes up between dates t and T, $S(T)$ is very high; the maximum of the two quantities will be $S(T)$ and the investor will have benefited from the rise in prices. Conversely, if markets crash, $S(T)$ is very low and the maximum will be equal to k.

Hence, instead of collapsing to zero as it would have if the portfolio P' had contained only S, the investor's wealth is equal to k. This simple but fundamental use of put options is called *portfolio insurance*, the put providing a protection against down moves. As of now, it is important to remember the rule *call for positive exposure, put for protection*.

Formula (4.2) satisfies the first two fundamental motivations of any investor:

1. Benefiting from a market rise if it occurs, which may also be expressed by a wealth utility with a strictly positive derivative.
2. Limiting his losses to reach a minimal wealth of k dollars in the case of a market decline. This floor satisfies the investor's risk aversion, a feature that has been exhibited in experiments conducted for a long time by sociologists and economists; risk aversion may be expressed by a concave utility function U (i.e., U has a negative second derivative).

Many equity products have been proposed along these lines to investors wishing to be part of a rise in stock prices without losing everything in the case of a bear market; unsurprisingly, these products have been/are very successful. It is clear that similar positions can be built with commodities and are being offered in commodity structured products; they will be discussed again in the last chapter. Note that for the desk that is selling the product P', the difficulty will be to hedge over the interval (t, T) the call held in a short position (or the long put); hence, for the bank, an assumption needs to be made on the dynamics of the spot price S of the commodity during the lifetime of the structured product. This is why the structured notes won't be issued for a maturity beyond three years, and still the choice of an appropriate model is challenging.

4.4 VALUATION OF EUROPEAN CALLS: THE BACHELIER–BLACK–SCHOLES FORMULA AND THE GREEKS

This section could cover hundreds of pages if we wanted to account for all valuable papers written on the subject since the early 1970s. We will limit ourselves, however, to the famous Black–Scholes model and will discuss a number of extensions later in this chapter and throughout the book.

Goal:
Price today the right to exchange at a fixed maturity T the amount of k dollars for the delivery of the asset S – hence, the reference problem is already the valuation of an *exchange* option, namely the right to exchange at a future date an amount of k units of a *numéraire* currency for an asset S that may be a stock, a bond or a commodity.

For this endeavor, the sole use of the no arbitrage assumption does not suffice and one needs a larger set of assumptions, namely a *model*. The first version was first produced by the French mathematician Bachelier. In his 1900 dissertation entitled 'Théorie de la speculation,' he introduced the *definition* of calls and puts and proposed to price them as *derivatives* from the underlying asset, making the dynamics of the underlying asset a key assumption in the model.

His single error was to choose for the spot price a stochastic process allowing for negative values.

The model presented below was developed in the parallel papers of Black–Scholes (1973) and Merton (1973). The model immediately became 'a self-fulfilling prophecy,' to quote the third author, because the assumptions were in alignment with the developments of the portfolio theory (Markowitz, 1958) and Capital Asset Pricing Model (Sharpe, 1964); because the derived formula was explicit, hence could be successively incorporated in calculators, computer software or iPhones; and more importantly because the assumptions of the model led to a *unique* price. When the price is uniquely recognized by the buyer and the seller of the call option, they can have a trade. The gigantic number of transactions made possible by the formula, in particular by hedgers who liked the protection provided by options versus Futures, was precisely recognized in the minutes of the Nobel committee who gave a Nobel Prize in 1997 to Merton and Scholes (naming also the late Fischer Black). The uniqueness of the price results from the market *completeness* resulting from the model (*two* non-redundant primitive securities continuously traded in a liquid market and a *single* source of risk represented by a 'well-behaved' source of randomness called a Brownian motion) and was not discussed in the early years as much as it deserved to be. This may have avoided the credit derivatives crisis and, later on, some gigantic losses experienced by traders who suddenly 'recognized' the non-uniqueness of the value of their position, making the market totally illiquid!

The assumptions (which include those used for the put–call parity) are listed below and will be discussed with respect to their extension to commodities:

   A1 Trading in the underlying stock takes place continuously.

   A2 Taxes and transaction costs are supposed to be negligible.

   A3 The underlying stock pays no dividend over the lifetime [0, *T*] of the option.

   A4 Interest rates are constant over the lifetime [0, *T*] of the option and will denote the continuously compounded rate.

   A5 There are no arbitrage opportunities in the markets.

   A6 The dynamics of the underlying stock price *S* are driven by the stochastic differential equation

$$\frac{dS_t}{S_t} = \mu \, dt + \sigma \, dW_t \tag{4.3}$$

where $\mu \in \mathbb{R}, \sigma \in \mathbb{R}^{+*}$.

We may also write

$$dS_t = \mu S_t \, dt + \sigma S_t \, dW_t \tag{4.3'}$$

The geometric Brownian motion driving S_t in equation (4.3) is discussed in great length in the literature and we will turn immediately to the problem of valuing a European call *C* written on *S*, with maturity *T* and strike *k*.

Obviously, the call price *C*(*t*) will vary with time, will depend on the current value of the underlying stock price *S*(*t*), and because of the Markov property satisfied by the choice of the process (*S*(*t*)), will not depend on any past value of the process *S*.

Hence, we can write

$$C(t) = C(t, S(t))$$

C appears as a function of two variables: the first one changes in a deterministic manner; the second one is driven by the stochastic differential equation (4.3). Using Itô's lemma, we obtain that the change in the call price between dates t and $t + dt$ is given by:

$$dC(t) = \frac{\partial C}{\partial t} dt + \frac{\partial C}{\partial S} dS_t + \frac{1}{2} \frac{\partial^1 C}{\partial S^2} [dS_t]^2$$

Replacing dS_t by its expression from formula (4.3') and $(dS_t)^2$ by $S_t^2 \sigma dt$, since all other terms in $(dS_t)^2$ are null, we obtain[2]:

$$dC(t) = dt \left[\frac{\partial C}{\partial t} + \mu S_t \frac{\partial C}{\partial S_t} + \frac{1}{2} \sigma^2 S_t^2 \frac{\partial^2 C}{\partial S^2} \right] + dW_t \left[\sigma S_t \frac{\partial C}{\partial S_t} \right] \quad (4.4)$$

So far, our arguments have been primarily mathematical. Now, having in mind equations (4.3) and (4.4), we build at date t a portfolio P containing one call and n stocks, where n is a real number fixed over the interval $(t, t + dt)$:

$$V_p(t) = C(t) + nS(t)$$

$$dV_p(t) = dC(t) + n\, dS(t)$$

$$dV_p(t) = dt \left[\frac{\partial C}{\partial t} + \mu S_t \frac{\partial C}{\partial S_t} + \frac{1}{2} \sigma^2 S_t^2 \frac{\partial^2 C}{\partial S^2} + n\mu S_t \right] + dW_t \left[\sigma S_t \frac{\partial C}{\partial S_t} + n\sigma S_t \right] \quad (4.5)$$

The change in value of the portfolio between dates t and $t + dt$ is random because of the second term involving dW_t. In the first term, all quantities have been observed at date t since, with a more precise notation, we should write for instance $\frac{\partial C}{\partial t}(t, S_t)$.

In order to make $dV_p(t)$ non-random, we ask that:

$$\sigma S_t \frac{\partial C}{\partial S_t} + n\sigma S_t = 0$$

The parameter sigma and the stock price S_t are non-null; otherwise, the option would not be traded. Hence, we need to choose:

$$n = -\frac{\partial C}{\partial S_t}(t, S_t) \quad (4.6)$$

For this choice of the real number n not only does the term in dW_t disappear but also the two terms containing μ in the first bracket cancel out and the quantity $dV_p(t)$ is reduced to:

$$dV_P(t) = dt \left[\frac{\partial C}{\partial t} + \frac{1}{2} \sigma^2 S_t^2 \frac{\partial^2 C}{\partial S_t^2} \right] \quad (4.7)$$

---

[2] We recall the 'fundamental rules' of Itô's calculus: assuming that any quantity in $(dt)^\alpha$ with $\alpha > 1$ is negligible, we have $(dW_t)^2 = dt$; $dt.\, dW_t = 0$. Itô's lemma is nothing but a Taylor expansion of the function denoted in our problem $C(t, S_t)$; a contribution in dt comes from the second partial derivative in S_t since $(dW_t)^2 = dt$.

The portfolio P, whose value changes in a non-random manner during the time interval $(t, t + dt)$, is *riskless*; more precisely, *locally riskless* since this property is true for the one-day (or half-day) denoted $(t, t + dt)$.

Using now for the first time the no arbitrage assumption, we state that the return of P over the interval $(t, t + dt)$ has to be equal to the risk-free rate r:

$$dV_p(t) = r \ V_p(t) \ dt$$

$$dV_p(t) = r\left[C(t) - S_t \frac{\partial C}{\partial S}\right] dt$$

Comparing this expression of $dV_p(t)$ to the one obtained in (4.7) we obtain:

$$\frac{\partial C}{\partial t} + r S_t \frac{\partial C}{\partial S} + \frac{1}{2} \sigma^2 \ S^2 \ \frac{\partial^2 C}{\partial S^2} - rC = 0 \qquad (4.8)$$

This relationship between C and its partial derivatives for any date t between 0 and T is called a partial differential equation (PDE). Moreover, the terminal value of C is by definition

$$C(T) = \max(0, S(T) - K)$$

The partial differential equation (4.8) is sufficiently 'well behaved' to provide with the boundary condition on $C(T)$ a unique solution $C(t)$ at all dates t in $(0, T)$. The discussion of the unicity together with the expression of that solution goes back to the work of Einstein at the beginning of the 20th century, who had studied the so-called *heat equation*:

$$\frac{\partial y}{\partial t} + a \frac{\partial^2 y}{\partial x^2} = 0$$

Classical results on PDEs (such as changes of variables and 'variation of constants') show how the solution of equation (4.8) can be obtained through the solution of the heat equation and lead to the price at the date of the European call option:

$$C(t) = S(t) \ N(d_1) - ke^{-r(T-t)} N(d_2)$$

$$d_1 = \frac{\ln\left(\frac{S(t)}{ke^{-r(T-t)}}\right) + \frac{1}{2}\sigma^2(T-t)}{\sigma\sqrt{T-t}}$$

$$d_2 = \frac{\ln\left(\frac{S(t)}{ke^{-r(T-t)}}\right) - \frac{1}{2}\sigma^2(T-t)}{\sigma(T-t)}$$

$$N(x) = \int_{-\infty}^{x} \frac{1}{\sqrt{2\pi}} e^{-t^2/2}$$

where $N(x)$ is the cumulative function of a normal distribution $N(0,1)$.

One of the remarkable features of the Black–Scholes model is that it provides the explicit value of the call price at date t, simply expressed in terms of the current price of the underlying stock $S(t)$; the volatility and the constant interest rate r; and the parameters k and T of the option.

It is particularly worth noticing that the first parameter μ defining the stock price dynamics in equation (4.3) is not present in the pricing formula: it disappeared when we made the portfolio P riskless.

A second proof of the Black–Scholes formula involving the so-called 'risk-adjusted probability measure' – denoted Q in the book – demonstrates that the call price should *not depend on the drift* μ of the stock price process, a property that is not necessarily intuitive at first sight. One may find in the Geman (2005) book the detailed proof of the construction of Q in the Black–Scholes setting, that illuminates the two economic and probabilistic pillars in exhibiting Q. This measure Q is today called the *pricing measure* since it allows one to write the price of any attainable contingent claim as the expectation of its discounted payoff (a beautiful property, very useful when Q is unique).

4.4.1 Consequences of the Black–Scholes formula

The consequences of the Black–Scholes formula are quite numerous and crucial and will be discussed in different parts of the book. For now, we will start with the most important ones:

1. Probably the most important consequence consists in observing that the price formula has been established *without any assumption on the preferences* and beliefs of market participants. The only economic assumption, A5, states that there are no ways of accumulating some wealth starting with no money and bearing no risk.
2. We established the put–call parity in section 4.3. Now that the call price is exhibited, we can derive:

$$P(t) = C(t) + ke^{-r(T-t)} - S(t)$$

$$P(t) = -S(t)\left[1 - N(d_1)\right] + ke^{-r(T-t)}\left[1 - N(d_2)\right]$$

which may also be written as (4.10):

$$P(t) = ke^{-r(T-t)} N(-d_2) - S(t)N(-d_1) \qquad (4.10)$$

3. Returning to the proof of the Black–Scholes formula, the portfolio P, which is riskless over the interval $(t, t + dt)$, behaves like the money-market account M:

$$V_p(t) = C_t + nS_t = -ke^{-r(T-t)}N(d_2)$$

and its evolution over the interval $(t, t + dt)$ can be written as:

$$dV(t) = -rke^{-r(T-t)}N(d_2)dt$$

Analogously, since:

$$C(t) = V_p(t) - nS_t = V_p(t) + S_t\frac{\partial C}{\partial S}$$

we obtain:

$$dC(t)_{(t,t+dt)} \approx \frac{\partial C}{\partial S} dS_t - \left[rke^{-r(T-t)}N(d_2) \right] dt$$

(4.11)

This formula exactly describes the replicating portfolio of the call C, i.e., the hedging portfolio one should hold after having sold the call. It consists in a quantity $\dfrac{\partial C}{\partial S_t}$ of the underlying stock S and a (negative) quantity of the money-market account M. The second term is less important since it is related to the *risk-free instrument* that any bank or firm holds in all cases.

We shall see below that the quantity $N(d_1)$ represents the partial derivative of the call price with respect to S_t, i.e., the quantity of the underlying stock one has to buy after selling the call to hedge the exposure to changes in the underlying S.

Hence, the Black–Scholes model provides in the same formula the valuation of the call as well as the hedging strategy for the holder of a short position in the call.

Once a trader has sold a call, he receives the premium $C(t)$ and borrows the amount K $\exp(-r(T-t))N(d_2)$ (negative investment in the money-market account), which added to the premium $C(t)$ allows him to buy $N(d_1)$ shares of the stock S.

As time t goes by, the quantity of S necessary to hedge the call changes. If this quantity increases at $t + dt$, for instance from 0.48 to 0.52, the hedge will be adjusted by buying an extra amount of the underlying S, namely 0.04 shares. This adjustment over the lifetime of the call option is precisely the *dynamic hedging* of the short position.

In the case of a weather derivative, let us observe that the paradigm of hedging a short call by the purchase of the underlying collapses because it is impossible to buy Celsius or Fahrenheit degrees. In the case of electricity, it is possible to buy at date t the appropriate amount of electricity to hedge a short position in a power derivative; however, it is not possible to carry the position to the following day $t + dt$ and since the hedging portfolio has immediately vanished, there is no adjustment to make at date $t + dt$. Hence, the concept of dynamic hedging has to be reformulated appropriately in the case of electricity derivatives and replaced, for instance, by the static hedge provided by the physical asset.

4.4.2 The Greeks

The Greeks are the partial derivatives of the call price with respect to the variables S and t and the different parameters involved in the option formula.

Delta
Delta is the partial derivative of the call price C with respect to the price S of the underlying stock and unsurprisingly plays a key role in computing exposure of a position:

$$\Delta = \frac{\partial C}{\partial S}(t, S_t) = N(d_1)$$

(4.12)

Hence, the delta is positive and the call price, at any date t, is an increasing function of S_t. At maturity T, the simple graph of the call value $C(T)$ depicted at the beginning of the chapter clearly indicates that it is an increasing function of $S(T)$. Formula (4.12) shows that this property holds at all times, in agreement with our intuition.

Let us note that, for a small change dS of the stock price (for instance, positive), the corresponding change in C is given by:

$$\delta C \approx \frac{\partial C}{\partial S_t} \delta S = N(d_1) \delta S$$

By dividing both sides by C/S and observing that $SN(d_1) > C$, we obtain that

$$\frac{\delta C}{C} > \frac{\delta S}{S} \qquad (4.13)$$

If we anticipate a rise of the underlying S, the return generated by any amount of money invested in the call is strictly higher than the return on the stock during the same time period. This is called the *leverage* effect in the use of derivatives and it allows investors to increase their returns when betting on a given move of the underlying: inequality (4.13) holds in absolute values and provides the same result for returns on short positions in the case of an expected decline of the underlying stock. It also shows that the loss will be greater in the case of a wrong expectation.

Note that, interestingly, some farmers who feel pretty confident in the quality of the coming crops buy call options on corn or soybean to be twice exposed to a rise in the commodity price at the time of harvest, and the second time in a *leveraged* manner. This is the opposite of hedging/protecting their revenues against an adverse weather event!

Gamma
Given the crucial importance of the delta of an option, it is not surprising that the gamma, derivative of the delta with respect to S, also deserves attention:

$$\Gamma = \frac{\partial \Delta}{\partial S} = \frac{\partial^2 C}{\partial S^2} = N'(d_1) \frac{1}{S\sigma\sqrt{T-t}}$$

$N'(d_1)$ represents the density of a normal variable $N(0,1)$ at d_1. Since a density distribution is positive everywhere, the gamma of the call $C(t)$ is positive and the call is a *convex* function of the underlying stock price S_t.

Again, this property was obvious at maturity just from the graph of $C(T)$ as a function of $S(T)$; it was not obvious that it is also true at all dates.

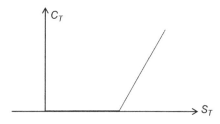

Moreover, the Black–Scholes formula shows that at all dates t, the call value is lower than the stock price (also obvious by super-replication arguments); hence, the graph is located in the lower first quadrant. Lastly, the call price at date t is zero if the stock price is zero (the company that has issued the stock S is gone). Hence, the graph of the call is quite precisely determined and displayed below:

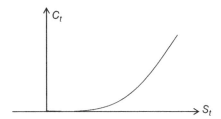

If we turn to the delta and gamma of the put, we know from the put–call parity that:

$$S(t) + P(t) = C(t) + ke^{-r(T-t)}$$

Taking the partial derivative with respect to S on both sides, we obtain:

$$1 + \Delta_{put} = \Delta_{call}$$

$$\Delta_{put} = -\left(1 - N(d_1)\right) \qquad (4.14)$$

Hence, the price of the put at date t is a decreasing function of S_t, extending the property of $P(T)$ being a decreasing function of $S(T)$.

Taking a second time the partial derivative in S in formula (4.14) we obtain:

$$\Gamma_{put} = \Gamma_{call}$$

The put price at date t is a convex function of S, as it is at date T; both put and call are convex functions of the underlying asset.

Let us consider, for example, a long position in a call option, denoted as C and write a Taylor's expansion of the option price between dates t and $t + dt$ when the underlying stock has moved from S_t to $S_t + dS_t$:

$$C(t+\delta t,\ S_t + \delta S_t) - C(t, S_t) = \frac{\partial C}{\partial t}\delta t + \frac{\partial C}{\partial S_t}\ \delta S_t + \frac{1}{2}\frac{\partial^2 C}{\partial S_t^2}(\delta S_t)^2$$

The left-hand side represents the P&L between dates t and $t + dt$. If we leave aside the term $\dfrac{\partial c}{\partial t}$ reflecting the passage of time, which is not large since its multiplier is small, we see that in order not to be exposed to a negative change in S_t, which would damage the P&L, one needs to add to the option a quantity $-\dfrac{\partial C}{\partial S_t} = -\Delta$ of the underlying stock S, i.e., delta hedge the long call.

Now the P&L of the *hedged long position* is (assuming for now no change in volatility):

$$C^{cov}(t+\delta t) - C^{cov}(t) = \frac{\partial C^{cov}}{\partial t}\delta t + \frac{1}{2!}\ \Gamma_{option}(\delta S_t)^2 \qquad (4.15)$$

The covered position will benefit from large moves of S_t through the *convexity* term $\frac{1}{2}\Gamma_{option}(\delta S_t)^2$.

More generally, for any position or portfolio of assets, one will try to hold *positive convexity* in order to gain from the big moves of the underlying; the same property has been exhibited many times in the context of bond portfolios where embedded options generate positive or negative convexity.

We shall see that physical optionalities are present everywhere in the commodities industry and must be recognized and hedged (if held short) or *monetized* if held long; this is something that producers or private equity funds buying *physical assets* are totally aware of, not only in the case of power plants but soybean crushers and warehouses as well.

Lastly, if one wanted to account for random changes in volatility as well, the hedged position will change according to the formula below:

$$C^{cov}\left(t+\delta t,S_t+\delta S_t,\sigma+\delta\sigma\right)-C^{cov}\left(t,S_t,\sigma\right)=\frac{\partial C^{cov}}{\partial t}\delta t+\frac{1}{2}\Gamma_{call}\left(\delta S_t\right)^2+vega_{call}\,\delta\sigma_t$$

Now, one has to monitor optimally both the positive gamma and vega of the hedged call, where the change in volatility brings a positive or negative multiplier to the vega (and leaving aside further terms).

This leads to the important message that the ownership of physical assets in the commodities world – which is the case of the big trading houses mentioned in Chapter 1 – results in large profits when there are large *changes in the commodity spot price and volatility*, not necessarily when prices increase. Regulators around the world tend to excessively focus only on food prices getting higher, which may happen as well, obviously. The two issues are important enough to deserve to be analyzed separately.

Theta

Theta is the partial derivative of the call price with respect to time:

$$\theta_{call}=\frac{\partial C}{\partial t}=-\frac{S\sigma N'\left(d_1\right)}{2\sqrt{T-t}}-rke^{-r(T-t)}N\left(d_2\right)$$

In the case of a put:

$$\theta_{put}=-\frac{S\sigma N'\left(d_1\right)}{2\sqrt{T-t}}+rke^{-r(T-t)}\left(1-N\left(d_2\right)\right)$$

Both quantities can be shown to be negative and represent the time decay of the option as it gets closer to maturity. One way to see it is to keep in mind that more time to maturity means more opportunities for random moves of the underlying. These changes may be upwards or downwards; since the option payoff cannot be negative, the net result of more randomness will be positive.

In order to clearly identify the time value of the option, practitioners introduce for the holder of the option the notion of *intrinsic value*, which is defined as the payoff of the European option were it exercised immediately – this value being zero if the current stock price is below the strike.

The remaining part is the *time value* and the option price can be decomposed as follows:

$$C(t) = \text{intrinsic value} + \text{time value}$$

When the option reaches maturity, the time value goes to zero and the intrinsic value is $S_T - k$ or zero.

Vega

The option vega is the partial derivative of the option price with respect to the volatility parameter. In the context of the Black–Scholes model, the expression of the vega (which is not a Greek letter) is:

$$Vega_{call} = \frac{\partial C}{\partial \sigma} = S\sqrt{T-t}\,N'(d_1)$$

and using the put–call parity, we easily see that the put has the same vega as the call with same strike and maturity:

$$Vega_{put} = \frac{\partial P}{\partial \sigma} = S\sqrt{T-t}\,N'(d_1)$$

Again, we may give the following intuition for these results: the greater the volatility, the higher the effect of the multiplier of dW_t in equation (4.3) and the bigger the random moves. The effect of the downward ones (respectively upward in the case of a put) is limited for the reasons mentioned above and the holder of the long position will overall benefit from a higher volatility.

4.5 THE MERTON (1973) FORMULA FOR DIVIDEND-PAYING STOCKS

As we will see, this formula plays an important role for options on commodities. For the time being, we describe the original Merton framework, namely that the underlying asset is a stock but in contrast to the previous section, the stock pays dividends over the lifetime $[0, T]$ of the option. All assumptions of the Black–Scholes model are kept except that the stock is supposed to make a continuous dividend payment at the rate g: the owner of a stock over the period $(t, t + dt)$ receives at date $t + dt$ the dividend $gS(t)\,dt$.

The European call price is then given by the Merton formula:

$$C(t) = S(t)e^{-g(T-t)}N(d_1) - ke^{-r(T-t)}N(d_2) \qquad (4.16)$$

where:

$$\begin{vmatrix} d_1 = \dfrac{\ln\left(\dfrac{S(t)e^{-g(T-t)}}{ke^{-r(T-t)}}\right) + \dfrac{1}{2}\sigma^2(T-t)}{\sigma\sqrt{T-t}} \\ d_2 = d_1 - \sigma\sqrt{T-t} \end{vmatrix}$$

Proof

Let us first comment in this framework the impact of a continuous dividend on the drift of the geometric Brownian motion, describing in equation (A6) the dynamics of the stock price. Denoting now this drift as μ', we can write:

$$\frac{dS(t)}{S(t)} = \mu'dt + \sigma\,dW_t$$

Note that in comparison with the case of no dividend payment, it has to be that

$$\mu' = \mu - g$$

For two firms with exactly the same activity and the same capital structure, the stock of the firm that distributes dividends will grow at a reduced rate, the difference accounting exactly for the dividends received – continuously in our model.

Note also that the buyer of the option is not entitled to these dividends; he will have the right at date T to exercise and get for k dollars a stock less pricey than in the case of no dividends. Hence, we expect the call price to be lower than in the case of Black–Scholes and this is indeed translated by the factor $e^{-g(T-t)}$, which multiplies the positive term in the pricing formula.

We follow the same line of reasoning as in the previous section: the call price can again be written:

$$\begin{cases} C(t) \equiv C(t, S_t) \\ where \ dS(t) = \mu S(t) dt + \sigma \ S(t) dW_t \end{cases}$$

We write Itô's lemma:

$$dC(t) = dt \left[\frac{\partial C}{\partial t} + \frac{\partial C}{\partial S_t} \mu \ S_t + \frac{1}{2} \sigma^2 \ S_t^2 \frac{\partial \ C}{\partial S_t^2} \right] + dW_t \left[\frac{\partial C}{\partial S_t} \sigma \ S_t \right]$$

and build the portfolio P at date t:

$$V_p(t) = C(t) + nS(t)$$

where again the choice $n = -\dfrac{\partial c}{\partial s}$ ensures that $dV_p(t)$ contains no random term:

$$dV_p(t) = dt \left[\frac{\partial C}{\partial S_t} + \frac{1}{2} \sigma^2 \ S_t^2 \frac{\partial^2 C}{\partial S_t^2} \right]$$

The portfolio P is now riskless and its total return over $(t, t + dt)$ has to be the risk-free short-term rate, minus the dividend $gS(t)dt$ received in cash on the stock.

We are led to a partial differential equation very similar to the one of the case of no dividend, except for an extra term in g, with the same boundary condition at date T, in turn yielding the price of the plain vanilla call option.

Hence, assuming a geometric Brownian motion for the dynamics of the underlying dividend paying stock S, we obtain formula (4.16), for the price of a plain vanilla call option, where the extra term g appears in $nC(t)$ and the two multiplier coefficients N.

1. Since we assumed a constant dividend rate g, it is not surprising that the structure of the proof and the choice for n in the riskless portfolio is the same as in the Black–Scholes formula.
   The Greeks will be derived using the same method as before, namely the computations of partial derivatives from the closed-form formula providing the option price.
2. Repeating the type of reasoning we used before, we can show that the put–call parity in the case of a stock paying a dividend y or a commodity with a convenience yield y becomes

$$S(t)e^{-y(T-t)} + P(t) = C(t) + ke^{-r(T-t)}$$

4.6 OPTIONS ON COMMODITY SPOT PRICES

A fundamental and immediate consequence of the Merton formula is that it provides the valuation of European calls written on commodity spots. We saw in Chapter 3 that we may view the commodity price behavior as the one of a stock paying a continuous dividend equal to the convenience yield. Hence, if *we assume that the geometric Brownian motion is an appropriate representation* of the commodity spot price, the price at date t of a European call written on the spot price S of commodity with a convenience yield y is obtained by replacing g by y in equation (4.16), that is

$$C(t) = S(t)e^{-y(T-t)}N(d_1) - ke^{-r(T-t)}N(d_2)$$ (4.17)

where:

$$\begin{cases} d_1 = \dfrac{\ln\left(\dfrac{S(t)e^{-y(T-t)}}{ke^{-r(T-t)}}\right) + \dfrac{1}{2}\sigma^2(T-t)}{\sigma\sqrt{T-t}} \\ d_2 = d_1 - \sigma\sqrt{T} \end{cases}$$

and S denotes the spot price of the commodity.

1. Again, any call option written on S has a unique price and replicating portfolio.
2. Dynamic hedging, a fundamental result, holds as long as the underlying commodity is storable and the hedging portfolio is rebalanced daily according to the delta of the call sold at date 0. Obviously, since electricity cannot be stored at a reasonable cost, the argument would not hold.
3. The approach can be easily extended to a mean-reverting process, continuous process or another diffusion, in which case the unicity of the price will continue to prevail.
4. This remarkably simple valuation formula holds as long as the convenience yield y is viewed as constant during the lifetime of the option (as well as interest rates, but if these ones are stochastic, the simple change is to replace the discount factor by the price $B(t, T)$ of a bond paying one dollar at date T).
5. If the option has a distant maturity, it becomes necessary to introduce a stochastic convenience yield in the problem to represent the changing supply/demand conditions in the underlying commodity.

An Ornstein–Uhlenbeck process is then used most of the time as it allows y to take positive and negative values and a choice of the parameter b equal to zero would imply a mean reversion around zero, which is the value that one should assume unless the economics of the commodity or the calibration say otherwise:

$$dy(t) = a(b - y(t))dt + \sigma dW_t^1$$

where the additional Brownian motion is possibly correlated with the one driving the spot price.

Note that in this case the seller of the option faces *two sources of risk* and would typically use two Futures contracts of different maturities to hedge his position.

The valuation of the option itself could be obtained through Monte-Carlo simulations performed in the case of two correlated sources of risk, as developed in Chapter 6.

6. In the case of an option written on the spread between two commodities, such as Arabica and Robusta coffee, this spread may be positive or negative over time depending on the respective supply/demand conditions in these two commodities, and the geometric Brownian motion proposed by Samuelson in 1965 should be replaced by the founding Bachelier (1900) model where the underlying is driven by an arithmetic Brownian motion – for which an even simpler pricing formula for a call option was exhibited as early as 1900.
7. For the addition of stochastic interest rates in all the situations described above, the exercise is purely mathematical and the reader is referred to Geman *et al.* (1995) or Geman (2005). In the current situation of low interest rates, their effect is of a second order and the focus should remain on the commodity price and volatility.

4.7 OPTIONS ON COMMODITY FUTURES: THE BLACK (1976) FORMULA

The Black formula is probably the most important in option pricing, because of its applications to Futures written on all kinds of underlying assets, and its crucial extension to the so-called 'market model' for the valuation of caplets and swaptions in the world of interest rates. In the world of commodities, they are much more liquid than options written on the commodity spot price since, as we saw in the previous chapters, most of the trading in commodities takes place in the form of Futures or forward contracts.

Fischer Black, in his 1976 paper, proposed the famous Black formula for options written on Futures. The Future itself may be written on a stock or on a commodity; its maturity T_1 has obviously to be greater than the maturity T of the option.

Assuming once again no arbitrage and a geometric Brownian motion for the dynamics of the Future/forward price process $(F^{T_1}(t))$ – and noting that a forward contract pays no dividend – it is easy to build again a riskless portfolio over the interval $(t, t + dt)$, comprising the call option and an appropriate number of Future contracts and derive the partial differential equation satisfied by the call price, leading to the Black formula:

$$C(t) = e^{-r(T-t)} \left[F^{T_1}(t) N(d_1) - k N(d_2) \right]$$

(4.18)

where:

$$
\begin{cases}
d_1 = \dfrac{\ln\left(\dfrac{F^{T_1}(t)}{k}\right) + \dfrac{1}{2}\sigma^2 (T-t)}{\sigma\sqrt{T-t}} \\
d_2 = d_1 - \sigma\sqrt{T-t}
\end{cases}
$$

and *the volatility is now one of the specific underlying Future contracts* of maturity T_1.

We can also observe that in the particular case where $T_1 = T$, the option written on the Future contract is equivalent to an option written on the spot price – if we assume no arbitrage between the spot and Futures markets $S(T) = F^T(T)$. This is confirmed by writing the spot/forward relationship at date t:

$$F^T(t) = S(t)e^{(r-y)(T-t)}$$

Plugging this quantity into equation (4.18) gives:

$$C(t) = S(t)e^{-y(T-t)}N(d_1) - ke^{-r(T-t)}N(d_2)$$

which is exactly the Merton formula (4.16) for options written on the spot price of the commodity.

Finally, let us observe that in the general case $T_1 < T$, the put–call parity for options written on Futures has the following form:

$$C(t) + ke^{-r(t-t)} = F^{T_1}(t)e^{-r(T-t)} + P(t)$$

and provides the price of the put written on the Future contract.

Comments

i) We observed that the volatility σ_{T_1} to be incorporated in formula (4.18) is the volatility of the Future contract F^{T_1}. For practical purposes, it will depend on the maturity T_1 of this contract: for instance, in the gas or electricity market, σ_{T_1} will be much higher for $T_1 =$ January than April. If we want to be even more precise we may introduce a function that depends on both arguments t and T. If this function is deterministic, it is easy to prove that formula (4.18) still holds as long as the variance v is defined by

$$(T-t)v = \int_t^T \sigma^2(u, T_1)du$$

ii) The proof written above applies best for an option written on a *forward contract* f_{T_1} since there would be for sure no intermediary cashflow in this case (see Geman and Vasicek, 2003).

4.8 MONTE-CARLO SIMULATIONS FOR OPTION PRICING

4.8.1 The founding result

A central result in probability theory – not very difficult to prove but fundamental for its application in different problems arising in insurance and finance – is the law of large numbers that we present below in its simple 'weak' form.

Law of large numbers

Let $X_1, X_2, \ldots, X_n$ be a sequence of random variables with the same mean m and variance σ^2 where σ^2 is finite, pairwise uncorrelated.

Then, the sequence of random variables (U_n) defined by $U_n = \dfrac{1}{n}[X_1 + X_2 \ldots + X_n]$ converges in probability to the constant m; equivalently for any $\in > 0$,

$$\text{Proba}(|U_n - m| > \varepsilon) \to 0 \text{ if } n \to +\infty$$

Remarks

1. The proof is derived in a straightforward manner from the Bienaymé–Tchebitcheff inequality applied to U_n, and from the fact that, by absence of correlation between the X_i, the variance will decrease in $1/n$.
2. If $X_1, X_2, \ldots, X_n$ have the same distribution, they will obviously have the same mean and variance (note that this variance has to be finite for the result to hold). In the same spirit, if $X_1, X_2, \ldots, X_n$ are independent random variables, they will be pairwise uncorrelated.

Fundamental consequence
If we consider a random variable X whose *true distribution* is *unknown* – which in practice is the case in finance, in insurance, or other applied sciences – we can still obtain an estimate of the first order moment $m = E(X)$ as long as we are able to perform N independent random draws, called Monte-Carlo draws, $X_1, X_2, \ldots, X_n$ of this variable X by applying the law of large numbers:

‘The exact value of the expectation m of X may be approximated by the arithmetic average of the numbers obtained in a large sequence of independent draws of this random variable.’

Generalization
In a famous paper, Metropolis *et al.* (1953) extended this result to the computation of $E[f(X)]$ where f is a fairly general real functional:

$$E[f(X)] = \text{limit of arithmetic average of the values of } f(X) \text{ over } n \text{ draws}$$

This result was greatly applied in insurance and in industrial engineering in the 1950s and 1960s. It did not appear in finance before the end of the 1970s, precisely at the time when the option price started being written as the expectation of its (discounted) payoff under an appropriate probability measure.

4.8.2 Monte-Carlo methods for plain vanilla options on non-dividend paying stocks

These have to be performed under the probability measure under which the derivative price may be written as the (discounted) expectation of its terminal payoff, hence the risk-adjusted probability measure (while Monte-Carlo Value at Risk would be performed under the real probability measure). As mentioned before, in the Black–Scholes setting, there exists a unique probability measure Q such that the dynamics of the non-dividend paying stock are driven by the stochastic differential equation:

$$\frac{dS_t}{S_t} = r\,dt + \sigma\,d\hat{W}_t \quad with \left(\hat{W}_t\right)_{t\geq 0} = Q - Brownian\ motion \tag{4.19}$$

and the call price is then

$$C(t) = E_Q\left[\max\left(0, S(T) - k\right)e^{-r(T-t)} / F_t\right]$$

Since interest rates are constant (as already expressed in the above formula), the discount factor may be pulled out of the expectation and we recognize that the computation of $C(t)$ is equivalent to finding the expectation of a function of $S(T)$:

$$C(T) = e^{-r(T-t)}\,E_Q\,[f(S(T)/F_t]$$

and

$$f(S(T)) = \max(0,\ S(T) - k)$$

Hence, we know that if we can perform *independent* simulations of $S(T)$, the results of the above paragraph will provide an approximate value for $E_Q\,[f(S(T)/F_t]$.

The problem now is reduced to simulating N times the quantity $S(T)$ in order to derive the corresponding values for the option payoff $\max(S(T) - k, 0)$.

Let us integrate equation (4.19) between the dates t and T:

$$S(T) = S(t)\exp\left\{\left[r - \frac{\sigma^2}{2}\right](T-t) + \sigma\,\hat{W}(T-t)\right\} \tag{4.20}$$

At date t, the current value of the stock or commodity $S(t)$ is fully observed, as well as the risk-free rate r. The key volatility parameter is estimated by the trader, from historical values of $S(t)$ or as an implied volatility derived from liquid options.

Hence, simulating $S(T)$ is equivalent to simulating $\hat{W}(T-t)$ whose distribution under Q is normal $N\left(0; \sqrt{T-t}\right)$.

The cumulative function F of $\hat{W}(T-t)$ is easy to represent:

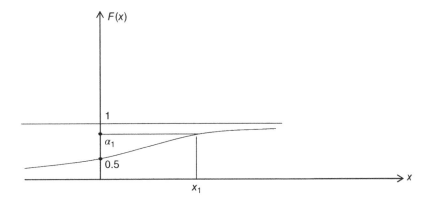

If we choose an arbitrary number α_1 between 0 and 1, it will define a unique x_1, which is a random simulation of $\hat{W}(T-t)$. In the above drawing, α_1 happened to be higher than 0.5, leading to a positive x_1. If we were to choose the second number α_2, we would tend to place it somewhere below 0.5, in order to reintroduce the symmetry exhibited by the density of $\hat{W}(T-t)$. This should destroy the feature of independence required for the draws. Hence, it is a random number generator installed on the computer that is going to produce the numbers $\alpha_1, \alpha_2, \ldots \alpha_N$ leading to N independent draws $x_1 \ldots x_N$ of $\hat{W}(T-t)$ (which can themselves produce N other ones by symmetry of the normal distribution). We plug each number x_i into (4.20) and obtain successively:

$$S^{(1)}(T) = S(t)\, \exp\left\{\left[r - \frac{\sigma^2}{2}\right](T-t) + \sigma x_1\right\} \tag{4.21}$$

$$S_T^{(2)} = S(t)\exp\left\{\left[r - \frac{\sigma^2}{2}\right](T-t) + \sigma x_2\right\}$$

...

leading in turn to the values $b_1, b_2, \ldots, b_N$ defined as:

$$\begin{cases} b_1 = \max\left(0,\ S^{(1)}(T) - k\right) \\ b_2 = \max\left(0,\ S^{(2)}(T) - k\right) \\ \ldots \end{cases}$$

and positive or null depending on the position relative to k of the simulated values $S^{(1)}(T)$, ..., $S^{(N)}(T)$. We then obtain as an approximation for the option price

$$C(t) \approx e^{-r(T-t)}\left[\frac{b_1 + b_2 + \ldots + b_N}{N}\right]$$

We note that our approach has been parsimonious since we simulated the only quantity we need in the context of plain vanilla options, namely the price $S(T)$ of the stock at maturity as opposed to the whole trajectory. When the number of simulations becomes very high, we can check numerically that, in agreement with the theory, the Monte-Carlo price converges to the Black–Scholes price. It is important to observe that the Monte-Carlo approach is a very simple and intuitive computation of the option price.

4.8.3 Monte-Carlo methods for plain vanilla options on the spot commodity

We observed in the previous section that for storable commodities, the convenience yield is analogous to a dividend yield y on a stock. Since this dividend reduces the growth rate of the stock (or the spot commodity), the dynamics of the spot price under the pricing measure Q have the following form, under the assumption of a geometric Brownian,

$$\frac{dS_t}{S_t} = (r-y)dt + \sigma \, d\hat{W}_t \tag{4.22}$$

Assuming the convenience yield y constant over the lifetime of the option (as well as the continuously compounded short rate r), we just need to change r into $(r-y)$ in equation (4.21) and nothing else is changed in the procedure, which provides the Monte-Carlo approximation of the option price.

Note that y is positive or negative, as discussed in Chapter 3. This quantity y links the prices of Futures and options written on S (both being *derivatives*).

Remark
As observed before, the numerical value of the convenience yield may be derived from the observation of the market prices of two liquid forward contracts and the fundamental relationship:

$$F^T(t) = S(t)e^{(r-y)T-t}$$

4.9 IMPLIED VOLATILITY, SMILE, AND SKEW IN EQUITY OPTION MARKETS

We have seen before that the option price is a strictly increasing function of the volatility parameter as

$$vega = \frac{\partial C}{\partial \sigma}$$

is strictly positive for the call (and the put as well). When a function is strictly monotonic in a variable, it may be inverted in this variable and the implied volatility is precisely defined by 'reverse-engineering' the volatility parameter in the Black–Scholes formula from the option market price. This market practice does not presume that the trader is using the Black–Scholes model. It defines a one-to-one relationship between the market price and the 'implied' volatility, and this exercise is conducted for a number of strikes k, one being the value of the underlying today and called ATM (at the money).

If the Black–Scholes (or Black) formula's assumptions were exactly reflected in the markets, the volatility parameter should be constant over time t in the interval $[0, T]$, should be independent of the maturity T, and independent of the strike k greater, equal to or lower than the ATM number. Moreover, the *ex-post* (or realized) volatility should be equal to the historical volatility or standard deviation – computed at date T from the data series of spot prices $S(t)$ observed during the period $[0, T]$. Following the formidable success of the Black–Scholes–Merton (1973) model, participants in equity markets started as of the early 1980s to compute the volatility implied in market option prices by the Black–Scholes formula.

If we place ourselves on a given date t and plot the volatility implied in a family of options written on the same underlying S, with same maturity T and various strikes k, we obtain a graph that is not a flat line:

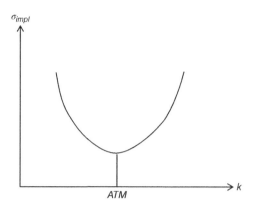

Moreover, a greater liquidity is empirically observed in the stock market for out of the money (OTM) options, namely calls for k greater than $S(t) = $ ATM (investors buying calls with large values of k in order to be positively exposed to the stock price and benefit from a great piece of news on the stock – a new drug in the case of a pharmaceutical company for instance); symmetrically, investors looking for protection against a large downward move of the market will buy puts with a low strike k.

Indeed, if one holds today a call with $k > S(t)$, the hypothetical immediate exercise of the call today would provide an *intrinsic value* of zero, hence the name OTM (and the option price is purely *time value*); symmetrically, for puts with strikes lower than ATM. Since a necessary condition for the market to be right is to be liquid, the graph of the implied volatility is built in equity markets and most markets by computing the implied volatility from call prices for $k > $ ATM and puts for $k < $ ATM (even though the pure Black–Scholes model assumes the same dynamics and volatility for calls and puts).

In the early years 1973 to 1980, the graph of the implied volatility was a flat half-line, exhibiting that the pricing formula was a 'self-fulfilling prophecy,' according to the famous statement made by Merton in 1974. From 1981 to 1987, this graph in equity option markets took the shape of a smile – with a minimal point equal to the ATM value of the underlying. The economic interpretation of the smile can be found in the risk aversion of the option's seller who wants a greater price reward to hedge an option in a market with possible large fluctuations in the underlying prior to maturity.

Accordingly, after the crash of 1987 the shape of the smile changed in the stock market to become a skew, translating the fact that option traders had understood that there is no symmetry in volatility between upward and downward moves of the market:

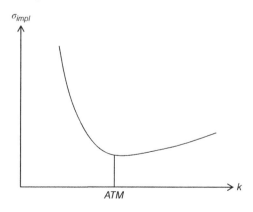

The explanation for this asymmetry is that the stock market as a whole is very averse to the occurrence of a new crash and prepared to pay a higher premium, i.e., a higher volatility, for puts with low values of k which precisely provide insurance against downward moves, as we shall review in the last chapter of the book. The increase of volatility in the presence of a collapse in this equity price is called leverage effect in corporate finance (since indeed the debt to equity ratio increases). It is not surprising that the same property be shared by the implied volatility, which is at date 0 an estimator of the realized volatility over the period $(0, T)$.

Returning to the equity volatility smile, its shape and curvature are more than ever the subject of an intense scrutiny in banks and financial institutions. Some practitioners use a so-called *local volatility* model – where the volatilty changes randomly but as a deterministic function of the spot price.

Another route to capture the smile/skew is the use of a *stochastic volatility* model for the dynamics of the underlying. The two approaches are described below:

1. If one views the volatility as non-deterministic but does not wish to bring in the complexity of an extra source of randomness in the volatility σ – not only mathematically but also in terms of the necessity of a hedging instrument for this new source of risk in order to avoid 'market incompleteness' – a simple route consists in writing sigma as a deterministic function of S_t, in which case the random changes in σ will occur through S_t (see Dupire (1994) and Derman-Kani (1994)). From a calibration perspective, the problem may be solved at each date t in a fairly simple manner, using for instance a low degree polynomial for the determinstic function as long as a large variety of strikes and maturities of traded options are available. Once the model volatility is calibrated on liquid plain vanilla options, it is used by practitioners to have a better approach to the valuation of exotic options, such as barrier or Asian options.

   This approach is quite appropriate in those commodity markets where no other instrument (such as a variance swap) is very liquid in order to hedge volatility as a source of risk in its own right. Note that the effect of seasonality in the spot price can be captured by a corresponding seasonality in the deterministic function sigma. It is the author's preferred approach to introduce stochastic volatility in commodity options.

2. Otherwise, if one views volatility as being a stochastic quantity in its own right, a stochastic volatility model needs to be chosen. The most popular one in the financial markets today may be recognized as the Heston (1993) model, where the dynamics of the stock price and volatility are described under the pricing measure Q by the equations

$$
\begin{cases}
\dfrac{dS_t}{S_t} = r\,dt + \sigma(t)\,dW^1(t) \\[2mm]
d\Sigma(t) = a\big(b - \Sigma(t)\big)dt + \gamma\sqrt{\Sigma(t)}\,dW^2(t) \\[2mm]
\text{and } \Sigma(t) = \big[\sigma(t)\big]^2 ; \; dW^1(t).\,dW^2(t) = \rho\,dt
\end{cases}
$$

The mean-reverting property in the second equation ensures that volatility remains bounded, a desirable property for a quantity always lower than 120% (a value sometimes reached by the volatility of electricity or shipping rates), while the presence of the square root term precludes negative values for Σ; the correlation is typically negative for equity options because of the leverage effect. Obviously, the mathematical complexity becomes higher but the greatest difficulty arises from the incompleteness of the model. We are now facing two sources of risk S and Σ and have only one asset, the stock or the commodity, to hedge a short position in an option. Again, one would need a particularly liquid option (typically the ATM plain vanilla call option), which can be viewed as a primitive instrument whose price is provided by the market. Hence, the hedging portfolio will consist of the underlying S and the option.

3. Lastly, the introduction of a jump component in a diffusion process (jump–diffusion process) or of a pure jump process (see Geman (2002)) immediately creates stochastic volatility from the random occurrence of breaks in the trajectories, which may be added to stochastic volatility.

4.10 VOLATILITY SMILE IN AGRICULTURAL COMMODITY MARKETS

4.10.1 Where is the liquidity in agricultural commodity option markets?

We can recognize essentially the physical options, such as the ones related to the valuation of flexibility in storage, delivery or exchange options, in which case the option is related to the spot price of the commodity and the owner of the option is the owner of the physical asset. Usually, these options are not traded as financial instruments *per se*, but used as collateral for trading activities.

The financial options traded by banks, before and after withdrawing from the commodity markets, are written on Futures contracts for obvious reasons: the underlying is traded with a great liquidity on an exchange and the techniques of dynamic hedging quite familiar to the bank apply with no further difficulties.

Hence, when repeating for commodities the exercise of computing the volatility contained in option market prices, we conduct it using options on Futures that have the further merit of being traded on an exchange as well.

4.10.2 Extracting the implied volatility from options on commodity Futures

Obviously, like in the case of options on the spot price of equities, we have the choice of the maturity T of the option contract, for instance $T = 3$ months or 6 months. Moreover, we now have the choice of the maturity T_1 of the Future underlying the option, which gives a second time dimension for the potential family of options to analyze.

In practice, the market extracts the implied volatility from options where the maturity of the Future is $T + 1$ month, meaning that at maturity the underlying Future will be the first nearby, with the double benefit of an underlying very similar to the spot for an option that one can dynamically hedge; and the great liquidity of the underlying all the way to the maturity of the option.

It is the approach we follow in the graphs of implied volatility displayed below for options on grains Futures.

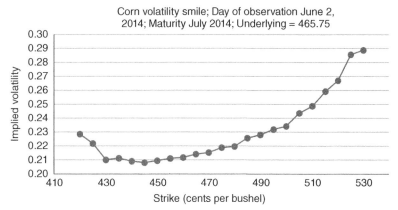

Figure 4.1   Corn volatility smile; day of observation June 2, 2014; maturity July 2014, underlying = 465.75

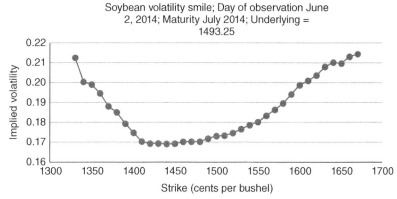

Figure 4.2   Soybean volatility smile; day of observation June 2, 2014; maturity July 2014; underlying = 1493.25

A final comment is the fact that the options on commodity Futures traded on an exchange are in fact American options, meaning that they may be exercised any day up to T, hence may have a greater value – in fact, the same value if the forward curve is in contango since one should not exercise early in a market where the commodity price is expected to go up.

In the case of a backwardated market, the early exercise may be desirable; depending on the conflicting effect of the downward trend that recommends exercising immediately and the volatility effect that argues in favor of the time value (we have a similar discussion in Chapter 5 in the comparison of the prices of a plain vanilla call and an Asian call). One can decide to neglect the American feature and extract the implied volatility from the option prices inverting the Black formula; otherwise, the so-called Whaley transformation can adjust the American price quoted on the exchange into a European one before inverting the Black formula.

From the graph in Figure 4.1, in June 2014, the corn implied volatility curve was clearly skewed to the right, in agreement with the 'inverse leverage effect' prevailing for commodities

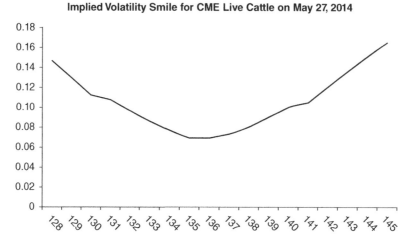

Figure 4.3   Implied volatility smile for CME Live Cattle on May 27, 2014

during the period 2002 to 2008 (see Geman (2005)) and expressing that buyers of calls were prepared to pay a high price to get a positive exposure to corn prices. We can note that between January and June 2014, news on corn prices had contradictory effects on prices: the annexation of Crimea pushing up wheat and corn prices, and good news on weather pushing them down. Call options allow investors to be positively exposed without buying the underlying corn (or rather, Futures on corn).

In the graph in Figure 4.2, also built in June 2014, we note a symmetric shape for the implied volatility in soybeans, suggesting that buyers of calls and puts pay roughly the same price for volatility. We can also observe that the curve is not very smooth compared to the one we would get from options on stocks, indicating a lower liquidity in the case of commodities.

Lastly, the graph in Figure 4.3 shows that the shape of the smile in cattle options is less regular, translating the lesser liquidity in this market where hedgers and 'speculators' essentially use Futures.

5

Commodity Swaps, Swaptions, Accumulators, Forward-Start, and Asian Options

'Everything should be made as simple as possible, but not simpler.'

Albert Einstein

5.1 SWAPS AND SWAPTIONS

Swaps in commodity markets have the same definition as in the interest rates markets and are nothing but a portfolio of forward contracts entered at the same price.

As usual, the current date is being denoted as t and the period covered by the swap is $(H, H + n$ years$)$ where H is a future date, $H > t$; n is typically an integer but may be a fraction of a year:

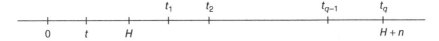

On the dates t_1, t_2, $\ldots$, $t_q = H + n$ years, which are usually equally spaced (e.g., quarterly, monthly), the buyer of the swap pays a fixed amount of G dollars – G is the guaranteed price of the swap – corresponding to a well-defined quantity A of the commodity underlying the swap contract:

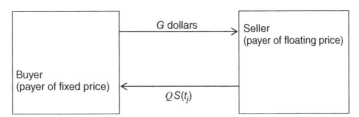

On the same date t_j, the seller of the swap pays the amount $QS(t_j)$, where Q is the number of tonnes of wheat and $S(t_j)$ denotes the spot price at date t_j of a unit quantity of this commodity as reflected by a major index (e.g., Platts index in the case of crude oil); hence, the importance of reliable and liquid indices in agricultural commodities and shipping markets discussed in Chapter 1.

It is clear that if the number of cash flow exchanges reduces to one date ($q = 1$), the swap reduces to a forward contract where the price G paid by the buyer was defined at inception of the contract and where the seller has to deliver the promised quantity. Note that commodity swaps are financially settled and do not involve any physical delivery. They are over the counter, customized transactions and perfectly suited for hedging activities. Again, the existence of a reliable index is crucial for the determination of each payment of the floating leg.

Unsurprisingly, following the colossal development of interest rate swaps, the swap market has exploded for commodities, in particular for gas, oil, and electricity.

As already done in the case of forward and Futures contracts, we are going to analyze the market value $V_p(t)$ of, let's say, a long position paying the fixed leg G in a commodity swap.

At the outset of the contract:

$$V_p(t) = 0$$

since none of the two parties makes any upfront payment and it is a fair zero-sum game between the two parties. After that date, the value of the position will change upon the arrival of news and we can write:

$$V_p(t') = \sum_{j=1}^{q} V_{p_j}(t')$$

where the position P_j corresponds to the exchange of cash flows at date j. These elementary positions are, as observed before, forward contracts (with maturities t_1, t_2, ..., t_q) which have the property to involve the same *price G* for each forward contract. We saw in Chapter 3 that the price at a date $t < t_j$ of a t_j maturity forward contract signed at date 0 is, assuming $Q = 1$:

$$V_{p_j}(t) = e^{-r(t_j-t)}\left[F^{t_j}(t)-G\right]$$

$$V_{p_j}(t) = e^{-r(t_j-t)}\left[F^{t_j}(t)-G\right]$$

Hence, the value of the swap at any date t is

$$V_{SW}(t) = \sum_{j=1}^{q} e^{-r(t_j-t')}\left[F^{t_j}(t)-G\right] \tag{5.1}$$

We can now see that G, the guaranteed price of the swap, is simply obtained by stating that $V_{swap}(t) = 0$

$$G = \frac{\displaystyle\sum_{j=1}^{q} e^{-r(t_j-t)} F^{t_j}(t)}{\displaystyle\sum_{j=1}^{q} e^{-r(t_j-t)}} \tag{5.2}$$

Note that a better version of formula 5.2 is obtained by replacing all discount factors in the numerator and denominator by the market prices of the zero-coupon bonds of the corresponding maturities.

This number G is also called the *swap price* (swap rate for interest rate swaps) at date t. In the case of oil and gas, the swap market is fairly liquid (very liquid for oil) and the swap price, for a given hedging period and frequency of cash flows, is given by the market. Any deviation between this market price and formula (5.2) would in principle allow uncovering quasi-arbitrage opportunities. In the case of agricultural commodities, swaps are becoming more and more liquid, even for commodities little known by the public such as fertilizers.

The remarkable feature of the swap is that its value is an *average of forward prices* (weighted by discount factors). This is straightforward, but from an operational perspective, this number captures the whole forward curve up to maturity of the swap. We see that this quantity has come back in the picture under various forms, in the model described in Chapter 3 and introduced by Borovkova and Geman (2006) as the first state variable replacing the spot price when modeling commodity forward curves, in the discussion of the first moment of the average spot price for Asian options, and now in the case of swaps.

In interest rates markets where swaps have experienced a huge growth in the 1990s, swaptions have become a very popular instrument over the last few years. They are experiencing the same success in commodity markets for the same reason, namely the great liquidity of commodity swaps.

Definition

A swaption, as indicated by its name, is an option on a swap, i.e., grants its holder the right to enter at a future date T a swap relative to the period (T, T_1) at a guaranteed price G fixed at inception t of the swaption:

Maturity of the swap

The swaption with maturity T is an option written on a swap and gives its owner the right to enter at that date a swap with a specified duration, frequency of payment dates, underlying commodity, and swap rate. The buyer pays at date 0 the price of the swaption to the seller.

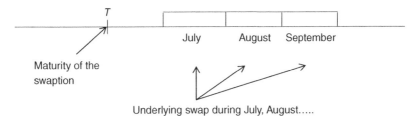

Underlying swap during July, August.....

In the above example, the maturity of the swaption is T = March 31, 2013; the payment dates of the swap are June, July, August, and September 2013.

The 'payer swaption' gives its owner the right to enter the swap as the payer of the fixed leg specified at date 0 – and receiver of the floating leg $S(j)$, where j = June 30, July 31...

The underlying swap volatility involves

- The volatilities of the forward prices associated to the maturities t_j.
- The correlations of these forward prices.

And an assumption needs to be made on the dynamics under the pricing measure Q of the market value of the swap. Since that quantity may take positive or negative values, one simple solution consists in representing it as an arithmetic Brownian motion (see the section on spread options in Chapter 6), which will lead to an explicit solution for the swaption price. A much better approach is to use the forward curve and formula (5.2) to represent the dynamics of the swap price.

Obviously, the buyer of the swaption will only exercise his right if the swap market value at date T is strictly positive, as is the case for all options.

Consequently, the payoff of the swaption at maturity T can be written as:

$$C_{swap}(T) = \max\left(0, V_{swap}(T)\right)$$

The price of the swaption at date t can be derived accordingly:

$$C_{swap}(t) = e^{-r(T-t)} E_Q\left[\max\left(0, V_{swap}(T)\right) / F_t\right]$$

where V is the swap value. As usual, the key quantity to assess will be the volatility of the swap price – analogous to the volatility of the swap rate in the case of swaptions on interest rates. This volatility may be found in forward-start options (discussed in this chapter), which are also becoming increasingly liquid in commodity markets and provide the implied volatility between two dates, as we shall see later on in Section 5.3.

The graph below is meant to emphasize the similarities and differences between forward-start options and swaptions, both used to hedge a period starting at a future date T and not pay the cost of the hedge/cost of volatility prior to

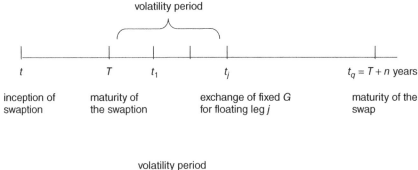

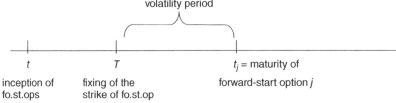

Since forward-start options are quite popular in commodity markets where different time periods in the future play different roles because of seasonality of seeding, news on harvests and storage, the above graph allows one to infer from liquid forward start options the price that the financial issuer will propose to a consumer wishing to buy a swaption.

5.2 ACCUMULATORS

These instruments came into existence in the world of equities, have lately become quite popular for agricultural commodities, and are traded between commodity producers and users.

Definition

An accumulator is a swap contract with physical delivery and a barrier feature. It is characterized by

- An inception date 0.
- A maturity T, for instance $T = 12$ months.
- A number of fixings, $N = 12$ for instance.
- A fixed price set at a value k usually lower by 10 or 20% than the forward price prevailing today for maturity T (for instance $k = 80$ if the forward price is 100).
- An upper barrier set at a value U strictly higher than $f(0, T)$, for instance 115.

At the end of each month, the buyer of the accumulator is committed to buy one unit of the commodity at the price k as long as the spot is below U.

If the spot price of the commodity is above the value U, the accumulator is knocked out and expires.

Example

An agrifood company has bought from a coffee producer a 12-month accumulator related to 1 tonne of coffee per month:

1. If commodity prices go up while remaining below the barrier U, the agrifood company makes profits through the accumulator by buying each month at a low price the coffee it needs.
2. If commodity prices go down, the agrifood company loses money on the accumulator since it is committed to buy each month at the price k.
3. If prices stay roughly flat, the situation is good for the agrifood company since k was set at a value lower than the forward price $f(0, T)$.

The pricing methodology will involve a standard swap with a barrier feature (see Geman and Yor (1996) for the valuation of barrier options – a fairly simple problem).

5.3 FORWARD-START OPTIONS (OR CALENDAR SPREAD OPTIONS ON THE SPOT PRICE)

These involve a single commodity S and allow traders at date t to take a view on (or hedge against) the evolution of S over a future period $[T_1, T]$, where $t < T_1 < T$ and t being the current date. The payoff of a forward-start call option is defined as:

$$C^{fs}(T) = \max\left(0, S(T) - S(T_1)\right) \tag{5.3}$$

whereby the fixed strike k of the plain vanilla call option defined in Chapter 4 is here replaced by the value of the commodity spot price at a future date T_1:

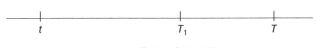

Fixing of the strike

Typically, the buyer of such a call wishes to hedge against a possible rise of the underlying price of the commodity between the dates T_1 and T: for instance the current date t is March 1, and the buyer seeks protection against an increase in corn prices between June 1 and July 1. Assuming for simplicity that the commodity price is driven by a geometric Brownian motion, its dynamics under the pricing measure Q are given by the following stochastic differential equation

$$\frac{dS_t}{S_t} = (r - y)dt + \sigma \, d\hat{W}_t \qquad (5.4)$$

It is clear that integrating between the dates T_1 and T gives a simple expression of $S(T)$ in terms of $S(T_1)$, namely:

$$S(T) = S(T_1)\exp\left\{ \left[r - y - \frac{\sigma^2}{2} \right](T - T_1) + \sigma \, \widehat{W}(T - T_1) \right\} = S(T_1)\exp U$$

$$U = \left(r - y - \frac{\sigma^2}{2} \right)(T - T_1) + \sigma \, \hat{W}(T - T_1)$$

Hence, we can extract $S(T_1)$ in the payoff of the forward-start option:

$$C^{fs}(T) = S(T_1)\max(0, \exp U - 1)$$

and write

$$C^{fs}(t) = e^{-rt} E_Q\left[S(T_1)(\exp U - 1)1_\varepsilon / F_t \right] \qquad (5.5)$$

where $\varepsilon = \{$states of nature where $S(T) > S(T_1)\}$.[1]

Note that the increments of the Brownian motion are *independent*, the quantities $S(T_1)$ and U (which are random variables viewed from date t) are independent and the computation involved in equation (5.5) is of the same type as the one developed in the proof of the Black–Scholes formula involving expectations under the pricing measure Q. Moreover, we use the fact that the T_1 maturity forward price is constant on average under Q. Observing that, we obtain

$$E_Q\left[S(T_1)/F_t \right] = E_Q\left[F^{T_1}(T_1)/F_t \right] = F^{T_1}(t)$$

Pulling this quantity out of the expectation in equation (5.5) and repeating for the product $(\exp U - 1)1_\varepsilon$, the computations conducted in Chapter 4, we obtain for the price at date t of the forward start option:

$$C^{fs}(t) = S(t)e^{-y(T-t)} N(d_1) - F^{T_1}(t)e^{-r(T-t)} N(d_2) \qquad (5.6)$$

$$\begin{cases} d_1 = \dfrac{\ln\left(\dfrac{S(t)e^{-y(T-t)}}{F^{T_1}(t)e^{-r(T-t)}} \right) + \dfrac{1}{2}\sigma^2(T - T_1)}{\sigma\sqrt{T - T_1}} \\ d_2 = d_1 - \sigma\sqrt{T - T_1} \end{cases}$$

---

[1] The mathematical formalism is kept to an acceptable minimum.

This interesting formula is the same as the Black–Scholes formula, except that the fixed strike k has been replaced by the *forward price* of the commodity prevailing at date t for the maturity T_1, the date at which the option 'really' starts. Equation (5.6) shows that, even though we assumed a constant volatility over the whole period $[0, T]$ in equation (5.4), the only volatility that matters in the problem is the one prevailing during the period $[T_1, T]$. This is the implied volatility embedded in this forward-start option reflecting the market view of the volatility for the future time period (T_1, T).

For example, in corn markets, a grower may wish to buy as of January a forward start put option (to protect his revenues against a collapse in prices) with respect to a strike equal to the spot price of corn in June, when part of the important information with respect to the new crop is being released. By doing so, he does not pay the cost of hedging between January and June. Forward-start options have become quite liquid in equity and commodity markets and traders are today looking for models that not only explain the volatility smile for plain vanilla options at some chosen maturities T but also the *'forward smiles'* involving pairs of maturities.

5.4 ASIAN OPTIONS AS KEY INSTRUMENTS IN COMMODITY MARKETS

These options appeared in the financial markets at the end of the 1980s and are particularly important today in currency and commodity markets.

1. In the case of FX markets, their validity can be explained in a simple example: consider a treasurer of a multinational company who knows that he will receive in a future period daily (or weekly) cash flows denominated in Japanese yen while he is based in Switzerland. In order to hedge his exposure to a decline of the Japanese yen, he needs to buy put options on the underlying JPY/CHF, the value of the yen relative to the Swiss franc. If he is to receive 100 cash flows, he may protect each of them by an ordinary put option. This very exact hedge of 100 options is likely to be expensive and cumbersome. A less precise but reasonable solution consists in buying a put option written on the arithmetic average of the 100 exchange rates, i.e., an Asian put option. In a symmetric manner, this treasurer will need an Asian call option written on the value of the Brazilian real with respect to the Swiss franc to hedge against a rise in the cost of the coffee imports from Brazil.
2. In the case of commodities and shipping markets, many indices are arithmetic averages of the underlying spot price in order to prevent momentarily wild fluctuation related to large exchanged quantities or volumes. In the case of oil, the quantity of time elapsed between the day a tanker leaves the production site and reaches its destination explains why oil indices (e.g., dated Brent) are arithmetic averages; accordingly, many financial options related to oil are Asian. Bunker fuel indexes are also defined as averages. In the shipping markets, most freight indexes are defined as averages over a calendar period to avoid manipulations by a big player – manipulating prices for many days is difficult and costly.
3. Whenever the underlying spot price is not easily identifiable (and this is particularly true for many agricultural commodity markets), the party losing money on a position in plain vanilla options may be tempted to sharply move the market on the date of maturity T in order to make the options expire worthless. A 'large player' can fairly easily push the market up or down on a given day. This price manipulation becomes impossible in the case of arithmetic-average option since many numbers enter into the computation of the average defining the payoff and the exercise of market power becomes more problematic.

Because of points (2) and (3), Asian options are particularly appropriate for commodity markets and, unsurprisingly, represent a large fraction of the options traded in these markets.

As mentioned before, if we assume a geometric Brownian motion for the dynamics of the commodity price, we have the following expression under the pricing measure Q:

$$\frac{dS(t)}{S(t)} = (r - y)dt + \sigma \, d\widehat{W}_t$$

where y is the convenience yield (positive or negative according to the period) and $\widehat{W}_t$ is a Q-Brownian motion.

As done many times at this point, we know that, viewed from date 0, the values of S at future dates $t_1, t_2, \ldots, t_n$ may be obtained by integrating this equation:

$$S(t_i) = S(0) \exp\left\{ \left(r - y - \frac{\sigma^2}{2} \right) t_i + \sigma \, \widehat{W}(t_i) \right\}$$

Hence, the average $A(T)$ over the period, defined by

$$A(T) = \frac{S(t_1) + S(t_2) + \ldots + S(t_n)}{n},$$

appears as a sum of exponentials, which is not a simple mathematical object.

It is important to remember that it is the simple distribution of $S(T)$ in the Black–Scholes setting, namely a log-normal distribution, which is responsible for the simplicity of the valuation of European calls. The situation is quite different here, since a sum (or average) of log-normal variables is not log-normal.

The problem represented a mathematical challenge at the beginning of the 1990s and, to a certain extent, still does. We are going to review the most tractable methods and their limits as well.

5.4.1 Approximation of the arithmetic average by a geometric average

Kemna and Vorst (1990) observed that, if one considers instead the geometric average,

$$A^{geom}{}_{(T)} = \left[S(t_1) \ldots S(t_n) \right]^{1/n}$$

then the log-normality is preserved, since the average appears as a product of exponentials.

They show that in this case, the Asian option price at date 0 is obtained by a Black–Scholes-type formula:

$$C(0) = e^{-\alpha T} S(0) N(d_1) - k e^{-rT} N(d_2)$$

$$\begin{cases} \alpha = \dfrac{1}{2}\left(y - r + \dfrac{\sigma^2}{6} \right) \\[2mm] d_1 = \ln\left(\dfrac{S(0)}{k} \right) + \dfrac{1}{2}\left(r - y + \dfrac{\sigma^2}{6} \right) T \Big/ \sigma\sqrt{\dfrac{T}{3}} \\[2mm] d_2 = d_1 - \sigma\sqrt{\dfrac{T}{3}} \end{cases}$$

Consequently, the geometric average call option written on a commodity S can be priced by the standard Black–Scholes formula where the volatility is divided by the square root of 3 and the convenience yield y replaced by the quantity α defined above.

5.4.2 Approximation of the distribution of the arithmetic average by a log-normal distribution

Levy (1991) and other practitioners proposed to approximate the true distribution of the arithmetic average by a log-normal distribution. In this case, it is important at least to incorporate in the representation of $A(T)$ by a log-normal distribution the true values of the mean and the variance, in order to avoid the addition of errors.

We are going to propose here an alternate route to the computation of the mean, which has the merit of being simple and illuminating some messages conveyed in Chapters 3 and 4. Recall that, for a large number of points in the average, we can write:

$$A(T) = \frac{1}{T} \int_0^T S(u)\, du$$

and we are interested in the expectation (or mean) $E_Q[A(T)]$ under the pricing measure.

Looking at the dynamics of S_t under Q in the previous chapter, we get

$$S(0) = E_Q\left[S(u)e^{-(r-y)u}\right] \tag{5.7}$$

expressing that the commodity spot price, discounted and compensated for the 'loss' of convenience yield, remains constant on average under the Q measure.

Using now the linearity of the expectation operator, we can write

$$E_Q\left[A(T)\right] = E_Q\left[\frac{1}{T}\int_0^T S(u)\,du\right] = \frac{1}{T}\int_0^T E_Q\left[S(u)\right]du$$

From equation (5.7), and because we assumed r and y constant, we can write for any u:

$$E_Q\left[S(u)\right] = S(0)e^{(r-y)u}$$

This integral is straightforward and provides the mean of the arithmetic average of $S(t)$ over the interval $[0, T]$:

$$E_Q\left[A(T)\right] = S(0)\frac{e^{(r-y)T} - 1}{(r-y)T} \tag{5.8}$$

This anticipated average value of the commodity price over the coming period $(0, T)$ relative to the current price $S(0)$ is defined by:

$$\frac{E_Q\left[A(T)\right]}{S(0)} = \frac{e^{(r-y)T} - 1}{T - t}$$

and an elementary expansion shows that it is smaller than 1 if $r - y < 0$, a situation of backwardation, or greater than 1 if $r - y > 0$, a situation of contango. Hence, the shape of the forward curve is reflected in the Q-expectation of the average of future spot prices, which is consistent with the expectation of a future spot price embedded in each Future contract. Lastly, it is interesting to observe that

$$E_Q\left[A(T)/F_0\right] = E_Q\left[\frac{S(t_1)+S(t_2)+...S(t_n)}{n}/F_0\right]$$

$$= \frac{E_Q\left[S(t_1)/F_0\right]+...+E_Q\left[S(t_n)/F_0\right]}{n}$$

$$= \frac{E_Q\left[F^{t_1}(t_1)/F_0\right]+...+E_Q\left[F^{t_n}(t_n)/F_0\right]}{n}$$

$$= \frac{F^{t_1}(0)+...+F^{t_n}(0)}{n}$$

which is the average of the current forward curve (represented here is the average computed over a finite number of days, which is the case in practice).

We see now the beautiful relationship between the *average value of the forward curve observed today*, introduced in 2006 by Borovkova and Geman and discussed in Chapter 3, and the expectation under the pricing measure of the average price defining the settlement at maturity of the Asian options very much used in commodity markets and often traded on exchanges.

Together with the swaps discussed in Section 5.1 of this chapter, we have necessary consistencies to identify in a book of forward contracts, swaps, plain-vanilla and Asian options, which have the merit of being *model independent*.

5.4.3. Monte-Carlo simulations for Asian options valuation

One of the most popular methods used today by practitioners to price Asian options is to use the Monte-Carlo approach described in Chapter 4 for plain vanilla options. A difference, however, with the previous situation is the fact that in the case of European calls and puts, one needed only to produce N independent simulations of the terminal value $S(T)$. Now, we will need N *trajectories* of the commodity price over the period [0, T]; each of them will lead to one simulated average A, and in turn to a simulated payoff of the Asian option. The partition $t_1, t_2, ..., t_n$ of the period must be fine enough to incorporate all the dates included in the average (and may be finer).

Again, the dynamics of the underlying commodity price $S(t)$ are under the pricing measure Q:

$$\frac{dS(t)}{S(t)} = (r-y)dt + \sigma\, d\hat{W}_t$$

Integrating this equation between dates 0 and t_1 provides, as seen many times:

$$S(t_1) = S(0)\exp\left\{\left(r-y-\frac{\sigma^2}{2}\right)t_1 + \sigma\,\hat{W}(t_1)\right\}$$

A random draw of $\hat{W}(t_1)$ will lead to one simulated value $\hat{S}(t_1)$.

Starting from this point – since we need to have 'consistency' in the construction point by point of the trajectory according to our chosen model – we obtain:

$$S(t_2) = \hat{S}(t_1)\exp\left\{\left(r - y - \frac{\sigma}{2}\right)(t_2 - t_1) + \sigma\,\hat{W}(t_2 - t_1)\right\}$$

Now, a random draw of $\hat{W}(t_2 - t_1)$ (whose distribution is the same as the one $\hat{W}(t_1)$ for equally spaced points t_1, t_2, ..., t_n over the period [0, T]) leads to a simulated value $\hat{S}(t_2)$. Proceeding piecewise, we simulate a first trajectory b_1 of the underlying commodity S over which we can compute a simulated average a_1:

$$a_1 = \frac{\hat{S}(t_1) + \,.... + \hat{S}(t_n)}{n}$$

and a simulated payoff $b_1 = \max(0, a_1 - k)$.

We repeat this procedure N times and obtain an approximated value for the Asian option at time 0:

$$C(0) \approx e^{-rT}\frac{b_1 + \,.... + b_n}{N}$$

This Monte-Carlo approach gives a very good approximation of the exact Asian option price because of the smooth nature of the payoff. However, since we have no explicit formula[2] for the price $C(0)$, we cannot take its partial derivative with respect to $S(0)$ to obtain the delta of the Asian option. A classical answer adopted by practitioners is to use a 'finite-difference method' and approximate the *delta* (slope of the tangent) by the slope of a segment centered in $S(0)$, the current price of the underlying commodity:

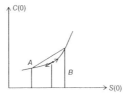

Using the same random draws as before for $\hat{W}(t_1)$, $\hat{W}(t_2 - t_1)$ ... $\hat{W}_t(t_n - t_{n-1})$, we now compute the Asian call price, but for a starting value $S(0) + \frac{h}{2}$; lastly, we use as a starting value $S(0) - \frac{h}{2}$, where h is a small number (for instance, of the order of $S(0)/100$). We then write an approximated value of the delta:

$$\Delta^{As} \approx \frac{C^{As}\left(S_0 + \dfrac{h}{2}\right) - C^{As}\left(S_0 - \dfrac{h}{2}\right)}{h} \tag{5.9}$$

_____

[2] One of the beauties of the BSM formula, as said before, is the existence of a closed-form expression for the call price, hence for all its partial derivatives.

5.4.4 Exact results (Geman and Yor, 1993)

Geman and Yor (1993) wish to address the exact issue, namely an arithmetic average for the expression of the underlying, in an exact manner (i.e., with no approximation for the distribution of this arithmetic average $A(T)$ or for the computation of the option price).

1. Using several probabilistic tools, including a stochastic time change, they are able to provide an exact formula for the Laplace transform with respect to maturity of the Asian option price. Because of the *linearity* of the Laplace transform, the same approach applies to the delta and other Greeks. Eydeland and Geman (1995) show how to invert this Laplace transform and also exhibit the loss of accuracy occurring in the computation of the different Greeks with approximate methods. Fast inversion procedures existing today for the Laplace transform (and the Fourier transform) provide the option and the Greeks within a very short time.
2. In the same paper, Geman and Yor underline that the valuation of the Asian option does depend on the date at which the pricing takes place relative to the averaging period. Supposing for simplicity that the averaging period coincides with the lifetime of the option:

At date 0, none of the values $S(t_1)$, $S(t_2)$... is known and the price $C^{As}(0)$ is related to the *expectation* of the average of all quantities. Now, suppose that the date t of analysis lies between the date t_j and t_{j+1}:

The values $S(t_1)$, ..., $S(t_j)$ are then *fully observed* at that point and the average may be written as:

$$A(T) = \frac{S(t_1) + ... + S(t_j) + \tilde{S}(t_{j+1}) + ... + \tilde{S}(t_n)}{n}$$

where the randomness resides only in the last terms, hence, diminishes to zero as one gets closer to the maturity date. We observe that if the values $S(t_1)$, ..., $S(t_j)$ registered prior to date t are large, it may happen that the quantity $(S(t_1) + ... + S(t_j))/n$ be larger than k.

Since the unknown quantities $S(t_{j+1})...S(t_n)$ are positive, it is already certain at date t that:

– the Asian call option will finish in the money
– $\max(0, A(T) - k) = A(T) - k$.

Hence, it becomes legitimate to write:

$$C(t) = e^{-r(T-t)} E_Q \left[\max\left(0, A(T) - k\right) / F_t \right]$$

$$C(t) = e^{-r(T-t)} E_Q\big[(A(T)-k)/F_t\big] \tag{5.10}$$

The linearity of the expectation operator allows one to obtain an explicit formula for the Asian call, in this particular case, namely:

$$C^{As}(t) = S(t)\frac{1-e^{-r(T-t)}}{rT} - e^{-r(T-t)}\left[k - \frac{S(t_1)+....+S(t_j)}{n}\right] \tag{5.11}$$

Geman and Yor observe that this formula has interesting resemblances with the Black–Scholes formula, where the strike k is adjusted for the already observed values and the coefficient of $S(t)$ can easily be shown to be positive and smaller than 1. However, the quantity in brackets is in fact negative since we are in the particular case where the past prices are very large, and the option price is the sum of two positive terms, exhibiting the high value of the Asian call in the particular case of analysis. Note that this formula may help in the valuation of weather derivatives, since these are formulated as Asian options.

3. When comparing the Asian call and plain vanilla call with the same strike and maturity, it is clear that the arithmetic average of n quantities $S(t_i)$ has a smaller volatility than a single quantity $S(t_i)$. Consequently, the common view is that an Asian call option should *always* be cheaper than the plain vanilla one with the same strike and maturity. Geman and Yor (1993) show that this statement is not true: even though volatility is a key component of an option price, it is not the only one.

To take an elementary example, let us consider an Asian option based on an average over 3 points t_1, t_2, $t_3 = T$ of a dividend-paying stock whose values are $S(t_1) = 80$; $S(t_2) = 60$; $S(t_3) = 40$. The average $A(T)$ is equal to 60 while $S(T)$ is equal to 40. Hence, for all strikes between 40 and 60, the Asian option has a positive payoff and the European one a zero payoff. Consequently, the price at date 0 of the Asian call option should be higher than the European one, even though the volatility of the average is lower.

This observation is particularly important in our situation, namely commodities: as seen many times in this book, the convenience yield plays the role of a dividend payment. If the convenience yield y is positive and very high, and more precisely if the *forward curve is backwardated*, $r - y$ is negative and the Asian call option *may be more expensive* than the European call with the same characteristics.

Geman and Yor show the following:

– If $r - y$ is positive, i.e., the forward curve is in contango, the Asian call option is indeed cheaper than the European one.
– If $r - y$ is negative, i.e., the forward curve is in backwardation, the answer is not clear and depends on the relative impact of the volatility reduction in the average versus the expected declining value of the underlying commodity spot price. Detailed results may be found in their (1993) paper.

An important conclusion of this discussion, beyond the specific case of Asian options, is to remember that the price of any option depends not only on the volatility parameter σ but also of the drift term $(r - y)$ of the price dynamics *under the pricing measure Q*, as exhibited in Chapter 4. For options written on commodities, this message is indispensable since $r - y$

may be positive or negative. It is interesting to observe that many practitioners, even if they are not focused on the details of the pricing measure Q, have an instinctive knowledge of these properties as the sign of $(r - y)$ has a direct impact on the *shape* of the forward curve as well as on the price of the Asian call option relative to the standard European call.

5.5 TRADING THE SHAPE OF THE FORWARD CURVE THROUGH FLOATING-STRIKE ASIAN OPTIONS

As indicated by the name, the floating-strike Asian options do not have a fixed strike, but instead the value of the underlying commodity at maturity, $S(T)$. The payoff at maturity reflects the relative value of the average spot price over the period $(0, T)$ with respect to the ending value of S at date T.

Since a call option has the property of giving a positive payoff when the underlying price goes up, a floating-strike Asian call option is defined by the following payoff at maturity:

$$C_{fl}^{As}(T) = \max\left(0, \, S(T) - A(T)\right)$$

Trading a floating-strike Asian call or put amounts to expressing at date 0 anticipations on the *average value of the spot price over the period (0,* T) with respect to its end point $S(T)$. It was said in Chapter 2 that anticipations on future values of the spot price were contained in the forward prices. And we know that the expectation of an average is equal to the average of the expectations. The latter is contained in the average forward curve, hence the trader of a floating-strike Asian option is essentially comparing the average forward curve currently observed for maturities extending to T to the forward price $f(0, T)$. Regarding the valuation of floating strike Asian options, Monte-Carlo simulations offer an easy answer.

An alternative consists in writing

$$C_{fs}^{As}(T) = S(T)\max\left(0, 1 - \frac{A(T)}{S(T)}\right)$$

and using the commodity spot price S as the *numéraire*, namely

$$\frac{C(T)}{S(T)} = \max\left(0, 1 - \frac{A(T)}{S(T)}\right)$$

We recognize on the right-hand side the expression of a plain vanilla put option written on $X = A/S$, with strike 1 and maturity T. Using the *numéraire* change theorem (Geman *et al.*, 1995), one can fairly easily finish the computation and obtain the call price at date t, as well as its Greeks (see the book by Geman (2005)).

6

Exchange, Spread, and Quanto Options in Commodity Markets

'All models are wrong, but some are useful.'

2010 – George Box, *An Accidental Statistician*

6.1 EXCHANGE OPTIONS

Exchange options, in the form of real options, have existed for ever in the world of commodities: the exchange was called *barter*. In the form of financial instruments, exchange options have existed for many decades in equity markets since the mid-1970s for investment purposes: by holding the stock S_2 and an option to exchange the stock S_2 for another S_1, an investor gets at maturity the best of the two stocks S_1 and S_2, which is obviously a desirable position for all investors.

The payoff at maturity T of an exchange option is:

$$C(T) = \max\left(0, S_1(T) - S_2(T)\right)$$

Margrabe (1978) provided in the Black–Scholes–Merton setting an exact pricing formula that has the remarkably symmetric form:

$$C(t) = S_1(t) N(d_1) - S_2(t) N(d_2)$$

where:

$$
\begin{cases}
d_1 = \dfrac{\ln\left(\dfrac{S_1(t)}{S_2(t)}\right) + \dfrac{1}{2}\sum^2 (T - t)}{\sum \sqrt{T - t}} \\[4mm]
d_2 = d_1 - \sum \sqrt{T - t} \\[2mm]
\sum = Vol\,\dfrac{S_1(t)}{S_2(t)} = \sqrt{\sigma_1^2 + \sigma_2^2 - 2\rho\,\sigma_1\sigma_2} \\[2mm]
\rho = Correl(S_1, S_2)
\end{cases}
$$

The proof can be obtained through a partial differential equation analogous to the Black–Scholes one or by computing the discounted expectation under the pricing measure of the final payoff.

Turning to commodities and assuming the dynamics of their prices driven by geometric Brownian motions, we have seen that under the pricing measure Q, the processes $(S_1(t))$ and $(S_2(t))$ satisfy the following stochastic differential equations:

$$\begin{vmatrix} \dfrac{d S_1(t)}{S_1(t)} = (r - y_1)dt + \sigma_1 d\hat{W}_t^1 \\[2ex] \dfrac{d S_2(t)}{S_2(t)} = (r - y_2)dt + \sigma_2 d\hat{W}_t^2 \\[2ex] Cov\left(d\hat{W}_t^1, d\hat{W}_t^2\right) = \rho\, dt \end{vmatrix}$$

The resulting price of the option to exchange one unit of the commodity S_2 for one unit of the commodity S_1 is given by the same formula as Margrabe's, with the addition of convenience yields y_1 and y_2, assumed to be constant in our setting:

$$C(t) = S_1(t)e^{-y_1(T-t)}N(d_1) - S_2(t)e^{-y_2(T-t)}N(d_2) \tag{6.1}$$

where:

$$\begin{vmatrix} d_1 = \dfrac{\ln\left(\dfrac{S_1(t)e^{-y_1(T-t)}}{S_2(t)e^{-y_2(T-t)}}\right) + \dfrac{1}{2}\sum^2 (T-t)}{\sum\sqrt{(T-t)}} \\[3ex] d_2 = d_1 - \sum\sqrt{(T-t)} \\[2ex] \sum = Vol\left(\dfrac{S_1}{S_2}\right) = \sqrt{\sigma_1^2 + \sigma_2^2 - 2\rho\,\sigma_1\sigma_2} \\[2ex] \rho = Correl(S_1, S_2) \end{vmatrix}$$

Note that:

1. Σ is the *volatility of S_1 relative to S_2*, i.e., of the price of S_1 expressed in the *numéraire S_2*.
2. The sensitivity of the value of the exchange option to the volatility of S_1 (respectively S_2) is not necessarily positive, in contrast to the vega of a plain vanilla European call. This is immediately exhibited by observing that

$$\frac{\partial C}{\partial \sigma_1} = \frac{\partial C}{\partial \sum}\frac{\partial \sum}{\partial \sigma_1}$$

The first quantity $\dfrac{\partial C}{\partial \sum}$ is a classical vega, hence positive; the second quantity $\dfrac{\partial \sum}{\partial \sigma_1} = \dfrac{1}{\sum}(\sigma_1 - \rho\sigma_2)$

depends on the sign of the parenthesis, which may be negative if the correlation is non-zero and the volatility σ_2 fairly high, which does happen in the case of natural gas. This situation does not occur in equity markets since the standard volatility there is around 18% and high volatilities are around 30%. Hence, we need to be careful as volatilities of energy or agricultural commodities can lead to counterintuitive situations (e.g., a negative vega in one of the two underlyings). In practice, this means that when we have a high correlation, the great variability of the price of gas or cocoa may create a negative exposure to the volatility of the electricity price or cocoa butter.

Lastly, let us note that, if we wish to introduce mean reversion in the dynamics of S_1 and/or S_2, the price of the exchange option as an explicit formula given in equation (6.1) no longer holds; however, Monte-Carlo methods or trees can easily provide an approximation of the option price.

Using the spot-forward relationship and the Futures of maturity T on the two spot commodities, formula (6.1) may be rewritten as

$$ C(t) = e^{-r(T-t)} \left[F_1^T(t) N(d_1) - F_2^T(t) N(d_2) \right] $$

where F_1^T and F_2^T denote the Futures prices for the same maturity T of the commodities S_1 and S_2. These numbers can directly be read in the market and avoid the explicit computation of the two convenience yields.

This formula also holds for an exchange option between two Futures contracts maturing at the maturity T of the exchange option.

Note that a proper convergence of Futures prices to spot prices at maturity allows using this formula, as mentioned earlier, for the option to exchange one commodity for the other at date S. The value of the above formula is that it involves only visible Futures prices, an important property both for pricing and hedging.

6.2 COMMODITY SPREAD OPTIONS AND THEIR IMPORTANCE IN COMMODITY MARKETS

These are particularly popular in *all* commodity markets, e.g., soy crush in the soybean market, wheat mill in wheat markets, and can be encountered under several forms that are described below.

The spread between two quantities is probably the most traded instrument in the world of commodities and energy commodities in particular. Spread options come into play in the valuation of oil refineries, silos and storage facilities, processors, and transformation plants, i.e., all the fundamental physical assets in the commodity industry, and will be used in the last chapter in the valuation of physical assets. Unsurprisingly, financial spread options are also traded as financial instruments in their own right as part of commodity portfolios – the owners of physical assets can sell them using the asset to back the option, hence avoiding any pricing model for the option once the physical asset has been purchased.

Spreads can be broadly categorized in the following way.

Spreads between two commodities
In the domain of agricultural commodities, this spread then represents a 'quality' spread, such as different types of wheat (winter wheat, Chicago wheat, etc.); different types of coffee (Robusta versus Arabica); or the spread between the phosphate rock and the DAP (di-ammonium of phosphate) in the world of fertilizers.

Futures calendar spreads with zero strike
These are very popular in commodity markets for another type of reason, namely seasonality. A typical payoff at maturity T is of the form

$$ C(T) = \max\left(0, \ F^{T_1}(T) - F^{T_2}(T) \right) $$

where $T < T_1 < T_2$, meaning that the option is in fact a Futures calendar spread on the same commodity. Unsurprisingly, this option arises in the valuation of storage facilities, such as silos and elevators, and also water reservoirs. There are fundamentally two ways of pricing calendar spread options:

1. Either the Futures contracts of different maturities are perceived as the prices of two different commodities, in particular because of the seasonal effect. Under the pricing measure Q, the two Futures contracts will then be written as martingales with different volatilities, and obviously a correlation coefficient. A simple example of such a representation has been seen before: in the case of geometric Brownian motion there is no drift term in the stochastic differential equation driving the future prices:

$$\begin{cases} \dfrac{d\,F^{T_1}(t)}{F^{T_1}(t)} = \sigma_1 d\,W^1(t) \\[2mm] \dfrac{d\,F^{T_2}(t)}{F^{T_2}(t)} = \sigma_2 d\,W^2(t) \\[2mm] d\,W^1(t).d\,W^2(t) = \rho\,dt \end{cases}$$

   For a valuation of such a spread see Section 6.1.
2. Or one prefers to incorporate all the relevant properties of the commodity under analysis in a single stochastic process $(F^T(t))$ featuring a term structure of volatilities $\sigma(t, T)$ and the spread option at time 0 is priced as the expectation of the discounted payoff $\max(0, F^T{}_1(T) - F^T{}_2(T))$.
   In this case, a detailed comprehension of the *dynamics of the forward curve* is
   necessary.
   In general, it is the first approach that is adopted since the calendar spread is mostly perceived by market participants as built upon two different instruments: wheat in May is viewed as a different commodity from wheat in September.

Forward-start options (spot calendar spread options)
As we saw in the previous chapter, these options allow investors to take a view on the price of the same commodity at two different points in time:

$$C^{fs}(T) = \max(0, S(T) - S(T_1)) \tag{6.2}$$

These options were discussed in Chapter 5 and are used to hedge an exposure starting in the future.

Commodity spread options
A spread option between two commodities S_1 and S_2 has the same type of payoff as a standard call option, except that now the underlying is the difference $S_1 - S_2$ (or $Q_1 S_1 - Q_2 S_2$, where Q_1 and Q_2 are quantities of the commodities S_1 and S_2) and the strike k is non-zero. These options naturally appear in the valuation of physical assets such as soybean crushers, units producing

di-ammonium of phosphate from phosphate rock and any processor transforming the raw commodity into a more refined form. Typically, the payoff of the spread option is of the form:

$$C(T) = \max\left(0,\, Q_1\, S_1(T) - Q_2\, S_2(T) - k\right) \tag{6.3}$$

where:

- Q_1 and Q_2 are positive constants (representing quantities);
- the strike k is strictly positive.

Whether the dynamics of $(S_1(t))$ and $(S_2(t))$ are driven under the pricing measure Q by geometric Brownian motions or by diffusion processes including mean-reversion and time-varying volatilities, there is no more an explicit formula for the option price at date t.

A first approximation approach was proposed by Kirk (1995): assuming that the quantity k is small, Kirk considers that the addition of k to the second term does not change its geometric Brownian motion behavior (nor its volatility) and recognizes again the setting of the Margrabe (1978) formula.

If k is not small and one does not like the above approximation, Monte-Carlo *simulations of the bi-dimensional process* (S_1, S_2) provide an easy-to-implement pricing approach.

We have seen in Chapter 4 how to build Monte-Carlo simulations of the trajectories of a single commodity price $(S(t))$ by discretization of the process S over the lifetime $[0, T]$ of the option. The same procedure applies here, except that consistency in the construction of the trajectories for S_1 and S_2 needs to be insured given the crucial importance of the *dependence structure* between the two price processes $(S_1(t))$ and $(S_2(t))$. To make things simple, let us suppose that both processes follow mean-reverting diffusions, for instance driven under the pricing measure Q by the stochastic differential equations:

$$\begin{cases} d S_1(t) = a\left(b - \ln S_1(t)\right) S_1(t)\, dt + \sigma_1\, S_1(t)\, dW_t^1 \\ d S_2(t) = c\left(e - \ln S_2(t)\right) S_2(t)\, dt + \sigma_2\, S_2(t)\, dW_t^2 \\ d W_t^1 \cdot dW_t^2 = \rho\, dt \end{cases} \tag{6.4}$$

We can immediately see that non-constant volatility parameters σ_1 and σ_2 may be incorporated in what follows. This may be done easily if:

- σ_1 and σ_2 are deterministic functions of time (for instance, exhibiting seasonality).
- σ_1 (respectively σ_2) is a deterministic function of the commodity spot prices S_1 (respectively S_2), e.g., increasing when the commodity price rises according to the inverse leverage effect characteristic of commodity prices, at least until 2007. Since 2008, this feature may occasionally have disappeared for energy prices, much less so for agricultural commodities.

Returning to equation (6.4), we see that the simulation of trajectories from the equation driving $S_1(t)$ alone takes us back to Chapter 4. But we need to make sure that the correlation property is correctly represented. In this order, we will write the second Brownian motion W_2 as

$$W^2(t) = \rho W^1(t) + (1 - \rho) W^3(t) \tag{6.5}$$

where $W^3(t)$ is a Brownian motion independent of $W_1(t)$:

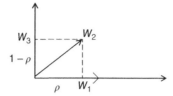

This geometric decomposition of W_2 is often referred to as the Cholesky decomposition, in particular in the Value at Risk literature where correlations absolutely need to be reflected in the analysis of the change in value of a position depending on several sources of risk $S_1, S_2, \ldots, S_q$. Figures 6.1 and 6.2 show the cloud of points generated by a bi-dimensional Brownian motion (W_1, W_2). In Figure 6.1 the correlation coefficient is equal to zero; in Figure 6.2, $\rho = 0.6$.

In order to build a first pair of trajectories $(Z_1^{(1)}, Z_2^{(1)})$ for S_1 and S_2 over the interval $[0, T]$, we first discretize it into n subintervals. The changes in S_1 and S_2 over the first subinterval are fully defined by the Brownian increments of

$$H_1 = W_1\left(0 + \frac{T}{n}\right) - W_1(0) \ \ and \ \ H_2 = W_2\left(0 + \frac{T}{n}\right) - W_2(0)$$

since we remember that the discretization of equation (6.4) leads to:

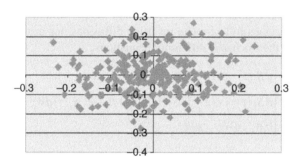

Figure 6.1   Simulations of pairs (W_1, W_2) in the case of zero correlation

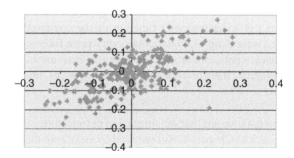

Figure 6.2   Simulations of pairs (W_1, W_2) when $\rho = 0.6$

$$S_1\left(\frac{T}{n}\right) - S_1(0) = a\left(b - \ln S_1(0)\right) S_1(0)\frac{T}{n} + \sigma_1 S_1(0) H_1$$

$$S_2\left(\frac{T}{n}\right) - S_2(0) = c\left(e - \ln S_2(0)\right) S_2(0)\frac{T}{n} + \sigma_2 S_2(0) H_2$$

For the quantity H_1 that is normally distributed with mean 0 and variance 1, a random draw $\widehat{H}_1$ is easy to obtain. To build a random draw denoted $\widehat{H}_2$ of H_2, we need first to create a random draw $\widehat{H}_3$ of the change over the same interval of an *independent* Brownian motion W_3 (same drift 0 and variance 1) and define

$$\widehat{H}_2 = \rho\,\widehat{H}_1 + \left(1 - \rho\right)\widehat{H}_3$$

in order to satisfy the correlation property.

Constructing 1000 pairs of trajectories for S_1 and S_2 in this manner, we obtain the corresponding terminal values $S_1(T)$ and $S_2(T)$ and hence 1000 simulated payoffs $u_1, u_2,..., u_{1000}$ by plugging these numbers into equation (6.3):

$$C(T) = \max(0,\, Q_1\, S_1(T) - Q_2 S_2(T) - k)$$

The Monte-Carlo price of the spread option at date 0 is consequently equal to

$$C^{MC}(0) = e^{-rT}\,\frac{u_1 + u_2 + ... + u_{1000}}{1000}$$

and is a very good approximation of the exact price $C(0)$ of the spread option.

Note that the methodology described above would readily allow us to handle *path-dependent* options written on S_1 and S_2 since *full trajectories* have been generated over the interval $[0, T]$.

6.3 COMMODITY QUANTO OPTIONS

The terminology of quanto options has been introduced in the context of equity markets for multi-asset options where one of the risk factors is the currency risk. These quanto options are obviously particularly relevant in commodity markets since producing regions export to various countries in the world. Consider a large Italian ice-cream maker (a subsidiary of Parmalat, for instance) that hedges its cocoa price exposure by entering a cocoa call option in London expressed in pounds sterling. Typically, the company will get at maturity T

$$C(T) = \max(0,\, S(T) - k)$$

where S denotes the spot price of the UK cocoa price in London. If cocoa prices go up, the positive payoff of the option will offset the increase in the cost of the raw material. However, in this process, currency risk appears since the possible decline of the British pound against the euro will impact the option payoff. The benefit of the hedge would be destroyed. Hence, a proper solution for the company is to buy from a bank, located in Italy, the UK or anywhere else, a *commodity quanto option*. The most appropriate one in the example under analysis would pay at maturity:

$$C(T) = \max(0, S(T)X(T) - k_d) \tag{6.6}$$

where $X(T)$ is the exchange rate prevailing at date T (number of euros per British pound) and k_d is the strike of the call option expressed in euros – the domestic currency of the ice-cream maker. The strike is chosen by the hedger at the level above which the cost of cocoa in euros would damage the benefits of the production of chocolate ice-cream.

Assuming that S, the spot price of cocoa in British pounds, and X, the exchange rate EUR/GBP both follow a geometric Brownian motion, the product $(S(t)X(t))_{t \geq 0}$ is also a geometric Brownian motion. Unsurprisingly, the price of the commodity quanto call at date t is given by a Black–Scholes-type formula, namely:

$$C(t) = S(t)X(t)e^{-y(T-t)}N(d_1) - k_d e^{-r_d(T-t)}N(d_2) \tag{6.7}$$

where:

- y is the cocoa convenience yield;
- r_d denotes the interest rate in the domestic economy

$$
\begin{cases}
d_1 = \dfrac{\ln\left(\dfrac{S(t)X(t)e^{-y(T-t)}}{k_d e^{-r_d(T-t)}}\right) + \dfrac{1}{2}\sum^2(T-t)}{\sum\sqrt{T-t}} \\[4ex]
d_2 = d_1 - \sum\sqrt{T-t} \\[2ex]
\sum = Vol(SX) = \sqrt{\sigma_S^2 + \sigma_X^2 + 2\rho\sigma_X\sigma_y}
\end{cases} \quad ;
$$

- σ_s and σ_x denote respectively the volatilities of S and X;
- ρ is the correlation coefficient between S and X.

We can note that except in the totally unlikely situation of a perfect correlation between the cocoa price in pounds and the exchange rate GBP/EUR, ρ is strictly smaller than 1 and the volatility of SX strictly smaller than the sum of the two volatilities. Hence, the price of the quanto option – and the cost of the hedge for the company – is strictly lower than the added premia of an option written on the cocoa price and an option written on the FX rate.

Proof

When one moves to a multi-economy problem, the no-arbitrage assumption needs to be extended to this new setting. It can be shown that the non-existence of arbitrage opportunities between the two economies implies, as long as the geometric Brownian motion is viewed as acceptable, that the dynamics of the exchange rate X under the multi-economy pricing measure Q has the following remarkable expression:

$$\frac{dX(t)}{X(t)} = \left(r_d - r_f\right)dt + \sigma_x \, dW_t^X \tag{6.8}$$

where:

- r_d (respectively r_f) denotes the domestic (respectively foreign) interest rate;
- σ_x denotes the volatility of the exchange rate.

Assuming now that the cocoa price *denominated in British pounds* also follows a geometric Brownian motion, the dynamics of S under the Q measure has an expression discussed before, namely:

$$\frac{dS(t)}{S(t)} = \left(r_f - y\right)dt + \sigma_s \, dW_t^S \tag{6.9}$$

where y denotes the convenience yield of the commodity S.

Introducing the correlation coefficient between the Brownian motions W^X and W^S, it is easy to see from equations (6.8) and (6.9) that the terminal value $S(T)X(T)$ is a log-normal variable. The drift of the process $(S(t)X(t))_{t\geq0}$ under Q is equal to $(r_f - y) + (r_d - r_f) = r_d - y$, hence leading to the pricing formula (6.7) through the developments proposed in both Chapters 4 and 5. Note that the expression of the volatility of SX translates the 'vector additivity' of the volatilities of S and X, which results in a norm smaller than the sum of the two norms:

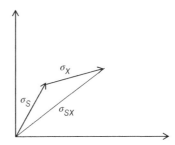

Many other types of commodity quanto options can be formulated. We will only describe another popular one, the 'commodity quanto struck in the foreign currency,' to paraphrase the terminology used in equity markets.

The call payoff at maturity T is

$$C(T) = X(T)\max\left(0, S(T) - k_f\right) \tag{6.10}$$

where now the strike is expressed in the foreign currency and the difference $S(T) - k_f$, if positive, is multiplied by the final value of the exchange rate to define the terminal value of the commodity quanto.

Note that since $X(T)$ is a random quantity at the date t when the call is purchased, the right-hand sides of formulas (6.6) and (6.10) cannot be reduced to the same quantity. Hence, we have indeed another form of commodity quanto and the buyer of the option will decide which one better suits his needs. The valuation problem in the case of payoff expressed in (6.10) is even simpler than in the example studied before. By arbitrage arguments, one can show that

$$C(t) = X(t) \text{ [price at date } t \text{ of a foreign call written on the commodity } S]$$

hence:

$$C(t) = X(t) \left[S(t) e^{-y(T-t)} N(d_1) - k_f e^{-r_f(T-t)} N(d_2) \right]$$

where:

$$d_1 = \frac{\ln\left(\dfrac{S(t) e^{-y(T-t)}}{k_f e^{-r_f(T-t)}} \right) + \dfrac{1}{2} \sigma_S^2 (T-t)}{\sigma_S \sqrt{T-t}}$$

$$d_2 = d_1 - \sigma_S \sqrt{T-t}$$

Accordingly, the hedging strategies will be different for the seller of these different options: the hedging portfolio will involve positions in the commodity and in the foreign currency but the corresponding quantities will differ according to the option. In both cases, however, the weights in S and the foreign currency are given by the pricing formula, which illustrates once more the remarkable virtues of the geometric Brownian motion setting. Lastly, note that the above results can be extended to stochastic interest rates in both economies, a generalization that becomes necessary for long-dated commodity quantos.

To conclude this chapter, note that the different categories of path-dependent and multi-asset options that experienced an exponential development in the stock market over the last 15 years are mostly relevant for commodity markets; commodities are in fact their 'raison d'être'...

7

Grain Cereals: Corn, Wheat, Soybean, Rice, and Sorghum

'But let the land be renewed and lie uncultivated during the seventh year!'

The Bible

7.1 INTRODUCTION

In this chapter are discussed corn and soybeans, which are usually referred to as 'feed grains' because of their primary use for animals; wheat and rice, which are referred to as 'food grains' since they are primarily directed to human consumption; and sorghum, a gluten-free cereal, mostly used for animals in developed countries and by humans in Africa, and is viewed by the author as having a great future because of its virtues for the human digestive system.

After the major drought in the USA in 2012 – the worst since the Dust Bowl years of the 1930s, with corn prices rocketing above $8 per bushel because of a decimated US crop – propitious growing conditions from Brazil to Ukraine to the USA in 2013 have raised hopes of a sharp rebound in world cereals stocks, reducing food security concerns. World corn, rice, soybean, and wheat production will break records in the agricultural year 2013–2014, according to the USDA estimates in August 2013. The International Grains Council in London expects grain inventories of major exporters such as Argentina, Australia, Europe, Russia, and the USA to rise by 40%. The US government forecast is a record domestic corn crop of almost 350 million tonnes, up by 28% from 2012, and the third biggest soybean crop of 88.6 million tonnes.

7.2 CORN

Corn was first cultivated in Central America about 5000 BC. At the time it was mainly used for human food. The cereal was brought to Europe and North America after the discovery of America, but remained poorly grown until the 19th century. Further development of strains of the plant led to a high-yield plant that could grow under different conditions and different climates. Plants were also modified to increase their content in proteins.

Corn must be planted no later than mid-June as it has to pollinate in the high heat of the summer in late July to mid-August. Late-planted corn is also vulnerable to an early frost in the fall. If corn is planted late, farmers may switch to a variety that has a shorter growing season.

The main competitors of corn as animal feed are wheat, sorghum, and bean meal. The first drawback of corn is its poor content in essential amino-acids, which are for instance higher in soybean. Corn production has been the subject of controversy in recent years. The use of genetically modified (GM) seeds that bear insecticide-producing genes or other modi-fied features has raised worldwide debate; some GM corns have for instance been qualified as improper for human food by the US Environmental Protection Agency (e.g., the Aventis StarLink product). Once in a while China sends back corn imports from the USA because of the way it was produced.

Indeed, almost 100% of US-grown corn today is made out of a genetically modified organ-ism (GMO), while countries in the European Union like France still strongly oppose these technologies on the basis of potential harm for human beings.

As was the case for the first known Central American populations, some regions in South America still use corn for human consumption. In Europe and the USA, it is mainly used for forage. In northern America, 75% of the corn produced is on average used for animal feed; this variety is called dent corn. About 8% is transformed into vegetable oil to be incorporated in food preparation; 6% is used for food, in particular proceeds from sweet corn, which pos-sess a higher quantity of sugars. Moreover, corn is used in alcohol distilleries, and in the production of alcohol for engines. (For an indication of the price of corn 1990 to 2013, see Figure 7.1.)

In February 2002, the Minneapolis Grain Exchange (MGEX), which was established in 1881, launched corn and soybean derivatives: Futures and options contracts respectively writ-ten on the National Corn Index (NCI) and National Soybean Index (NSI) started trading, while the MGEX launched at the same time its new electronic trading platform MGEXpress. NCI and NSI Futures and options trade exclusively on this platform. They were the first cash-settled grain and oil seed Futures and options and also represent the industry's first exclusively electronically traded contracts.

The NCI and NSI are indexes composed of country elevator bids. As such, they tend to track prices where grain is originated – the cash market – more closely than corn and soybean contracts traded at the CBOT, which are based on delivery at a few major elevators.

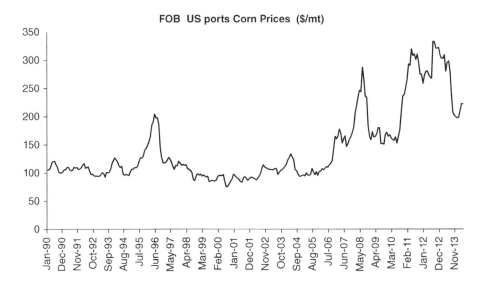

Figure 7.1   Corn prices FOB US ports 1990 to Dec 2013 (World Bank Pink Sheet)

08/29/2008 C=568^2 -19^2 O=587^4 H=605^0 L=485^4 Mov Avg 3 lines

Volume 5253214.00 Open Interest 1173301.00

Created with SuperCharts by Omega Research ® 1997

Figure 7.2   Price of the first nearby corn Future: a very large trading activity and a dramatic rise in 2007/2008

The indexes are calculated by Data Transmission Network (DTN), an electronic commerce and information services company that collects bids from roughly 1500 elevators, and in turn calculates the indexes. These indexes are based on bids in the country, hence they tend to correlate closely with cash prices, making the Futures contracts an effective tool for risk management.

The indexes also reflect a broad spectrum of cash market participants, which precludes the possibility of manipulations; for instance, the single largest bidders for corn and soybeans represent respectively 3.3% and 3.6% of the index, and more than 90% of US elevators are represented. The contract size is 5000 bushels (60 pounds in a bushel) for both NCI and NSI Futures.

Corn is a well-traveled commodity. Even if more ethanol plants are built to consume thousands of bushels locally – in Brazil in particular – most corn still travels by rail, road or waterway for hundreds and thousands of miles to reach its final destination.

- US exports make up 60% of the world's corn trade.
- Typically, corn from Minnesota is trucked to a barge on the Mississippi, then heads south to the Gulf of Mexico and on to South America, or northern Africa, or the Pacific Rim.
- In the case of the US corn, the main export destinations are:
  - Japan
  - Mexico
  - Egypt (which is also the largest importer of wheat in the world)
  - Syria
  - Algeria.

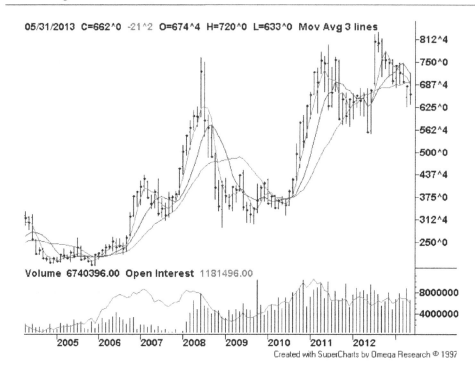

05/31/2013 C=662^0 -21^2 O=674^4 H=720^0 L=633^0 Mov Avg 3 lines

Figure 7.3 CBOT first nearby corn prices from 2005 to May 2013: the time of turbulence

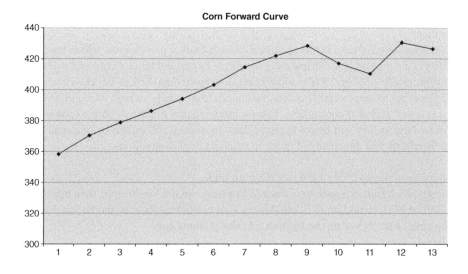

Figure 7.4 CBOT corn forward curve in October 2009: a steep contango after a respite in spikes

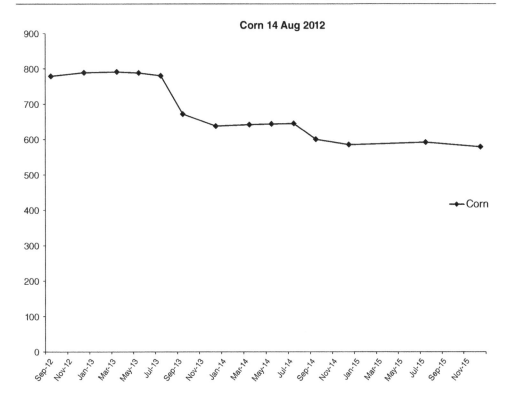

Figure 7.5   Corn forward curve in August 2012: back to backwardation

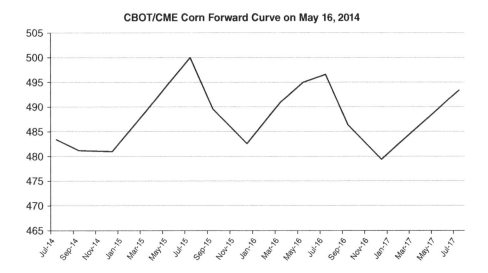

Figure 7.6   The liquidity of the forward curve now extends to 36 months

Chart created with NeoTicker EOD © 1998-2007 TickQuest Inc.

Figure 7.7 Corn prices went up by 12% during the week following the Crimea events because of tensions around Ukraine, the third world exporter of corn

For the agricultural year 2013–2014, the biggest imports forecast by the USDA are to be 15 million tonnes for Japan, 8.5 for South Korea, 8 for Mexico, 7.5 for the EU, 7 for China – up from 3 million in the crop year 2012–2013, 5 for Egypt, 4 for Taiwan and Iran, and 3.7 for Colombia and Malaysia.

7.3 WHEAT

A grass similar to wheat was cultivated in the Middle East more than 8000 years BC. Its culture in the region called the 'Fertile Crescent' at that time probably constituted the birthplace of agriculture. Wheat is the oldest commodity contract and started trading around 1850 on the CBOT. It represents food for humans as well as for animals. For many nations, wheat is an important part of daily food.

7.3.1 Wheat trading

Wheat is traded on three different US exchanges: the CBOT, the Kansas City Board of Trade (KCBOT), and the Minneapolis Grain Exchange. Chicago wheat is a soft winter wheat. It is planted in the fall and harvested in the late spring and early summer. It is grown primarily in Tennessee, Arkansas, Missouri, southern Illinois, Indiana, and Ohio. It is a low-grade wheat used as animal feed and for flour used in cheap bread and pizza dough. It is often exported to third-world countries because of its low price.

Kansas City wheat is the largest crop. It is a hard, red, winter wheat and is grown in Texas, Oklahoma, Kansas, eastern Colorado, and southern Nebraska. It represents prime bread and pizza dough wheat. About half of this crop is exported. Like Chicago wheat, it is planted in the fall and harvested in the spring and summer. Chicago wheat and Kansas City wheat account for 60 to 75% of the wheat grown in the USA. Minneapolis wheat is grown in the northern states of Montana, Dakotas, northern Nebraska, and Minnesota. It is a high grade wheat, planted in the spring and harvested in the fall, and is used for pastry but is not exported.

In the USA, the harvest generally begins in June in Texas and continues north through the summer until it is completed in September in Minnesota. Storage facilities exist to store approximately half of the wheat; the rest is sold immediately. This produces a temporary oversupply, depressing the market until all the wheat can be used or sold abroad. So every year, wheat is depressed during the summer harvest. When the harvest is complete, the selling pressure decreases in the market and the price gradually rises throughout the fall until supplies become available from the southern hemisphere around December.

Hence, a regular seasonal pattern in prices is realized that is exhibited by observed price trajectories. The fundamentals that produce this pattern are rather clear: if the price is approaching the bottom third of the historical trading range for wheat during the months of May, June or July time period, it is likely that this will be the low for the year. The combination of approaching historically low prices at the right seasonal timeframe can be a buying signal for technical analysis speculators. These observations are part of the elements that enter into the technical analysis rules often used in the trading of agricultural commodity Futures, by CTAs in particular.

Note that 75% of the wheat grown in the USA is winter wheat, which is planted in the fall. It germinates and sprouts, then is covered with snow and lies dormant for the rest of winter. In late winter or early spring, it resumes growing and is ready to harvest by early summer.

Futures contracts on soft red wheat are the most liquid among the various wheat contracts, and are also traded by European farmers because of that liquidity and despite the 'basis risk,' i.e., the difference between the commodity used for the hedge and the one produced.

7.3.2 Global wheat

Competitors of the USA in wheat production are most of the European countries, along with Argentina, Canada, and Australia. The main customers are Egypt, Morocco, Pakistan, India, Russia, and China. Wheat is grown in almost every part of the globe, including Saudi Arabia.

Wheat is a resistant plant and the only danger to wheat crop is the loss of yields and quality due to too much rain at the end of the crop cycle.

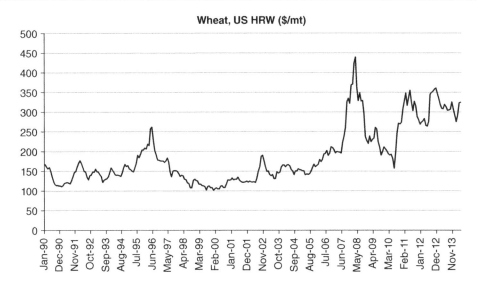

Figure 7.8   Hard red winter wheat FOB US ports (World Bank Pink Sheet)

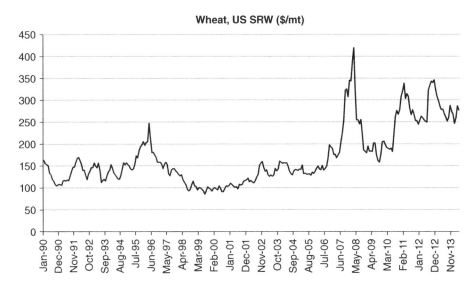

Figure 7.9   Soft red wheat prices, FOB US ports 1990 to Dec 2013 (World Bank)

Egypt consumes twice the amount of wheat that the USA does and imports more than half of its consumption, besides subsidizing its local production. Unfortunately, a significant part of domestic production is lost because of storage inefficiency.

7.3.3 The wheat supply chain

The grains go from the fields to the elevator that provides cleaning and silos, are then loaded onto trucks, barges or vessels to reach the country of destination where the grains are processed.

Figure 7.10   CBOT wheat prices Jan 2001 to Dec 2009, with a spike in 2008; large liquidity, but lower than corn's

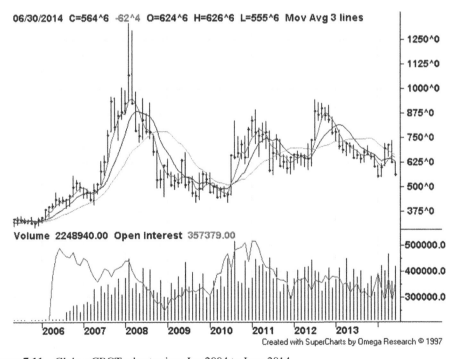

Figure 7.11   Globex CBOT wheat prices Jan 2004 to June 2014

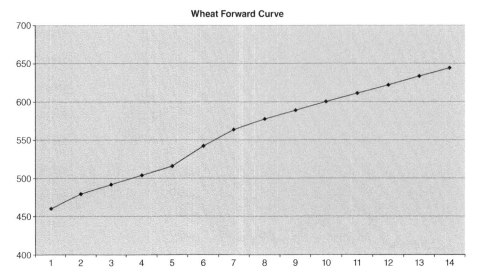

Figure 7.12   Wheat forward curve in October 2009: a sharp contango after the 2008 spike and decline

Figure 7.13   Wheat prices went up by 25% during the week following the annexation of Crimea: the effect of country risk

Wheat Futures went to a one-year low of 550 cents per bushel in February 2014 and bounced to 700 cents in early March after the Crimea events because of fears of the markets regarding the production in Ukraine, the breadbasket of Europe.

7.4 SOYBEANS

Soybeans were used in China more than 4500 years ago, and first appeared in France in the middle of the 18th century. In the USA, soybeans were first used in the east and southeast of the country, with culture appearing around the end of the 19th century. At the time it was mostly used as animal feed, with plants originating from eastern Asia.

Soybean production has been increasing strongly throughout the 20th century in the USA; one reason for this expansion is its similarity with corn's. Beans are planted in the spring, generally April and May, but they can be planted as late as early July. A late-planted crop runs the risk of being caught by an early frost in the fall and may have difficulties flowering and setting pods in August. Soybeans are known as the 'miracle plant' because of their remarkable resilience. Still, Monsanto, the world's largest seed company, is bringing forward more high-tech soybean seeds that boast built-in protection against insects and weed-killing sprays as farmers in countries like the USA and Brazil are heavily planting oilseed, perceived as a more profitable alternative to corn.

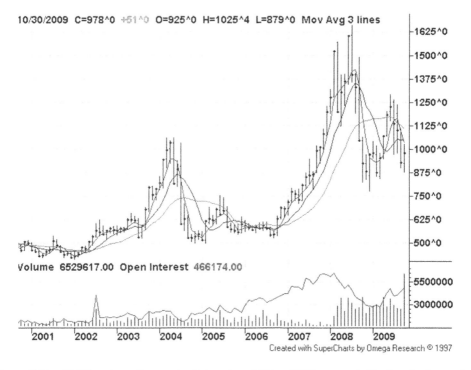

Figure 7.14 CBOT soybean first nearby Future from 2001 to 2010: a remarkable rise of prices and a very large trading activity (more than 6.5 million contracts in one day)

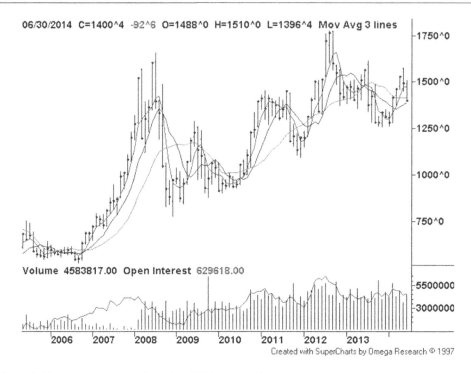

06/30/2014 C=1400^4 -92^6 O=1488^0 H=1510^0 L=1396^4 Mov Avg 3 lines

Figure 7.15   Soybean first nearby prices 2006 to June 2014

Prior to the 1970s, the USA was the only place to buy soybeans and bean products, and was responsible for more than three-quarters of world production. In the 1960s, because of a feed shortage in proteins, soybean growing skills were communicated to Brazil and Argentina, through firms like Archer Daniels among others. Today, these two countries combine to produce almost as many soybeans as the USA does, with 36% of world production against 45% for the USA. A few years ago, their combined production represented only about half of US production. Total South America soybean production from 1985 to 2003 has undergone a four-fold increase, with Paraguay entering the market in the mid-1990s.

Brazil supplanted the USA in 2012 as the world's largest bean exporter. Moreover, Brazil has over 100 million acres of uncultivated grasslands in the center and north of the country that are ideal for bean crops. Plantations there are producing as much as 50 bushels an acre, these yields being on a par with US yields. In the near future, the Brazilian government envisions seeing this area fully cultivated. At present, what these regions mostly lack for massive production is an adequate transportation system. These 100 million acres are a larger area than that of the Corn Belt. If Brazil is successful in developing its agricultural land for bean crops, then the growth of expected world demand for beans will be easily met. Imports of soybean to the European Community mostly arrive in the ports of Rotterdam and Saint Malo. As a percentage of total supply, the USA exports more than the two other producers combined (30% versus 20%), but the consumption represents roughly the same proportion in the three countries. Thus, exports alone explain the fact that the ending stock in the USA accounts for a smaller part of total supply: 10% compared with 20% in the two other countries. Note that

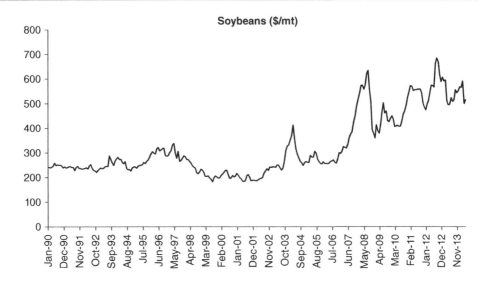

Figure 7.16 US Soybean Prices – CIF Rotterdam (World Bank Pink Sheet)

over the last five years, Brazil has exported much more and consumed less in percentage, with no significant change in ending stock percentage.

Agricultural products, soybeans in particular, accounted for almost half of Argentina's $83 billion of exports in 2013, making them the country's single most important source of foreign currencies.

Soybean acreage in the USA increased from 1.5 million in 1924 to 26.4 million in 1961 and a record 72.7 million in 2000. Cultivation takes place in most central and eastern states, from Wisconsin to Alabama, with Iowa and Illinois predominating, each having more than 10 million of acres of culture. Today, soybean represents the number one US export crop.

As mentioned in Chapter 3, an extensive study of soybean inventory and its relation to price volatility over the period 1990 to 2005 can be found in the article by Geman and Nguyen (2005).

Historically, soybeans were mainly used for their seeds, which were processed into different types of food products. Today, soybeans account for more than half of the total fats consumed in the USA. Indonesian consumers are also turning to this source of proteins and fats, with a sharp increase in their imports over the past decade. Soybeans are also traded under the form of soybean meal and soybean oil; the three forms constitute what is called the 'soybean complex.'

Soy meal and soybean oil
Crushing soybean leads to meal and oil. The crush spread is the expected gross margin of soybean processing. It is a very popular agricultural spread and traded by the simultaneous purchase (sale) of soybean Futures and the sale (purchase) of soybean oil and soybean meal Futures; the spread can be directly traded as a Future on the CME Globex. Meal makes up 75 to 80% of the content of a bean and is used for animal feed as a direct competitor with corn. It is a higher quality protein than corn and, as such, exhibits a premium over corn.

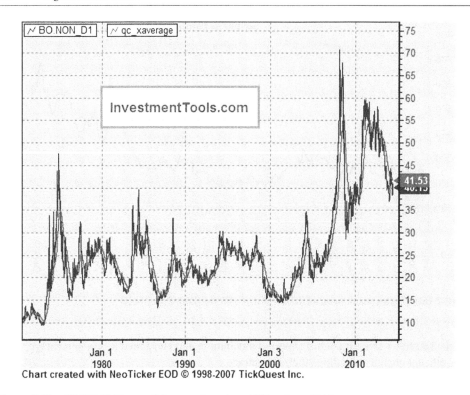

Figure 7.17   CBOT/ CME soy oil first nearby prices 1970 to June 2014

Factors affecting meal prices include: availability of meal from crushing operations; the price of fish meal, produced from anchovy fished off the Pacific coast of South America and in decline (see Chapter 8); and the price of corn and the size of livestock herds.

Soybean oil is mostly used for cooking. Its competitors range from India's groundnut oil to Canada's canola oil, as well as sunflower oil and palm oil, mostly produced in Indonesia and Malaysia. An important product extracted from soybean oil is lecithin, used in many food preparations as an emulsifier. If meal demand is high and oil demand is not, processors will crush at an increased pace while oil stocks build up.

Options on this spread are accordingly traded between participants in these markets. Each month the US Census Bureau and the National Oil Processor Association (NOPA) release estimates of the crush rate and the stock of meal and oil.

7.5 RICE

Rice provides 20% of the world's dietary energy supply and is the most important grain with respect to human nutrition.

Asian countries represent 90% of world production, with China and India accounting for more than 50%. China converted during the 1990s from a rice exporter into a rice importer,

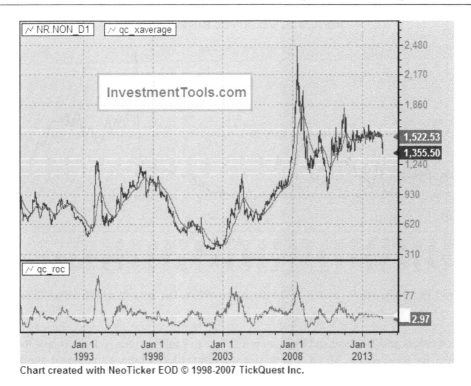

Chart created with NeoTicker EOD © 1998-2007 TickQuest Inc.

Figure 7.18   CBOT/ CME first nearby rice prices from 1988 to June 2014

while India did the opposite. At the world level, imports shifted from Asia to the Middle East, Africa and Latin America, as many South and Southeast Asian importers increased their production.

Thailand, Vietnam, the USA, India, and Pakistan are the major five exporting countries. On the demand side, more than 90% of rice is consumed in Asia, with China, India, and Indonesia accounting for 75% of total consumption. The rapid population growth in the low-income countries is causing an increase in rice consumption. The proportion of rice production that is traded internationally is small because the major rice-producing countries are also major rice consumers.

The Thai rice subsidy program has cost more than $4 billion a year since it was launched in late 2011 by the new government, which pledged to buy rice from farmers at 40 to 50% above market prices. This led to a gigantic overproduction and during the month of February 2013 alone, the Thai government was trying to sell more than 900,000 tonnes through two tenders.

A total of 20.5 million tonnes of milled rice were produced by Thailand in 2013–2014, out of which 8.5 million tonnes were exported. Still, Thailand lost to India its position as the world's top rice exporter. The glut of rice drove prices down by 23% in 2013, which was good news for big rice importers in Africa and China. India exported 10 million tonnes and Vietnam 7.7 million tonnes in 2013–2014; and in 2012–2013, India's exports were 11

Figure 7.19   White rice 5% broken – FOB Bangkok – 1990 to Dec 2013 (World Bank Pink Sheet)

million tonnes and Thailand and Vietnam were close to 7 million tonnes. India is now the top supplier for sub-Saharan Africa, a large rice importer, while China, a traditional purchaser of Thai rice, has been buying from Pakistan and Vietnam. In February 2014, China scrapped an agreement to buy 1.2 million tonnes of Thai rice because of a corruption probe in the purchasing scheme.

Consumers in some of the biggest rice-producing nations, including Thailand and India, continue to pay higher prices while surplus supplies sit in government warehouses – Asia's surplus has little impact in the USA, which produces different varieties of rice. This situation is the result of good weather and government programs that encourage rice growing. The Cereal International Council has announced that rice world production would be 476 million tonnes for the production year 2013–2014, up 1.6% from the previous production year, and up nearly 20% from the 400 million produced worldwide in the production year 2004–2005. This means that the carry-in stocks would increase for the ninth year in a row. Thailand, which is the third world producer, would have record inventories of 15.2 million tonnes in 2014, roughly half the world's total trade value in rice. The Thai government, which had announced in June 2013 a reduction of its purchase price from farmers, backtracked after street protests. India, the world's largest exporter, is expecting near record harvests as is Pakistan. Meanwhile, demand from large importers, including the Philippines and Nigeria, is dropping.

The 'Vietnamese 5% broken rice' price, which is used as an international benchmark, went down from $430 per tonne in November 2013 to $390 per tonne in February 2014 – but not to the lows of $360 per tonne reached in June and August 2013 when news of Thailand's rice stockpiles first surfaced.

7.6 SORGHUM

Sorghum, a gluten-free cereal grain, is the fifth most important cereal crop in the world, largely because of its natural drought tolerance and versatility as food, feed, and fuel. It is a plant full of nutrients, which can grow with a small amount of water. In Africa and parts of Asia, sorghum is primarily a human food product, while in the USA, it is used mainly for livestock feed and in a growing number of ethanol plants. However, the USA is starting to see the gluten-free benefits of sorghum for human beings.

Out of Africa

Sorghum is an ancient cereal grain that was grown 8000 years ago in southern Egypt. It was then introduced in Ethiopia and Sudan, and from there moved throughout Africa where it remains an important cereal. Sorghum likely traveled to India during the first millennium, taken as food on ships for the voyages. Then, it continued to be dispersed along the silk trade routes. It most probably arrived in the Americas in the 19th century with slave traders from Africa.

Today, different varieties of sorghum are grown in Asia – including India and Indonesia – and in the Americas. Sorghum kernels vary in color from white and pale yellow to deep reds, purples, and browns. The colored varieties contain excellent tannins to dye leather.

Moreover, in the current healthy/trendy gluten-free diet, sorghum has been adopted by many who recognize its nutritional benefits. Sorghum does not contain traits that can be enhanced through biotechnology, making it non-transgenic (non-GMO). Most varieties are high in antioxidants, another extremely valuable property. Sorghum can be easily substituted for wheat in a variety of baked goods because of its neutral flavor. In the Middle East, sorghum is used for flatbread; in some parts of Africa, one can find 'sorghum porridge.'

In the USA, sorghum grows on dry lands, the 'sorghum belt' stretching from South Dakota to west Texas through Kansas, Nebraska, and Oklahoma. Sorghum is among the most efficient crops for use of water. More than 8 million acres of sorghum are planted in 21 states across the country, making the USA the largest producer of sorghum. One third of it is used for ethanol. Because sorghum can grow with much fewer fertilizers and irrigation than corn, fuel production is much more efficient than in the case of corn ethanol.

Many of the world's poorest populations depend on sorghum as their main source of food, especially in Africa. Sorghum easily survives extreme heat and drought, as said before; Nigeria, Sudan, Ethiopia, and Burkina Faso account for nearly 70% of the sorghum grown in Africa.

The same amount of land produces a larger amount of sorghum than corn, according to a formula that roughly goes as follows:

Number of bushels of sorghum per acre = 50 + 0.5 number of bushels of corn

Hence, a very rich land that produces 150 bushels of corn per acre should continue to do so; as soon as the yield goes below 80 bushels of corn per acre, sorghum becomes a valuable alternative, with water being saved.

The selling price of sorghum in 2013 was $262 per tonne, with a yield comprising between 70 and 100 tonnes per hectare. The US yellow grain sorghum was selling at $8.66 to 9.29 per CWT (centum weight, roughly 45.39 kilos).

Sorghum has to be planted at a temperature of 60°F, versus 50°F for corn. Wheat can be planted under different temperatures depending on its type. The harvest of sorghum takes place 125 days later, which means that multiple crops are possible if the temperature is appropriate.

The main exporters of sorghum are

- USA
- Argentina
- Australia
- Sudan
- China.

The main importers are

- Mexico
- Japan
- Israel
- Taiwan.

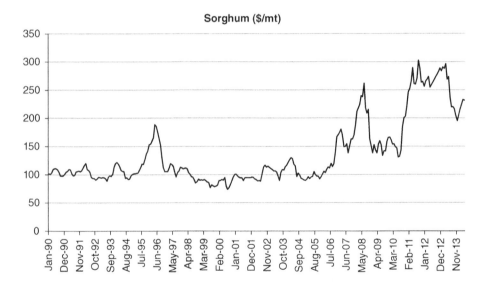

Figure 7.20   FOB US Gulf ports sorghum prices 1990 to Dec 2013: a sharp rise as of 2010

According to the USDA report of April 2014, US sorghum exports are projected to be at the level of 180 million bushels for the agricultural year 2013–2014, up from 63 million in 2011– 2012 and 76 million in 2012–2013. The ending stocks are projected at 19 million, down from 23 and 15 million respectively. The sorghum planted area in the USA is estimated at 8.1 million acres, up from 5.5 and 6.2 million respectively for the previous agricultural years.

A sorghum field in East Africa

8
Sugar, Cocoa, Coffee, and Tea

'If this is coffee, please bring me some tea; but if this is tea, please bring me some tea.'
Abraham Lincoln, 1809–1865

Unlike the cereals market where growers are increasingly large and sophisticated businesses, many of the soft commodities rely on small-scale farms in developing countries.

8.1 SUGAR

Sugar cane can be traced back to around the Southern Pacific Ocean approximately 8000 years ago. Most probably indigenous of New Guinea, sugar cane moved to Southeast Asia and India. In 100 BC, Chinese farmers were already cultivating and refining sugar cane and, by the sixth or seventh centuries, Persians traders were trading a sugar that was refined through a chemical process.

Sugar was discovered by Europeans at the very end of the 11th century. The Arabs had acquired the secret for the extraction of sugar from sugar cane after their invasion/conquest of Persia in 642. On the American continent, sugar cane was first introduced to the Caribbean during Christopher Columbus' second trip, in 1493. From the Caribbean, sugar rapidly expanded to the rest of the continent, due to the ease of its culture under this climate. Two thousand sugar mills were active in Brazil by 1540.

In the 17th century, the British began to grow sugar cane in Barbados, which by 1665 was exporting 7000 tons of sugar to England. In response to the English blockade of sugar from the Caribbean to France, Napoleon encouraged farmers to plant sugar beet and in a period of two years after Napoleon's decree supporting sugar beet production, France was producing 35,000 tons of sugar.

Sugar is a carbohydrate produced from various fruits and vegetables. There are three types of sugars: monosaccharides, disaccharides, and polyols. Examples of monosaccharides are glucose, fructose (found in fruit), and galactose (found in cows' milk). Glucose is the sugar used by the human body; its chemical formula is $C_6H_{12}O_6$. Sucrose, lactose, and maltose are the three types of disaccharides, with sucrose or saccharose – $C_{12}H_{22}O_{11}$ – being used as table sugar, often after being refined. Note that the 'low calorie' artificial sweeteners are more and more proven to be bad for the health (and quite fattening in fact).

The main sources of sugar are sugar cane and sugar beets, both plants containing sugar in large quantities. Sugar cane is a tall perennial grass growing in tropical and semi-tropical climates, which requires large amounts of water and a warm climate. It stores sugar in its stalk, and takes approximately 16 months to mature from planting. Planting is done from stalk cuttings and the plant can be cut several times, with decreasing yields after each cutting. The

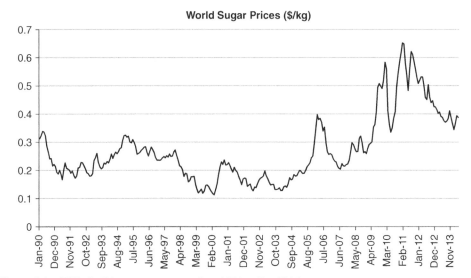

Figure 8.1   FOB Caribbean ports sugar prices 1990 to Jan 2014

main constraint of sugar cane processing is that its sugar content quickly deteriorates after harvesting. Therefore, the distance between the sugar cane field and the refinery has to be optimized. Many developing countries that have correct weather conditions and land available for the planting of sugar cane currently lack the necessary infrastructure for its rapid processing.

Sugar beet, on the other hand, is a small tubular plant with a white taproot that grows best in temperate climates but can be planted in a wide variety of climatic conditions. It stores the sugar in its root for a short while only before processing.

The composition of refined sugar is close to 100% sucrose, be it from beet or cane. Sugar cane is usually washed and ground within 24 hours from harvesting. The cane juice obtained from the grinding process is boiled until it becomes syrup, and then crystallizes to sugar particles. These particles are separated in a centrifuge from the clarified concentrated cane juice and the molasses left from the first boil is stored in large tanks to be shipped to distillers. The refining of sugar beets is usually done in a single stage of purification, concentration, and drying.

Raw sugar is the crystallized sugar obtained from the evaporation of the clarified cane juice and it is tanned to a brown color. Raw sugar is usually processed from the sugar cane at a sugar mill and then shipped to a refinery where it is further processed. Centrifugation washes out the surface molasses and gives it a light tan.

8.1.1 Links of sugar with other commodities

In Asia, Africa, and Latin America, sugar is a vital ingredient and a common sweetener used for cooking and the making of pastry and alcoholic drinks. In countries like Thailand, palm sugar is used as a cheap, healthier substitute for refined sugar.

One of the main competitors of refined sugar is corn syrup. Corn syrup contains dextrose and other saccharides and it is used as a sweetener by the food industry. Corn syrup was developed in the 1970s as a reply to soaring cane sugar prices, and is nowadays very popular in the United States among food and beverage manufacturers.

8.1.2 Sugar trading

Only 30% of world sugar is traded on the markets, and private companies dominate a large part of this trading activity. There are two world benchmarks for sugar prices, one for raw sugar and one for refined sugar. The Sugar No. 11 contract is the world benchmark for raw sugar trading. It is an FOB index at Caribbean ports including Brazil. The Futures contracts are traded on the ICE; sugar options and swaps are also available. The No. 407 contract traded on the NYSE LIFFE is the world benchmark for refined sugar. It recently replaced the No. 5 contract and is based on the spot price of refined sugar FOB in European ports.

Sugar is a distorted market because most countries have some form of protectionist policy. This implies that for many players in the sugar market, producers, end-users, and merchants, domestic prices represent a more accurate benchmark for their risk management needs. In the United States, the Sugar No. 16 contract – also traded on the ICE – plays this role for raw sugar. This contract includes physical delivery of US or foreign origin raw cane sugar with duty paid, in New York, Baltimore and Galveston, New Orleans or Savannah ports.

Other countries also offer sugar Future contracts in their domestic markets. Sugar is traded in Brazil on the Brazilian Mercantile and Futures Exchange, in India on the Multi Commodity Exchange (MCX) and the National Commodities and Derivatives Exchange (NCDEX), in Pakistan on the Pakistan Mercantile Exchange Limited, in China on the Zhengzhou Commodity (CZCE) Exchange, and in Japan on the Kansai Commodities Exchange (KEX).

Figure 8.2 ICE Sugar No. 11 first nearby prices from 2005 to June 2014 – large open interest and trading volume observed in June 2014 (and before)

Organizations such as the IMF, the World Bank, and FAO track sugar prices. The FAO Sugar Price Index consists of the prices from the International Sugar Agreement. The International Sugar Organization was founded in 1968 in London as an intergovernmental body in charge of administering the 'sugar agreement' but has no power over quotas, tariffs or prices. Its main purpose is to promote the trade and consumption of sugar.

The S&P GSCI Sugar Index is a sub-index of the S&P GSCI and is based on the Sugar No. 11 contract. It is part of the wider S&P GSCI-based ETFs. Exchange Traded Certificates (ETCs) are also on offer for this sub-index. In 2008, the Dow Jones-UBS Sugar Sub-index was introduced; it is part of the wider DJ-UBS Commodity Index. This index consists of Futures contracts on the physical commodity. Exchange Traded Notes (ETNs) and ETCs are available on both the main index and the sub-index.

8.1.3 The European Union

The European Union is one of the main exporters and producers of sugar from sugar beet, ranking first and third. Also, the EU-27 is on average one of the largest holders of ending stocks, displaying 8.3% of world ending stocks.

The Common Agricultural Policy (CAP) mechanisms to support sugar prices are import taxes, export support, and domestic intervention. This system is unique in the sense that it involves several levels of support depending on the volume of production eligible for each type of support.

8.1.4 Special relations of the EU with other countries

The EU has one of the longest traditions in protectionist sugar policies. From the inception of the EU Sugar regime in 1968, the adhesion of each country to the EU followed a change in sugar policy to adapt to the previous agreements these individual countries had, usually with former colonies.

The Uruguay Round Agreement in Agriculture, which came into effect in 1995, did not reduce the level of protection of sugar in the EU. However, in the early 2000s the WTO ruled against the EU for excessive exports and the EU subsequently decided to curb them.

8.1.5 The United States

The United States is one of the main producers and importers of sugar because of its large consumption. The USA produces both beet and cane sugar. Beet sugar mainly grows in the Great Lakes region, Great Planes, Upper Midwestern, and Far Western states while sugar cane is produced in Louisiana, Florida, Texas, and Hawaii.

The US sugar program, established in 1981, went through several modifications since its inception and its core policies include minimum prices and restrictions on domestic marketing. The minimum price is often called the loan rate because farmers can use sugar as collateral for loans from the USDA, hence effectively giving a set price for the sugar put as collateral.

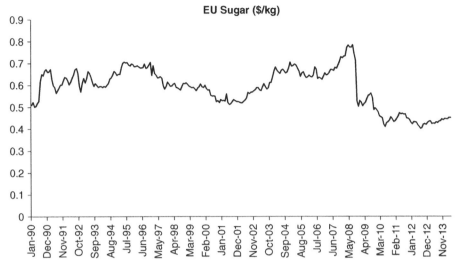

Figure 8.3   CIF European ports sugar prices – Jan 1990 to Dec 2013

8.1.6 Special relations of the USA with other countries

From the 1980s, the USA had in place a system of quotas and domestic price guarantees for Caribbean Community (CARICOM) sugar-producing countries, which have been progressively reduced in absolute value. Under the North American Free Trade Agreement (NAFTA), Mexico attained limited access to the US market, which was increased progressively from 2000 to 2008, followed by no more import restrictions on Mexican sugar.

The embargo imposed on Cuba by the United States started in October 1960 and became a near-total embargo by February 1962. In 1996, the USA passed the Cuban Liberty and Democratic Solidarity Act, which strengthened the embargo imposed on Cuba. The embargo applies to foreign companies trading with Cuba and restricts US citizens from doing business in or with Cuba.

8.1.7 Brazil

Brazil is the largest producer of sugar cane and sugar in the world, as well as the largest exporter of sugar. In 1975, the Brazilian government started the program 'Proalcool' to promote the production of fuel from sugar cane. As a direct consequence of this program, government policies for sugar cane and ethanol production became the main determinants of sugar output. Due to its long tradition of use of sugar cane, both for sugar production and ethanol, Brazil has established itself as one of the most efficient producers of sugar.

Some experts mention the so-called 'ethanol parity,' namely the price at which it is more profitable for sugar producers in Brazil to turn sugar cane into ethanol, creating in practice a floor for the export sugar price. In its international policy, Brazil controls ethanol imports and is the second largest quota holder to the US market. Domestically, Brazil defines the ratio of blending gasoline and ethanol, therefore affecting directly the ethanol parity price.

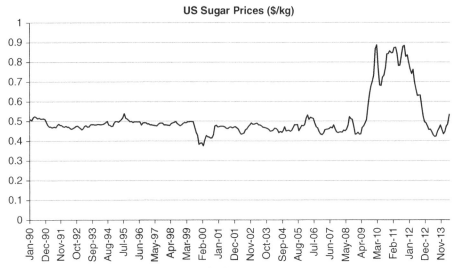

Figure 8.4   US CIF sugar prices 1990 to Dec 2013 (World Bank)

8.1.8 China

China operates a system of trade tariffs, quotas, and domestic support of its agricultural markets. A wide range of public and governmental organizations is involved in all aspects of
agricultural development and trade. China's accession to the World Trade Organization in
2001 implied the acceptance of a wide variety of reforms in its agricultural policy. Under the
three pillars of the Uruguay Round Agreement on Agriculture, China had to commit in all
three areas: market access (reducing the barriers to agricultural imports); eliminating export
subsidies; and capping domestic support.

China has experienced a rapid increase in productivity of its sugar industry over the last
few years. Starting in 1995, a large proportion of mills established long-term supply contracts
with the farmers, providing them in advance with fertilizers and pesticides. Since 2006, the
Chinese government has eliminated taxes directed to farmers, allowing them to invest in better
fertilizers and varieties of sugar cane, which has directly translated to an increase in yields.
Additionally, public investments in biotechnology and better technology for mills have been
contributing factors. Local governments have also set up a range of policies including access
to loans to farmers and sugar mills, and large infrastructure projects both for 'sugar cane
villages,' which take advantage of economies of scale, and for better irrigation of crops. Despite these advances, the cost of production in China is much higher than in other countries
due to high supply costs.

8.1.9 India

India is one of the main producers, importers, and exporters of sugar and has the largest ending stocks. India has a very fragmented sugar market with more than 50 million farmers and
500 mills. As with other agricultural commodities in India, yields have been decreasing due

to an incorrect use of fertilizers and almost no use of pesticides. This low use of agricultural inputs is directly linked to the poor profitability of Indian sugar farmers.

The Indian government actively intervenes in sugar prices. It does so by establishing a statutory minimum price factories have to pay to the farmers, by restricting sugar quantities in the markets, by imposing restrictions on sugar factories to sell below market price in public distribution centers, and by limiting exports and private stockholdings.

India is one of the countries usually quoted as a source of volatility in the sugar markets (FAO, Agricultural Outlook 2011–2020) due to the cyclical nature of its production with periods of two to three years of surplus followed by two to three years of deficit. Trade reflects this pattern with large imports during the deficit phase followed by large exports during the surplus phase.

8.1.10 Thailand

The sugar industry is a major element in Thailand's economy, which is second in world exports and third in ending stocks. Although Thailand has been changing to a more industrialized country, the sugar industry is still highly dependent on human labor in all the steps of sugar cane farming.

Politics have played a fundamental role in the sugar industry in Thailand. From the 1930s, the government has been involved in the relationship between sugar mill owners and farmers. As of the 1960s, the emergence of sugar associations shaped sugar policy due to their political influence.

Thailand has a price support program for sugar. This is a two-step process where the government acts as a mediator for sugar mills and farmers to agree on a price for sugar at the beginning of the growing season. This initial price allows farmers to receive payments and invest in fertilizers and equipment.

8.1.11 Australia

Australia is one of the top 10 producing countries and third exporting country of sugar. Most sugar cane is cultivated in the river valleys of Queensland. It is a very efficient industry with domestic prices linked to world prices. The regulatory framework for the sugar industry was established in 1999 but later on, central controls and import tariffs were greatly reduced. This government deregulation has been accompanied by an expansion of the industry as sugar cane farmers do not have the support or protective subsidies that farmers from other countries enjoy.

8.1.12 Guatemala and Cuba

Guatemala is the largest sugar producer in Central America and a large proportion of its production is exported to Mexico. Cuba has suffered from the US embargo since the 1960s but it kept long-term agreements for the supply of sugar with other countries, such as China. Due to the decrease in yields because of its aging technology, Cuba has been losing its position as a major exporter in the sugar market.

8.1.13 Sugar cane in Mauritius

The island's transport and most of its power stations rely on fuel imported from India or South Africa, but the cane industry already supplies 20% of the nation's electricity from sugar mill waste that is burnt to produce steam-generated power. According to locals, sugar cane could provide all of the island's energy with gasification of the biomass.

At the same time, the area of land cultivated for sugar cane has been shrinking at an alarming rate for the last decade as young people move to better-paid city jobs.

Sugar cane generates an irrigation system, among other positive features. During the Second World War, Mauritius was the first country to replace petrol and diesel with ethanol. Mauritius belongs to the International Sugar Cane Bio-Mass Utilisation Consortium.

8.2 COCOA

Cocoa, or *Theobroma cocoa*, was grown in South and Central America over 2000 years ago. In the Maya culture, cocoa was a highly valued drink, which was obtained after fermentation, roasting, and grinding. The drink, which was appraised for its nutritional and aphrodisiac properties, was also used in religious services. As for the beans, they were also used as an exchange currency. Though first brought back to Europe by Columbus amid presents he received from indigenous chiefs, it was Hernan Cortes who first realized the value of both the beans and the drink among local elites. Cocoa was exclusively grown by Spain in its colonies around the equator in the second half of the 16th century. It later spread over Europe as a drink consumed in cocoa and coffee houses, which was obtained after the addition of spices such as vanilla or cinnamon, and sugar. Under Louis XIV in France, cocoa was a renowned drink, which was praised, along with tea and coffee, for its healthy properties. The first Swiss grocery store dedicated to cocoa was created in 1825 by Louis-François Cailler; 'Maison Cailler' still exists now as part of the Nestlé Company. In the early 20th century, Rudolph Lindt

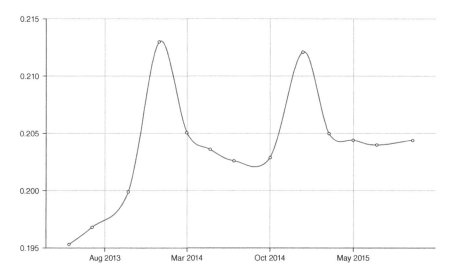

Figure 8.5   ICE Sugar No. 11 forward curve on March 22, 2013

discovered a process that gave birth to the solid chocolate tablets, and in 1907 the Buitoni family in Italy created the first candy-like form of chocolate under the name Perugina. In the USA, Hershey's chocolate was founded in 1905, while Mars Co. was created in 1922, both still having a large share of the cocoa market today.

European countries launched cocoa cultures in their near-equator colonies, such as São Tomé for Portugal, Java and Sumatra for the Dutch, Nigeria for the United Kingdom, and Ivory Coast for France. Production spread in the Horn of Africa, with Ghana and Cameroon also turning into big players. From around 1910 to the mid-1970s, Ghana was the main cocoa bean producer, with about a third of world production. In South America, the main producers are also located near the equator line, with Brazil ahead of smaller countries such as Ecuador and the Dominican Republic. In 2010, the main producers of cocoa beans were Ivory Coast (1301 kt), Indonesia (845 kt), Ghana (632 kt), Nigeria (399 kt), Cameroon (264 kt), and Brazil (235 kt). Yields over these countries are spread out, Ivory Coast's yield being about 1.5 times that of Brazil or Ghana, and 1.2 times that of Indonesia. In Togo, which produced about 101 kt in 2010, thus ranking 8th in world's production after Ecuador, the yield per hectare is 1.5 times that of Ivory Coast.

Cocoa is a tree crop that provides a livelihood for millions of small farms where the family works together, in more than 50 countries located in Africa, Asia, the Caribbean, and Latin America. In many of them, cocoa serves as the main source of income. It is, for instance, estimated that over 40% of the population in Ivory Coast lives on cocoa-related income.

In September 2013, the total net long position held by fund managers who were bullish on cocoa in London and New York had a combined record number of 165,555 lots, making it larger than the annual crop of Ivory Coast, according to a large commodity broker. This

Figure 8.6   ICE first nearby cocoa prices Jan 2005 to May 2014 (large activity, less than in sugar)

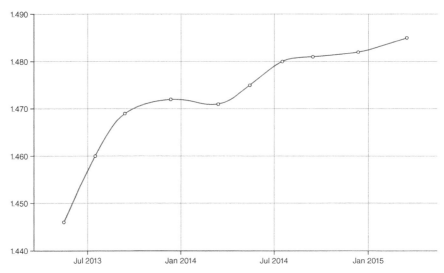

Figure 8.7   NYSE/ LIFFE cocoa forward curve – March 22, 2013

reflected the strong demand from North America and Europe, because of fears related to unusually dry weather patterns in West Africa. The combined effect was a rise of 17% in cocoa prices between early July and mid-September of 2013. For several years, prices had been sluggish because of large crops in West Africa. This led to a decline in the output from Indonesia, a leading producer in Asia, where a number of farmers had switched to palm oil and rubber, hoping to get better yields and returns. By the end of summer 2013, the supply and demand balance was expected to shift to a deficit comprised of between 130,000 and 170,000 tonnes, with a sharp rise in demand for 'cocoa butter,' which is obtained by the grinding of cocoa beans.

Countries recognized as cocoa producers are Ivory Coast,[1] Ghana, Indonesia, Cameroon, Nigeria, Brazil, Ecuador, and Malaysia, among others. According to the ICCO (International Cocoa and Coffee Association), the shares of the largest cocoa-producing continents are: 73% for Africa, 14% for Asia and Oceania, and 13% for the Americas (essentially South America). We have already mentioned, as it matters for the discussion of seasonality, that the main producers are either immediately close to the equator – on both sides – or in the southern hemisphere, like Brazil. This implies that harvests are greatly spread over the calendar year. In all cases, the pods that produce the beans that make chocolate need sufficient moisture to mature.

In all these countries, except to a small extent Malaysia and Indonesia, production comes from small farms that do not exceed four hectares (800,000 of them in Ghana alone). Production from countries like Togo, Malaysia, Dominican Republic, Peru, and Mexico is individually insignificant, but taken together constitute 10% of world supply.

---

[1] The Ivorian cocoa industry has been suffering from chronic underinvestment. Ivorian cocoa trees, planted more than 25 years ago, have already passed their peak of productivity with many farmers switching to more lucrative rubber. Without new planting, production in the country is likely to drop in a steady manner, tightening the global market as demand rebounds.

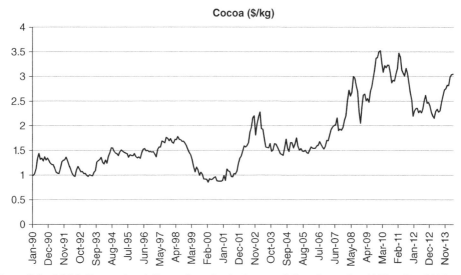

Figure 8.8   ICCO (International Cocoa Organization) cocoa daily prices – Jan 1990 to Dec 2013

Apart from Ghana and to some extent Cameroon, where production levels have bounced back from the 1990s slowdown, the output from most other countries has been on the decline due to aging cocoa trees, lack of necessary investments in the cocoa sector, and competing opportunities in the rubber and oil palm plantations (e.g., in Ivory Coast). The result is an increase in the geographical concentration of world production.

Crinipellis perniciosa, commonly referred to as witches' broom, is a fungal cocoa disease that has for the past decade caused a decline in yields of cocoa beans in Brazil. Though a new resistant variety has been found, production levels are, however, not expected to reach the level achieved during the 1980s because some producers, discouraged by the low cocoa prices over the 1990s, have already switched to alternative crops.

In Ecuador, Latin America's second largest cocoa bean producer after Brazil, cocoa production has been on the increase due to the successful introduction of the new variety resistant to the witches' broom disease, which had also affected its cocoa production areas. Still, the growth is expected to be limited, because of the increasing costs of production and lower returns to growers.

Production in both Indonesia and Malaysia takes place mostly on large plantations either privately or state owned. A downward trend in Malaysian cocoa production has been observed since the early 1990s, when the outbreak of disease coincided with the deterioration of the country's macro-economic conditions. In addition, farmers switched production from cocoa to more lucrative crops, such as palm trees, in response to the fall in world cocoa prices during the 1990s. The downward trend in the Malaysian cocoa sector is expected to continue due to the expansion of urban settlements. Therefore the production levels that were observed a couple of decades ago are unlikely to be observed soon.

Government policies in Indonesia in the 1980s–1990s have encouraged the expansion of production. Most of the increase during the last two decades was bulk cocoa coming from hybrid trees. While the expansion in Indonesia has slowed down since the late 1990s, yields in the country are still the highest among major cocoa producing countries in Asia. As in Ghana,

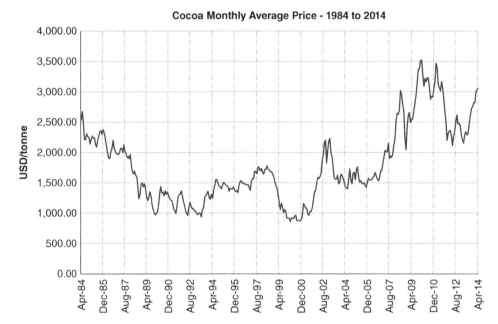

Figure 8.9   Monthly average price on which most options (hence, Asian) are written

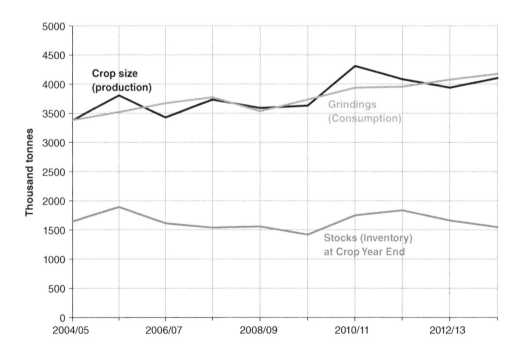

Figure 8.10   Cocoa production, consumption and stocks

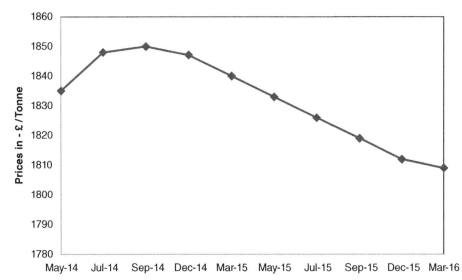

Figure 8.11   LIFFE cocoa forward curve April 30, 2014

Figure 8.12   ICE cocoa prices April 2012 to June 2014: an irresistible ascension since August 2013

where producers' selling prices are linked to world market prices, cocoa farmers in Indonesia receive a high proportion of the market price, which encourages reinvestment in cocoa inputs, and contributes to improvement in yields.

Over the 2000s, Africa has established itself as the leading cocoa supplier, increasing its production at an annual rate of 2.7%. Much of this growth came from Ghana, which in 2010 reached the status of second biggest cocoa producer in Africa after Ivory Coast, with 21% of the world production – West and Central Africa accounting for more than two-thirds of global production.

The major companies that grind cocoa beans are Archer Daniels, Mars, Cargill, and Nestlé.

There is currently an organic cocoa market but this represents a very small share of the total cocoa market. The ICCO estimates organic cocoa supplied to the world market to be less than 0.5% of total cocoa production. Production of certified organic cocoa is also estimated to be about 15,500 tonnes and sourced from countries including Madagascar, Tanzania, and Uganda.

8.3 COFFEE

Coffee is cultivated in tropical regions, even though Arabica trees need a more temperate climate. It is produced in more than 70 countries, primarily in Central/South America, Southeast Asia, and Africa. Its commercial utilization only began in the middle of the 19th century. Coffee is with tea one of the most consumed drinks in the world.

There are two types of coffee seeds. Arabica is traded in New York and Robusta in London. Arabica is considered a high quality coffee, but is heterogeneous. Robusta coffee is resistant to the coffee leaf rust but has a bitterer taste. Arabica trees need a more temperate climate.

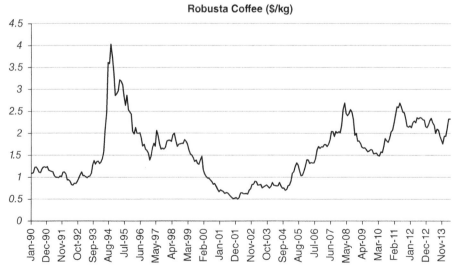

Figure 8.13   FOB/Marseille Robusta coffee prices (World Bank)

05/31/2013 C=127.05 -7.90 O=136.00 H=147.65 L=125.05 Mov Avg 3 lines

Figure 8.14   ICE/NYBOT first nearby Arabica coffee prices reached a 14-year high in 2011 because of a severe frost in Brazil

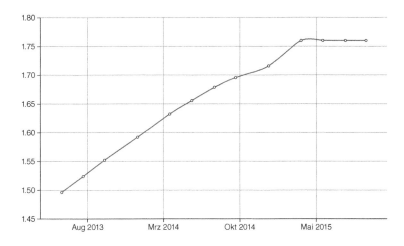

Figure 8.15   ICE coffee forward curve on March 22, 2013: a sharp contango

Harvesting coffee beans from plants is commercially viable only four to five years after plantation. The beans (called green coffee) go through dry processing. After that, the green coffee is sold to roasters who will roast the beans (and grind them in the case of powdered coffee). Both activities take place in general near the consumption areas.

The green coffee beans, held in airtight bags of 60 kg, can last roughly for one year.

The biggest coffee producers are Brazil and Colombia in South America, Uganda in Central Africa, and Vietnam and Indonesia in Southeast Asia.

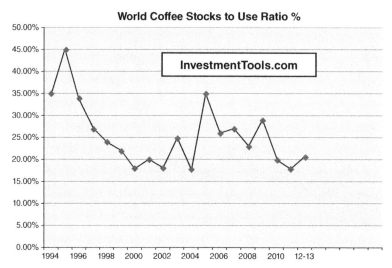

Figure 8.16   Decline of world coffee inventories

Figure 8.17   Spike of Arabica coffee prices in 2014 because of a long drought in Brazil in the first semester of 2014

Brazil produces 37% of total production, with a few countries in Central and South Africa producing another 60%. Hence, weather events in one of these countries have major consequences, as happened in 2010 and 2011, and weather derivatives, described in Chapter 12, can be a valuable hedging instrument for the farmers.

8.4 TEA

Kenya is the world's largest producer of black tea, bringing to the country $1 billion in hard currencies. It is followed by Sri Lanka and India. Other East African countries such as Malawi, Uganda, and Tanzania are also top tea exporters. The largest tea grower is McLeod Russell, an India-based plantation group; another important producer is Williamson Tea Kenya. The leading tea traders are Kenya-based Global Tea & Commodities, Cargill or Van Rees based in the Netherlands. Tea packers include Unilever, which sells the popular Lipton brand, or companies such as Finlays, whose activities go along the supply chain from plantations to packaging. Tea prices have plunged by 34% in 2013 compared to 2012 to $2.64 a kilogram, the lowest value since mid-2010 for the wholesale price of Kenyan medium-quality tea known as Pekoe Fanning 1 (PF1). Tea production is also crucial to several East African economies. The crisis in Egypt, the world's fifth largest importer, has cut demand just as global production has rebounded after several years of bad crops. In Kenya, the production was 194.9 million kilos in the first five months of 2013, up 52% from the same period in 2012. In Sri Lanka, the world's second exporter, it hit a five-year high.

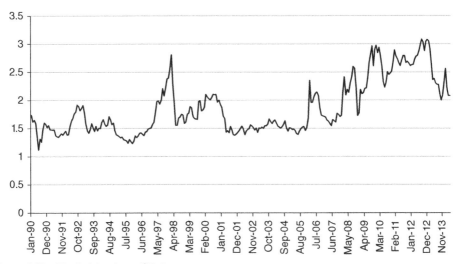

Figure 8.18   Tea in Mombasa ($/kg)

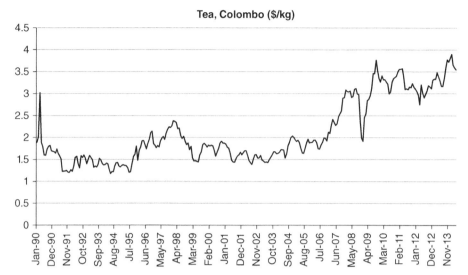

Figure 8.19   Sri Lankan tea, Colombo auctions (World Bank Pink Sheet)

Medium-quality tea prices hit a record high of $4 a kilogram in 2009 when droughts in key exporting countries significantly reduced supplies. Unlike coffee, tea does not trade in a Futures exchange and prices are based on physical deals at regular auctions. The weekly auction held at the port city of Mombasa, Kenya, by the firm Tea Brokers East Africa sets global benchmark prices. It is interesting to note that despite/because the non-existence of tea Futures markets, hence financial players, tea volatility as observed on the Mombasa price PF1 quality for instance and prices have been quite high since 2001, essentially driven by political and weather events, i.e., supply events. The largest black tea importers in 2011 were

Figure 8.20   Tea, average three auctions ($/kg)

Russia with 180,000 tonnes, followed by the UK with 150,000, the USA with 130,000 tonnes, Pakistan with 95,000 tonnes, and Egypt with 80,000 tonnes. The largest exporters are Kenya with more than 400,000 tonnes exported in 2011, followed by Sri-Lanka with 310,000 tonnes, China with 300,000 tonnes, India with 230,000 tonnes, and Vietnam with 130,000 tonnes.

At the time of writing, buyers in Cairo and Karachi, the Pakistani port city that serves as the country's commercial center, were stocking tea again after emptying their inventories for most of the year.

Tea's health benefits are largely due to its high content of flavonoids, plant-derived compounds that are antioxidants. Green tea is the best source of catechins, which in test tubes are more powerful than vitamins C and E in halting oxidative damage to health (Harvard Health Letter). Studies have found an association between consuming green tea and a reduced risk of a number of cancers as well as heart disease.

Finally, note that, according to Abraham Lincoln's early finding, medical research suggests today that both coffee and tea help in avoiding Alzheimer's disease.

The Mombasa port on the Indian ocean

9

Cotton, Timber and Wood,
Pulp and Paper, Wool

'There is no time in modern agriculture for a farmer to write a poem or compose a song.'

Masanobu Fukuoka, microbiologist, farmer, and philosopher

9.1 COTTON

Cotton is a hot-weather crop. In the USA, cotton production stretches from Georgia through Arizona and California and covers more than 14 million acres. California cotton is among the best-quality cotton in the world. Cotton is also grown in Latin America and Asia. Cotton exporters include a variety of nations such as Kazakhstan, Pakistan, and Australia. China also produces a large quantity of cotton and alternates from being an importer to an exporter depending on its crop size and domestic usage. China is today the world's biggest producer and consumer of cotton and the USA is the top cotton exporter.

Cotton prices in the USA are affected mostly by world prices, but they are also subject to government programs such as the US 'Step I: Export Subsidy Program.' This program is variously applied as it must be voted each year by Congress.

Because cotton is such an important US crop, the USDA gives a very complete report that includes supply and demand figures for the USA and the rest of the world.

Cotton is used primarily for clothing fiber and is used more in developing countries as their economies improve:

- For decades, only US grown cotton used to be accepted for the physical settlement of the ICE Cotton Futures contracts; it is not the case anymore. This is going to impair US supremacy in cotton markets since this contract is the one traded by farmers and merchants as well as hedgers and investors/speculators around the globe.
- Industry groups wish to boost supplies by adding reliable exporters such as Australia and Brazil to the list of eligible cotton origins and potentially making bales deliverable at ports in Southeast Asia and South America.

At the end of November 2013, the Chinese government decided to sell part of its 10 million tonne stockpile of cotton via auction with a minimum price of 18,000 yuan a tonne, or $1.34 a pound, according to a notice posted on the website of the China National Cotton Information Center, a government-run cotton industry body. China National Cotton Reserves held daily auctions from January through July 2013, but mills bought just 25% of the cotton offered because of the high prices offered by the corporation. The price of the November auction was about 70% higher than the US cotton nearby Future, the market benchmark.

Figure 9.1
Source: A cotton office in New Orleans, by Edgar Degas (1873).

The estimate of total Chinese cotton reserves of 10.3 million tonnes was provided by the International Cotton Advisory Committee, a Washington-based group that advises cotton producing countries. This number represents 40% of the world production in 2012.

Cotton production

Before cotton can be processed into one of many products, it must be planted, irrigated, nurtured with fertilizers, and protected from unwanted weeds and insects. Enriching nutrients such as nitrogen, phosphate, and potassium are added to the soil before planting.

Planting may be done by hand, but in developed countries, mechanical planters are used; these may cover as many as 12 seedbeds (rows in which the cotton seed is planted) at a time. In regions where soil erosion is a problem, *conservation tillage* is used. In this system, crop residues from the previous crop are left on the soil surface to protect the soil from heavy rains and winds; a special planter is then used to place the seed without destroying the protective cover.

Water is delivered to cotton fields from natural rainfall or through irrigation that can take three forms:

1. Furrow irrigation takes place by running water down a seedbed furrow.
2. Sprinkler irrigation sprays water over the area.
3. Dry tape irrigation is a relatively new method using buried tubing that releases water into the soil beneath the plant.

After a spike in cotton prices in 2011 because of a drought in major producing countries such as Australia and Pakistan, prices have been declining steadily, due to the increasing competition of better polyester fibers, which is unfortunate for the developing countries producing natural cotton.

Cotton A Index ($/kg)

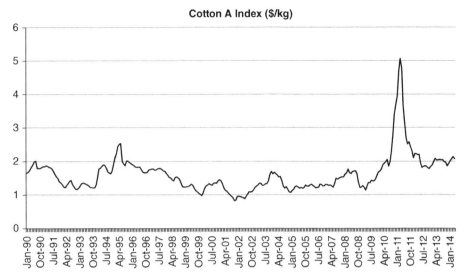

Figure 9.2   Cotton prices CIF Far East 1990 to 2013 (World Bank)

Chart created with NeoTicker EOD © 1998-2007 TickQuest Inc.

Figure 9.3   Cotton prices from 1974 to 2014; stagnant prices except for a spike in 2011 due to a drought in Pakistan and Australia

06/30/2014 C=79.21 -7.06 O=86.27 H=91.43 L=79.10 Mov Avg 3 lines

Volume 571116.00 Open Interest 169129.00

Created with SuperCharts by Omega Research © 1997

Figure 9.4   ICE Cotton No. 2 first nearby prices from 2006 to June 2014; a fairly large trading activity

9.2 LUMBER AND WOOD

Lumber (also known as timber) is wood in any of its stages and has a variety of uses, from structural material in construction and furniture-making to wood pulp for paper production. Lumber takes the form of either softwood or hardwood. Softwood trees include spruce, pine, fir, cypress, redwood, and conifer trees. Hardwood is more expensive, comes from broad-leaved trees, and is used for construction, flooring, furniture, and utensils.

The price of lumber is primarily influenced by the number of new houses under construction, and this exposes the industry to downturns.

The USA leads the world in softwood lumber production. The Wood Markets' annual survey of 2013 shows that US softwood lumber production increased by 6.3% to 28.5 billion board feet (bf); Canadian production increased only by 0.4% to 22.6 billion bf while corporate acquisitions and catastrophic mill fires altered the production landscape; the same flat Canadian output prevailed through August 2013. China surpassed Japan in 2013 to become the world's largest importer of hardwood chips. Its imports of softwood logs and lumber recovered to new heights in the second quarter of 2013. China imports lumber from Chile and the Nordic region.

Australia's consumption of primary wood products is forecast to increase strongly through to 2050. Japan and South Korea are likely to import more wood pellets and energy chips over the next 10 years.

Logging always played an active role in environmental debate. Cutting down large pieces of forests has damaged various species, ecosystems, and plants in a world increasingly affected by global warming. It has been estimated that deforestation is responsible for 17% of annual global carbon, a number higher than the one of emissions from transportation.

In the USA, standard lumber sizes were established at the beginning of the 20th century. The Chicago Mercantile Exchange introduced the first lumber Futures contracts in 1969. There are no exchange-traded funds (ETFs) related to lumber Futures. Those that exist are related to global timber companies such as the Guggenheim Timber ETF called CUT and iShares Global Timber & Forestry called WOOD. CUT includes companies from the USA, Japan, and Brazil; WOOD is 47% USA, 11% Canada, and 9% Brazil. Both of them gave large returns in 2013, in particular because of the recovery of the US economy.

Wood pellets

These are highly combustible, and 100 times easier to ignite than coal. Some power stations are switching from coal to wood pellets to meet their emission targets. As a major example, the large power station Drax, which currently produces 7% of the UK electricity, is converting three of its six coal units to run on biomass. The UK says that bioenergy, which includes biofuels for transport, could provide 8 to 11% of the UK primary energy demand by 2020. The pellets burnt by Drax, though, are shipped from Canada and the USA and critics say that once factored in the carbon cost of growing, harvesting, and processing the wood to make pellets and delivering them thousands of miles away, the new fuel for Drax is not really green. The project is still qualified as 'low carbon' and recognized as a cheap renewable because it does not require expensive back-up power like wind energy. The delivered cost of this biomass is £8 per gigajoule, nearly three times more expensive than coal.

The rise of biomass in Europe is a direct consequence of EU policy, specifically its commitment to produce 20% of its energy from renewables by 2020.

According to experts, there were at the end of 2013 23 gigawatts of biomass-to-electricity capacity in Europe, 2.5% of the total. This is much less than wind, at 106 GW, but still encouraging. In the USA, some utilities are co-firing coal and wood, in anticipation of new rules from the Environmental Protection Agency on CO_2 emissions. Biomass is being developed in the Netherlands, Denmark, Belgium, and Poland, but the UK is leading the group as it had some of the oldest power plants in Europe. Up until 2017, its Drax project will receive from the UK government a subsidy in the form of a 'renewable obligation certificate' (ROC) valued at about £43 per megawatt hour above the market price for electricity. After 2017, ROCs will be replaced by fixed price, long-term contracts for electricity. According to the *Financial Times* (December 10, 2013), Drax was promised by the UK government that its next two converted units will be guaranteed a fixed price of £105 per megawatt hour, twice the British wholesale price of electricity at the end of 2013.

Europe is emerging as the world's largest importer of wood pellets, receiving in 2012 two million tonnes from the USA and one million from Canada, a four-fold increase in four years.

World production currently stands at 35 million tonnes per year, and Europe's power generators consume one-third of it, creating a tight supply. Note that wood pellets are obviously dangerous to store and storage facilities – domes that can each hold 70,000 tonnes of pellets must be equipped with sensors and available nitrogen and carbon dioxide – squeezing out the oxygen, which could start a fire and cool the pellet pile if necessary. According to the *Financial Times*, Drax is spending £225 million on two pellet manufacturing plants in the southern USA, and a harbor in Baton Rouge, Louisiana, where the pellets would be stored (pellets need to be protected from the moment they are processed, in particular from humidity, which makes them unusable as fuel) and shipped from.

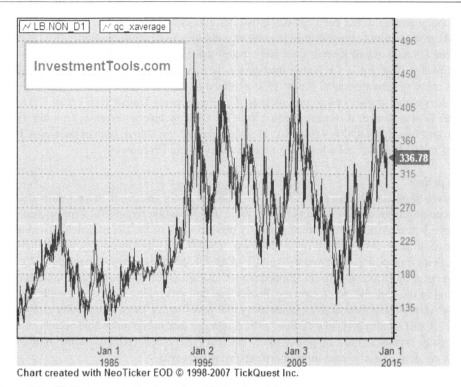

Figure 9.5   CME first nearby lumber prices 1975 to June 2014

Note that the environmentalist group Dogwood Alliance says that the biomass industry is causing an increase in deforestation and driving the destruction of wetland hardwood forests in the USA, as mentioned before.

The group has warned about the loss of biodiversity and the impact on water resources of 'clear-cutting,' i.e., felling all trees in a given area. Drax replies that its biomass comes from sustainably managed forests where the rate of growth exceeds the rate of extraction, avoiding depletion of the carbon stocks of the forests. Obviously, monitoring sustainability among the hundreds of pellet producers across the world and distinguishing good biomass from bad biomass is not an easy matter; hence, the environmentalists' view that biomass is not a truly green source of energy.

9.3 PULP AND PAPER

Pulp is a fibrous material obtained by extracting cellulose from wood, fiber crops or waste paper. Wood provides about 90% of pulp production, and 10% comes from plants. Pulp is one of the most abundant raw materials in the world. It is essentially used to manufacture paper, but also textiles, food, and many other industries. Paper-making used to be through cotton and linen fibers and paper was a relatively expensive commodity. The use of wood to make paper started in the 19th century with the development of mechanical pulping in Germany (Wikipedia). Two competing processes, one called sulfite pulping, the other Kraft process, were developed at the end of the 19th century. Canada is today the largest producer of wood pulp – also called pulpwood – followed by the USA; this pulpwood comes from softwood trees such as spruce and pines and hardwoods such as eucalyptus or birch.

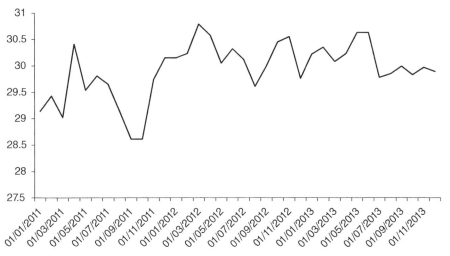

FOEX-PIX Pellet CIF Nordic E/MWh

Figure 9.6   Prices of CIF Nordic sea pellet – Jan 2011 to 2014

A pulp mill is a manufacturing facility that converts wood chips or other fiber sources into a board that can be shipped to a paper mill, before possible bleaching. The methods of pulping are chemical or mechanical pulping, the latter one being better for the environment but consuming more energy. All types of paper are made out of 100% wood. This includes newspapers and magazines. One of the dangers of harvesting wood for pulp mills is that it reduces the biodiversity of forests. Ninety percent of pulp today comes from reforested areas. Bleaching takes place afterwards in order to obtain white paper, using chlorine or ozone.

Crop fibers and agricultural residues are ways to protect forests from paper production; they also use fewer chemicals.

9.3.1 Pulp NBSK and BHKP indexes

- The price is for a minimum amount of 100 metric tons of prime quality Northern Bleached Softwood Kraft in USD and Bleached Hardwood Kraft Pulp market pulp (eucalyptus or birch) in euro/ECU.
- Terms of delivery: CIF North Atlantic or North Sea port (European port).
- Terms of payment: 30 days net or the most frequent.
- Price for pulp intended to be delivered within the current month or latest during the month following the trade.
- Price against free market pulp trades only – no prices against integrated shipments or prices tied to PIX or any other index.
- Standard dryness, i.e., 90% air dry.
- Standard strength characteristics.
- Brightness 88 or higher (for standard ECF/TCF).

9.3.2 Pulp US NBSK index

- The price is for a minimum amount of 100 metric tons of prime quality NBSK in USD.
- Terms of delivery: delivered to customer/customer's warehouse in the USA.
- Terms of payment: 30 days net or the most frequent.
- Price for pulp intended to be delivered within the current month or latest during the month following the trade.
- Price against free market pulp trades only – no prices against integrated shipments or prices tied to PIX or any other index.
- Standard dryness, i.e., 90% air dry.
- Standard strength characteristics.
- Brightness 88 or higher (for standard ECF/TCF).

9.3.3 Pulp BHKP China

The price is for a minimum amount of 100 metric tons of prime quality Bleached Hardwood Kraft Pulp (eucalyptus, acacia or birch) in USD.

- Terms of delivery: CIF Shanghai or equivalent Chinese port.
- Terms of payment: 10–14 days with cash discount, 30–60 days net, 90 days L/C, or other common terms.
- Price for pulp intended to be delivered within the current month or latest during the month following the trade.
- Price against free market pulp trades only – no prices for integrated shipments or prices tied to PIX or any other index.
- Standard dryness, i.e., 90% air dry.
- Standard strength characteristics.

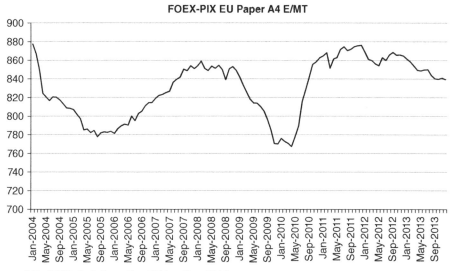

Figure 9.7   EU Pulp Index – Jan 2004 to Dec 2013

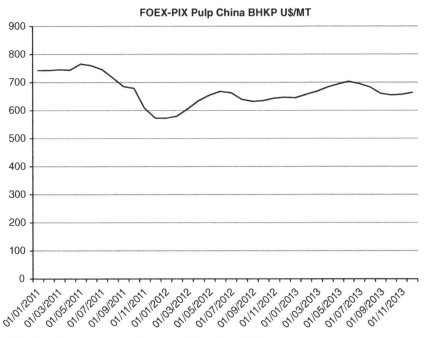

Figure 9.8 CIF Shanghai Pulp Index – Jan 2011 to Dec 2013

9.3.4 Pulp NBSK China

The price is for a minimum amount of 100 metric tonnes of prime quality commodity grade Northern Bleached Softwood Kraft Pulp in USD.

- Pulp of North American or European origin.
- Terms of delivery: CIF Shanghai or equivalent Chinese port.
- Terms of payment: 10–14 days with cash discount.
- Price for pulp intended to be delivered within the current month or latest during the month following the trade.
- Price against free market pulp trades only.
- Standard dryness, i.e., 90% air dry.
- Standard strength characteristics.

9.3.5 When bank notes go plastic

China invented paper money 900 years ago; later on, some countries used linen together with paper for their bank notes. Worldwide, governments spend nearly $10 billion annually to produce new bank notes. Today, paper money is receding in some countries as plastic/polymer notes are gaining attraction. Britain announced early in 2014 that it would begin replacing paper bills with flexible plastic polymer film – starting with the 5 and 10 pound notes that have been printed on cotton-based paper for more than 300 years. Doing so, it followed Canada, Australia, and smaller countries like the Kingdom of Bhutan. This change

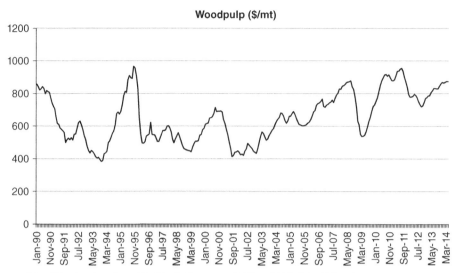

Figure 9.9   Wood pulp prices CIF North Sea ports 1990 to 2013 (World Bank)

in the evolution of money retains the virtue of 'tangibility' compared to credit cards or bit-coins. Moreover, plastic ages better than paper, is cheaper, and more difficult to counterfeit. In a study of the public health effect of new currency materials by Australia's University of Ballarat, it was evidenced from the analysis of bills used in coffee shops and cafeterias in 10 countries that fewer bacteria were found in general on polymer bills than on cotton-based ones, as a polymer note is not absorbent.

Polymer bills were introduced in 2011 in Canada and recognized by the Bank of Canada as sustaining temperatures as high as 284°F and as low as −103°F. Canada's primary stated motive was to make counterfeiting difficult because of the complex protection involved in polymer bills.

The US one-dollar bill, printed on a cotton/linen blend, lasts little more than 21 months.

9.4 WOOL AND CASHMERE

Wool production fell by one-third between 1990 and 2009, probably because of competition from naphtha-derived clothing.

The five largest exporters of wool are Australia, then New Zealand, which exports roughly four times less wool (in terms of weight) than Australia, followed by Uruguay, Argentina, and South Africa each representing one-fourth of New Zealand exports.

The Australian Wool Exchange (www.awex.com.au) was founded in 1993 and provides the major industry setting for the exchange of wool in Australia. It represents 95% of first-hand wool purchased in Australia each year and includes wool brokers, exporters, private merchants, processors, and wool producers.

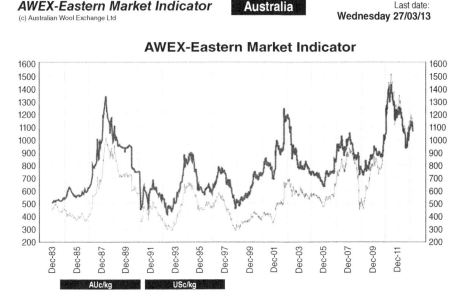

Figure 9.10   Australia Wool Prices – 1984 to 2013

There are more than 30,000 woolgrowers in Australia. Total wool production for the 2012–2013 season was estimated at around 345 million greasy kilograms shorn from 78 million sheep. Wool production is influenced by drought and economic factors. Eighty-five to 95% of shorn wool is offered by woolgrowers through an auction system (like in diamonds) via a selling broker. The rest is privately purchased from the farm through wool brokers or through treaties with private merchants.

The value of wool and cashmere largely depends on three characteristics:

- Fiber diameter, measured in microns. The thicker the fiber, the heavier and coarser the cloth woven from it will be. Hence, thick fibers are left for carpets, bags, and insulation.
- Staple length refers to the length of the fiber. Short fibers are difficult to spin, hence longer fibers are more highly priced.
- Fleece weight is a measure of the amount of fiber per animal.

9.4.1 Cashmere

Cashmere is an ultra-fine fiber, with a diameter no larger than 18 microns. It is finer than the finest Merino wool.

Kyrgyzstan is one of the places in the world where some of the finest cashmere comes from, produced by a local breed of goats. In the springtime, the owners shear them and sell the fleeces to local town traders, who in turn sell them to Chinese wholesalers, who sort them into quality lots before selling them to factories in China or Turkey for processing. Non-profit organizations have been very present in the development of cashmere projects in Kyrgyzstan.

9.4.2 From the Kashmir Goat to high quality yarns

There are four primary steps to cashmere production:

- Collection: cashmere fibers are collected by either combing or shearing the animal during the molting season, a several week period in the spring, and leading to 150 grammes per goat.
- Sorting: hand sorting for coarse hair takes place. After sorting, the fiber is washed to remove dirt and vegetable matter gathered during the collection process.
- Dehairing: this step removes grease and the coarse outer hair.
- At the end of this process, the cashmere is ready to be spun into yarns for weaving or knitting.

The countries that produce commercial quantities of cashmere are China with 70% of the world's output, Mongolia 15% and Afghanistan 10%. Small weights of cashmere are produced in the central Asian countries of Kyrgyzstan, Tajikistan and Kazakhstan. The world production is 7000 tonnes of 'pure cashmere'.

While most of China's production is shipped to fabric and garment makers in Italy, Japan and the UK, the Chinese textile industry has begun to also make cashmere garments for export. Mongolia produces the finest fiber, with a diameter lower than 19 microns.

10

Orange Juice, Livestock, Dairy, and Fishery

'I feel it is an obligation to help people understand the relation of food to agriculture and the relationship of food to culture.'

Alice Waters, chef and author

10.1 ORANGE JUICE

It is an old and important Futures market in the USA – orange juice is denominated as OJ – made famous by the movie *Trading Places*, which illustrates that agricultural commodity markets are central to the lives of human beings and that early information on weather plays a crucial role when trading agricultural Futures. In the same vein, the interesting paper 'Orange Juice and Weather' by R. Roll (1984) demonstrates in a statistical manner that orange juice Futures prices at a given moment are better predictors of the weather in Florida than the contemporaneous information releases of the Meteorology Office in the USA. Citrus represents a very important group in world fruit production. It constitutes roughly a quarter of the total fruit volume. Brazil, the United States, China, and Spain account for 53% of world production, and the first 10 countries for 71%.

The international market for citrus is divided into two types of products: fresh fruit and juices. One-third of citrus world production is transformed into juices. Brazil (the state of Sao Paulo) and the United States (the state of Florida) are the number one regions in the world for citrus juices, in particular orange juice, and account for 75% of the transformed citrus volume. Italy and Mexico for orange juice, Argentina for lemon juice, and Cuba for grapefruit juice complete the world offer. The European Union has slightly reduced its imports in the recent past while the United States has increased its imported volumes, and no significant change has happened in Asia.

A recent and fundamental evolution in juice consumption is a shift of interest to 'not from concentrate' orange juice. The market share of the 'not from concentrate' juice in the USA is currently 52% and should increase at a rate of 3 to 5% per year. Accordingly, many plants in Florida are transforming their entire capacity into the production of 'not from concentrate' orange juice.

Frozen concentrate orange juice (FCOJ) became seriously traded around 1947. Innovations in packaging and transportation permitted the emergence of an international market. In 1966, the New York Board of Trade (NYBOT) launched FCOJ Futures contracts; options on Futures appeared in 1985. Both instruments translated the importance of the weather effect on the commodity price, and in turn its risk: production in Florida is very sensitive to frost while orange trees in Brazil suffer from a dry climate.

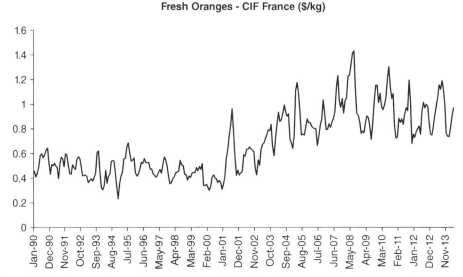

Figure 10.1   Orange prices – CIF EU/ Paris – 1990 to Dec 2013 (World Bank Pink Sheet)

The quality of orange juice is measured by two criteria: 'brix' and acidity (brix represents the fraction of sugar in the juice). The taste of the fruit is determined by the sugar-to-acid ratio.

In April 2014, orange juice prices jumped by 7.2% in the course of a week to reach their highest level in two years, on the expectation of a limited crop from Florida, the source of most oranges used in US juice. The frozen concentrated orange juice nearby contract on the ICE Futures exchange rose to its highest value since March 2012.

The move followed a report by the USDA cutting down its previous estimate by 12%, which would represent the smallest orange harvest in three decades; the reason was a bacterial disease that had spread to every orange-growing county in Florida.

At the same time, Brazil, the world's largest orange exporter, is experiencing the worst drought in decades, resulting in two simultaneous poor crops for the world's two largest producers.

Independently of these events, demand for OJ has been sinking over the last few years, because of the attraction of 'healthy' drinks such as cranberry, pomegranate or vegetable juice, as well as 'energy drinks.'

10.2 LIVESTOCK

In her 2014 book *The Big Fat Surprise: Why Butter, Meat and Cheese Belong in a Healthy Diet* the journalist Nina Teicholz makes the case for animal fats and advocates for the presence of red meat, whole milk, and other sources of saturated fats in a healthy diet, and against biscuits, cereals, and confectionery, often containing palm oil or other inexpensive polyunsaturated vegetable oils and produced at a low cost by food companies. The case against high carbs is certainly deserved.

06/30/2014 C=140.80 -18.60 O=159.50 H=166.00 L=140.35

Figure 10.2   ICE orange juice first nearby prices 2005 to June 2014. A small volume and open interest

Cattle raising can be traced back at least 8500 years in Europe and the Middle East, as mentioned in the Bible (see Investopedia). They were brought to the USA by European settlers in the 17th century. Cattle are used for milk, leather, meat, and agricultural labor.

In 1964, the CME introduced the first Futures contracts on livestock, allowing meat buyers and suppliers to hedge their exposure to the seasonal risk that live cattle trading creates.

Calves require a nine-month gestation period, and then grow from a weight typically comprising between 55 and 100 pounds at birth to as much as 1900 pounds, with a lifespan of roughly 15 years. Hence, it is a long-term horizon activity.

The world has about 1.3 billion head of cattle: India has 400 million, Brazil and China together 300 million, Africa 200 million, and the USA 100 million head. The USA alone produces 25% of world beef production with only 10% of world cattle. It is still a net importer because of its large consumption.

Over the last decade, and particularly since a 2008 conflict between the government and farmers around export taxes on beef, Argentina's cattle inventory has shrunk by 10 million to 48 million in 2011. The country has fallen from its position as the world's third biggest beef exporter to 12th place, behind Uruguay and Paraguay.

10.2.1 Livestock markets

Unlike grain markets where almost half is exported, the livestock markets are much more domestic. Exports have become a more important factor but represent only 10 to 15% of total use. The advance of agribusiness is noticeable in the livestock markets. Producers now sell their production directly to packers and this may lead to the demise of livestock Futures markets. For the time being, cattle and hogs are still auctioned on the open market.

10.2.2 Cattle

As suggested by Nina Teicholz, grass-fed beef grazing on pastures is good for the health because of the proper type of fat it provides, and better than beef fed in the barn with corn or other grains.

The USDA releases its 'cattle-on-feed' report every month; this shows the supply and demand numbers of cattle on feed, the placements and marketing. Cattle on feed means the total number of cattle in feedlots. Placements are the number of cattle placed in feedlots and marketing is the number of cattle marketed by these feedlots.

The USDA also releases a 'cold storage' report that includes pork, beef, and orange juice in cold storage throughout the country. At the end of January, the USDA releases its annual cattle inventory report, which is the best indicator of supply in the coming year, but also of increasing or decreasing production in the long term. But the total number of calves (and their ages)

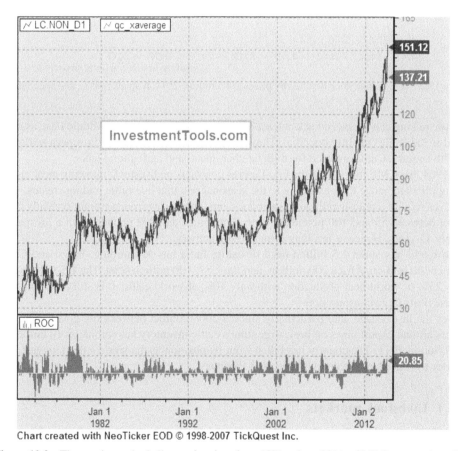

Chart created with NeoTicker EOD © 1998-2007 TickQuest Inc.

Figure 10.3   The consistent rise in live cattle prices from 1971 to June 2014 – CME first – nearby prices

Figure 10.4   New Zealand whole frozen sheep carcasses – London prices – Dec 1990 to Dec 2013

is not enough to describe the supply: the price of feed (corn) makes a big difference since animals are fed longer if corn is cheap. On the contrary, when the price of corn approaches $4, the market is flooded with large numbers of animals. Over the last 14 years, cattle prices plunged when corn prices were $3.25 or higher.

The demand for cattle is more elastic than the supply and when the public experiences the 'feel-good' factor, a preference for beef is observed.

Studies show that when the number of available cattle is tight, producers tend to try to hold their cattle so they can get a higher price for their animals. Likewise, if a period of high supply is about to be observed, they will try to sell their cattle while prices are still good.

To trade feeder cattle, one has to watch the feeder cattle market, the cattle market, and the corn market at the same time. As a consequence of the quantity of necessary information, there is a lack of liquidity in the cattle market.

10.2.3 Hogs

The cycle for hogs is significantly shorter than the cycle for cattle. Hogs are taken to the market when they weight around 230 lb, i.e., at the age of six months. The USDA's quarterly Hogs and Pigs Reports are filled with important details regarding the nation's hog supply. As mentioned earlier, another important report is the monthly 'cold storage' report.

10.2.4 Pork bellies

Pork bellies are the flanks and ribs of hogs and are largely used to make bacon. They may be stored up to one year when frozen and represent the underlying of the CME contract. The hog Futures contract represents 40,000 lb of carcass and (unsurprisingly) is cash-settled against an index of prices collected by the USDA. The belly Futures contract represents 50,000 pounds of frozen bellies; each point move (one-hundredth of a cent) represents $5 per contract. There is a 300-point limit in the belly market, which is known for numerous 'limit moves.' The reason usually given for this high volatility is the high percentage of speculators – as opposed to hedgers – in this market.

Note that a 'limit move' is the maximum change in the price of a Future contract during a given trading session. No orders can be filled outside the up-and-down limits. The Exchange sets the 'limit move', consistently with the choice of the margin deposit.

10.2.5 The US live cattle contract specifications

Ticker symbol	LC (CME) for Open Outcry; LE (Globex) for Electronic Trading
Contract size	40,000 pounds
Contract months	Feb, Apr, June, Aug, Oct, Dec
Trading hours	CME Mon to Fri 9 to 1 pm CST; eCBOT Sun to Fri 6 am to 4 pm CST
Last trading day	Last business day of the contract month
Last delivery day	Up to 7 business days of the month following the contract month
Price quoted	Cents per pound
Tick size	0.00025 per pound = $10 per contract
Daily price limit	A three-cent/pound above or below the previous settlement price (LME)
Deliverable grades	55% choice, 45% select yield grade 3 live steers as defined by USD standards
Initial margin	$1013 per contract in Dec 2013
Position limits	6300 contracts in any non-spot month; 300 for the spot month

If a trader sells (or buys) a live cattle using the quotation LC15Q@101.50, he offers to sell a Future contract for delivery August (Q) 2015 resulting for him in a total selling price of

$$(\$101.50/100)\times 40,000 = \$40,600$$

Futures on live cattle are traded on the CME and BM&F Bovespa (the Brazilian Futures Exchange located in Sao Paulo). Details on the relative moves of the two Futures families can be found in Geman and Vergel (2014).

According to the UN, cattle farming contributes at least 18% to greenhouse emissions. The primary pollutant is methane, which is largely produced by the digestive systems of cattle and considered to be worse than CO_2 because its warming effect is at least 23 times greater.

Bovine spongiform encephalopathy (BSE) – also known as mad cow disease – periodically impacts the live cattle industry and results in the necessary destruction of thousands of livestock. In 2005, Japan, the largest importer of US beef, banned US cattle after the discovery of BSE in Texas. It was an opportunity for Brazil and its neighboring countries to start expanding their cattle industry.

10.2.6 Australia

Australia is the world's third biggest beef exporter but has suffered a terrible two-year drought. 2013 was the hottest year since records began and the persisting drought raised questions on the viability of farming in parts of Queensland, in the northeast of the continent and home to almost half of the country's 27 million cattle.

Australia's dry weather coincided with a severe drought across big cattle ranching states in the USA, causing a global supply crunch just as demand in China was rising rapidly. The FAO bovine meat price index went from a level of 122 in 2009 to more than 200 at the end of 2013.

The level of financial assistance provided to farmers in Australia is low by international standards, with subsidies representing 2.1% of gross farm receipts, well below the 7% in the USA and 19% in the EU. With little grass available in the very dry conditions, farmers are forced to buy feed for their animals in the form of grains, which are expensive because of the drought. The number of cattle slaughtered in the last three months of 2013 hit a record number of 2.2 million, 15% more than the previous year. In the same quarter, live cattle exports surged to 275,000 tonnes, up 230%. Together, a record 596,000 tonnes of beef were produced, out of which 155,000 tonnes were exported to China (and its 1.3 billion potential consumers), up from 30,000 in 2012. This resulted in a rise of cattle prices of 60% between June and December 2013.

10.2.7 The USA

In the USA, the world's largest beef producer, severe droughts (mentioned above) in Texas and California have cut cattle numbers to 87 million, their lowest level since 1951. This has pushed up US beef prices, which are viewed by the experts as the floor for global beef prices.

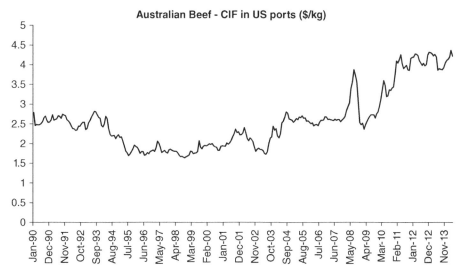

Figure 10.5 Frozen boneless beef from Australia/New Zealand – CIF US East Coast ports (World Bank)

10.3 DAIRY

World demand for milk and milk-derived products has lately been increasing by 2 to 2.5% a year, while the demand for milk powder or whey protein powder has jumped by 30% over the period 2010–2013. Needs from emerging countries and China are the key explanatory factor. And the giants of milk drying towers' production, such as Tetra Pak from Sweden or GEA from Germany, have seen their activity grow by 10% in the sole year 2012. Producers of milk cisterns and 'chaudronnerie agro-alimentaire' such as Bio-Inox from France forecast an acceleration of orders up to 2015.

The French cooperative Sodiaal has joined forces with the Chinese Synutra to build new drying towers for milk.

The Danish-Swedish giant Arla Foods reached in 2012 a production of 13.5 billion liters of milk and revenues of 9 billion euros, becoming the first milk cooperative in Europe, ahead of Friesland Campina from the Netherlands and Sodiaal from France. In 2012, Arla Foods merged with Milch-Union, the German leader, which transforms 1.3 billion liters of milk per year; and with the British specialist of cheddar cheese Milk Link; and more recently with the German dairy firm MUH. Arla Foods is building an immense milk processing plant near London, which should produce more than 1 billion liters of 'pasteurized' milk per year. However, the downside of being a cooperative is that Arla Foods has to pay all its members a uniform price, hence the highest one among the producers; its merger with MUH has generated an increase of 4 cents per liter in Germany.

Regarding China, the projected growth of sales of dairy products into China over the period 2013–2018 is 21% for cheese, 16.7% for baby-milk formula, 13.5% for yogurt and sour-milks products, and 8.5% for milk, making an average annual growth rate of 9.7% for total dairy consumption. Not part of the traditional Chinese diet, milk and cheese are minor luxuries that the Chinese consume more when they move to the cities and join the middle class. The company China Huishan Dairy Holdings saw its revenues rise by 92% in the year ending in March 2013 and in September 2013 was planning an IPO in Hong Kong. The company offers better safety assurances to consumers than its major competitors because it controls the whole production chain, down to the growing of alfalfa that cows eat. It was, at the time of the projected IPO, the largest alfalfa producer in China, with a 28% share of output.

New Zealand has become a major player in the 'white gold' market. It used to be described as a country with 20 sheep per person, but today cows have replaced the sheep. China has made New Zealand the world's biggest milk supplier and transformed its US$175 billion economy. China is New Zealand's largest trading partner and exports to China have risen by 45% from 2012 to 2013 to the value of US$8.3 billion, attracting investors to New Zealand pastures.

Experts estimate the rise in annual output to reach 3.4% in 2014, driven by surging dairy exports.

Milk is changing the face of New Zealand: since 1980, their dairy herd has more than doubled to 6.5 million cows while the number of sheep has halved. At least 300,000 hectares have been transferred to dairy use from other types of farming and forestry over the past decade, causing a jump in agricultural land prices. The dairy industry is driving the boom, with NZ$1 billion in dairy plants under construction together with other related infrastructure projects, such as fleets of trucks and new ports. Obviously, the country is quite exposed to a drop in dairy prices or a reduced Chinese demand.

Since a 2008 event that killed six infants and made 300,000 sick because of Chinese-made baby milk that was tainted with the chemical melamine, Chinese parents prefer to turn to well-established Western brands. The baby-formula market has been surging, from a level of $770 million in 2000 to a predicted value of $29 billion in 2018. As of 2013, international companies have gained an important presence: Johnson covers 11.1% of the market, Nestlé 10.6% and Danone 10.3%. Recently, the firm Synutra International, one of the top 10 Chinese baby-formula makers, bought a plot of land in Brittany, France – a region where excellent quality milk is produced – and is investing $125 million in order to build the first baby-formula plant totally managed by a Chinese company. The plant will send its entire output to China and consume 300,000 liters of local milk per year and 30,000 tonnes of whey that will be processed into dried baby milk.

France is the second dairy producer in Europe behind Germany and already exports to China a large amount of its dried milk used for infant formula, with shipments growing by 41% between 2012 and 2013.

Chinese companies are also investing in other European countries such as Germany, Ireland, and Denmark to secure their milk supply and benefit from international know-how in the milk industry that does not quite exist in China yet.

10.4 FISH MARKETS

The best-known fish market is the fresh salmon market in Norway. The company Fish Pool ASA does not offer trade of physical fish products but has established a synthetic market price, named the Fish Pool Index™, to reflect the actual spot price of Atlantic fresh salmon.

The exchange Fish Ex provides trading and clearing services for Norwegian salmon *forward derivative contracts*. The underlying has SALNO as ticker code; the quoted currency is the euro.

The forward contracts have weekly maturities, and four weeks for the 'block contracts.' The block contracts are cascaded into week contracts (as for electricity forward contracts traded in the Nordpool). The contract size is 1000 kg for the week contract and 4000 kg for the block contracts (in agreement with the cascading rule). The trading model is continuous trading via the Internet.

Nord Pool Clearing (NPC) has entered a cooperation agreement with Fish Ex whereby NPC provides clearing services for fish derivatives contracts traded at the Fish Ex. This allows Fish Ex to benefit from the notoriety acquired by Nord Pool in electricity derivatives. This means that NPC acts as the counterparty in all contracts traded on the Fish Ex.

The collateral consists of cash deposits in a pledged bank account and/or on-demand bank guarantees. The daily margin call is calculated for all open positions on the clearing accounts based on daily closing prices. All NPC settlement banks in the electricity market are also available for the Fish Ex market. The delivery settlement is a financial settlement against the trading price as reference price. The clearing fees are included in the settlement amount.

A sharp shift to farmed fish is a new trend and the expression of a strong demand for seafood in a context of health awareness in the developing world and benefits of fish in a diet (source of omega-3 fat acids) expressed in particular in the growing popularity of sushi. World salmon production has risen from 1566 thousand tonnes in 2008 to 2189 thousand tonnes in

2013. For Norway – the largest producer of farmed salmon – salmon exports have grown from NOK18 billion in 2008 to NOK40 billion in 2013, representing an increase of 35% over the previous year and the second resource of Norway after crude oil. Salmon prices went over NOK50 ($8.50) per kilo in 2013 because of a strong demand coming from the USA and Brazil, as well as higher prices of fish feed like anchovies due to climate change. Oslo-based Marine Harvest, the largest farmed salmon grower with operations in Norway, Chile, and Scotland, saw its earnings multiply by six (*Financial Times*, May 9, 2014) and Norway Royal Salmon reported the best results in its 21-year history.

Wild-caught fish grow on a natural diet (plankton, small fish, insects, aquatic plants), which keeps them healthy and free of disease most of the time. Farm-raised fish, on the other hand, including trout, salmon, and catfish, are fed the same diet as cows and chickens are fed in industrial farming: corn, soy, and rice, hopefully mixed with fish.

According to the UN Food and Agriculture Organization, farmed fish consumption per human being is forecast to increase by 4.4% to an annual consumption of 10.3 kg in 2014 compared to 2013, rising for the first time above the corresponding number for wild fish, which is expected to fall by 1.5% to 9.7 kg.

We can note that a number of consumer groups, such as the association Green Warriors of Norway, correctly resent the gigantic growth of fish farming, as well as the lice attacks and antibiotics and pesticides to fight them. In order to answer the protests, Marine Harvest announced in April 2014 that it would from now on feed its salmon with fish oils properly cleaned and devoid of possibly contaminating material.

In Denmark, some experimental aquaculture farms have started raising salmon in a closed environment where water is recycled to avoid parasites, and fish cannot escape and contaminate the fjords. This could be a way to go for fish farming in the future, together with an upper bound on the number of fish per farm.

10.5 POULTRY AND EGGS

Total US chicken meat exports were 3.2 million tonnes in 2013, in a steady growth from 2 million tonnes in 1999.

The top five importers of US chicken meat are:

- Mexico for 600,000 tonnes
- Russia for 280,000 tonnes
- Angola for 200,000 tonnes (this oil-rich African country can afford to consume poultry)
- Canada for 160,000 tonnes
- Cuba for 130,000 tonnes.

The US company Pilgrim's, acquired in 2009 by the Brazilian meatpacker JBS, saw its income triple in 2013 to a record $550 million as its sales rose 3.6%, helped by investment in automated machinery two years ago.

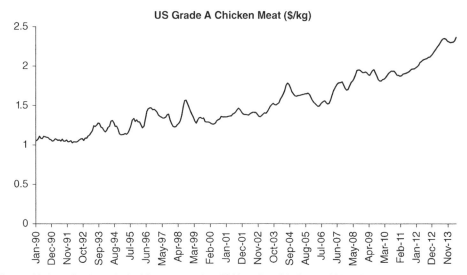

Figure 10.6   USDA grade A chicken meat Jan 1990 to Dec 2013 (World Bank)

Eggs

Eggs are viewed by some experts as the greatest of all foods, containing all nutrients to create life in a powerful combination of proteins, amino acids, fat acids, antioxidants, minerals, and vitamins. By source of proteins, eggs are the cheapest nutrient.

Unsurprisingly, eggs from hens raised on pasture are far more nutritious than eggs from confined hens in factory farms. Compared to the latter, eggs from hens raised on pasture may provide four to six times more vitamin D, three times more vitamin E, 25% less saturated fat, 33% less cholesterol, and twice as much omega-3 fat acids.

11

Rubber, Palm Oil, and Biofuels

'If you're using first-class land for biofuels, then you're competing with the growing of food. And so you're actually spiking food prices by moving energy production into agriculture.'

Bill Gates

11.1 RUBBER

Hevea brasiliensis, better known as rubber tree, is the primary source of natural rubber. As indicated by the name, it is native to Brazil (parts of the Amazon Basin and Matto Grosso), but most of the world's rubber today comes from Asia.

Although rubber is still tapped from wild trees in the Amazon Basin, production in South American plantations is once and a while hampered by a fungal disease.

Hevea brasiliensis is the only species planted commercially and is the primary source of natural rubber. The milky latex, produced by a specialized secretory system in the phloem, is the raw material for natural rubber and can be sustainably tapped without harming the tree.

Rubber is water resistant, does not conduct electricity, is durable, and, most importantly, is highly elastic. Natural rubber is used today in play balls, latex gloves, and many other industrial applications. It is more suitable than synthetic rubber for the tires of aircraft and space shuttles.

- Rubber is one of the most important products to come out of the rain forest. Like maize, rubber owes its existence to South America where it was used to make play balls, shoes, and waterproof clothes. It was brought back to Europe when the American continent was discovered.
- Rubber is a polymer consisting of hydrogen and carbon and is elastic in nature. It is found in the fluid of *Hevea* trees, which are tapped. These plants live in general 32 years but may live up to 100 years. Synthetic rubber is produced through polymerization of various monomers.
- Now, rubber grows mostly in Asia – Thailand (first), Indonesia, and Malaysia account for 94% of world production; India is another big producer and also the fourth largest consumer. China is the leading consumer worldwide.
- Synthetic rubber accounts for approximately 55% of demand, and natural rubber the remaining 45%.
- The listed Asian plantation groups that dominate the sector are running out of land to extract the liquid gold from squat green trees, spawning risky competition for space in equatorial Africa (the place it imported plants from when the Asian industry started in the 1960s).
- Malaysia, responsible for 40% of production, has very little plantable land left due to a mixture of reasons including infrastructure problems and restrictions on land use.

Thailand, Indonesia, and Malaysia control 70% of the world supply of natural rubber.

The Bangkok-based International Rubber Council, in order to stop the 60% fall in rubber prices that had taken place since their February 2011 peak, decided in September 2012 to reduce their supply, in a move that was damaging to tire makers, the largest consumers of rubber.

Vietnam, the world's fourth largest producer, is not part of the Council.

Rubber latex makes up 60% of the cost of medical gloves and Top Glove Corp, the world's largest exporter of rubber gloves, said the company will make more gloves from synthetic materials in a first stage; it also bought an Indonesian company with about 74,000 acres of plantation land.

The price of natural rubber hit a record high of 528 yen per kg in February 2011, and then fell because of construction slowdown in China and Brazil. Prices in August 2013 had fallen 60% from that high point of $6.40 to $2.50 per kg, because of the combined effect of a global slowdown and a surplus of rubber. In Thailand, the world's largest producer and exporter of natural rubber, this price collapse led farmers to demonstrate in order to get from the government price guarantees for raw rubber sheet, rubber cup lump, and latex at above-market prices, as well as loans to invest in rubber processing and machinery upgrades. The Thai government had just spent $18 billion to fund controversial rice subsidies in which the government had bought rice from farmers at 50% above global market prices. This rice program had built up $4.4 billion in financial losses and 17 million tonnes of rice in storage, the equivalent of two years of the country's exports. In 2012, Thailand joined Indonesia and Malaysia to cut exports by a collective 300,000 tonnes of rubber to boost prices, but this was fairly ineffective. According to the FAO, China, India, Indonesia, Myanmar, and Vietnam contributed to an overall production increase in millions of tonnes of rubber over the past decade, challenging Thai farmers who had accumulated heavy debt during the good years. After Thailand got the lead in global rubber production in 1990 when it overtook Malaysia, it is now contributing to one-third of the world total.

Several exchanges are trading rubber: the Singapore exchange (SICOM), the Tokyo Commodity Exchange (TOCOM), and the Osaka Mercantile Exchange (OME) are the major ones. OME merged in August 2006 with the Central Japan Commodity Exchange (C-COM).

Contracts with different quality specifications are also offered on the Kuala Lumpur Commodity Exchange (KLCE), the Shanghai Futures Exchange (SHFE), and the National Multi-Commodity Exchange of India (NMCEI).

Volume traded in SHFE natural rubber was booming in the mid-2000s, with for instance a growth of 403% in volume between March 2005 and March 2006, accounting for more than 40% of total business of this exchange in some years.

There are few rubber companies and most big players are located in China, Thailand, or Malaysia.

Rubber prices declined by 25% in 2013 as an excess supply of 384,000 tonnes depressed prices. In the first two months of 2014, prices lost another 13% in a context of reduction of China growth and the decline continued over the whole first semester of 2014.

The International Rubber Consortium advised its members not to sell in a situation of 'unreasonably low prices.' Thai exporters confirmed they would not sell below their production costs.

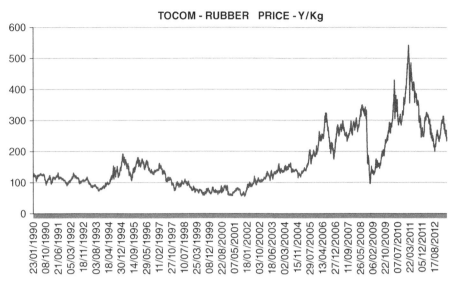

Figure 11.1   Rubber first nearby prices in Tokyo in yen/kg 1990 to 2013

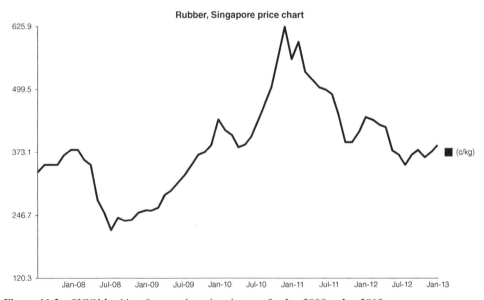

Figure 11.2   SICOM rubber first nearby prices in cents/kg Jan 2008 to Jan 2013

A Note on cement

Cement is usually manufactured from sand and stones. In the near future, however, biocement could be made out of rubber and linen. The Franco-Belgian cement company Alkern is also looking at 'miscanthus,' a plant similar to bamboo, used in the production of biomass and which has the merit of growing annually and nearly everywhere. Obviously, these alternative sources of cement would reduce the environmental impact of this industry.

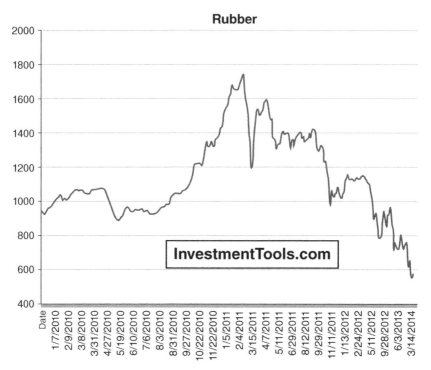

Figure 11.3   The recent collapse of rubber prices

11.2 PALM OIL

African oil palm is a native palm from West Africa, hence its name of *Elaeis guineensis* refer-ring to Guinea, one of the countries where it originates. Although archeological evidence of the use of palm oil was found in Egypt in the tomb of Abydos, dated 3000 BC, the use of palm oil from the African oil palm may have been part of the food supply in West Africa from much earlier times and was brought to Egypt by Arab traders. There is recorded evidence of farmers in West Africa producing palm oil for their own food consumption but also for export in the early 19th century. Palm oil acquired a much more prominent role during the British industrial revolution when it was used as a lubricant for machinery and also for candle-making.

The listed Asian plantation groups that dominate the sector are running out of land to ex-tract the liquid gold from squat green trees. Malaysia, for instance, responsible for 40% of world production, has very little agricultural land left due to a mixture of reasons including infrastructure problems and restrictions on land use. In fact, 66% of Malaysia is still covered by forest, compared to 25% in Europe and Western countries in general. Similarly, Indonesia, which produces 45% of global supplies, has plenty of land, but most of it is virgin forest the country has promised to preserve.

This pressure on available land causes ferocious competition for space in equatorial Africa, from where plants were originally imported when the Asian industry started in the 1960s. For instance, Olam has a joint venture in Gabon, where Wilmar also owns a plantation that used to belong to Unilever. Other countries of interest are Ivory Coast, Sierra Leone, Nigeria, and

Uganda. The costs are high and the risks enormous, in particular given the civil wars that have hurt most of these countries over the last decades.

Strong demand for palm oil comes from India and China where increasing prosperity induces a growing interest in processed food products, many of which contain palm oil, like pastries, chocolate, and ice-cream.

11.2.1 The oil palm and palm oil

The African oil palm *Elaeis guineensis* comes in several varieties: the thick-shelled dura, the shell-less pisifera, and the tenera palm, which is a hybrid of the two. Tenera plants are exceptionally thin shelled and have high oil content but are rarely found in the wild. After 1945, the establishment of large-scale programs for the breeding of the tenera variety started to provide positive results. Nowadays, it is common to refer to tenera as DxP, since the fruits produced through pollinating the pisifera onto the dura flowers give the tenera hybrid, which is the commercial oil palm used for the production of palm oil. Although the yields produced by the tenera variety depend on their genetics, they give the highest yield of oil per hectare compared to any other crop. Two varieties of oil are extracted – palm oil and palm kernel oil. Palm kernel oil lacks carotenoids, is not red, and has 81% saturated fat content, whereas palm oil obtained from the pulp of the fruit has a high content of carotenes, a distinct red color, and a much lower content (41%) of saturated fat.

The oil palm was first introduced in Southeast Asia in 1848, when seeds from West Africa were planted in a botanical garden in Java. Later, in 1902, with the invention of hydrogenation – a process by which polyunsaturated fats are transformed into saturated and transfats and thus converts liquid vegetable oils into solid or semi-solid fats – palm oils were used for the making of margarine. In 1905, the agricultural engineer Adrian Hallet went to Sumatra and noticed that the palms in that region were more productive than the ones in West and Central Africa. Since these palms were descendants from the seedlings brought to Java in 1848, their product was quite uniform. This gave planters the advantage of high yields with lower risks from a number of pests, as they were far away from their original habitat. In the 1920s, oil palm seeds were introduced from Malaysia and West Africa respectively to Panama and Guatemala, where the first commercial planting took place in 1940, successfully expanding to Honduras.

There were more technological advances in the refining of palm oil that allowed its liquid form to be used in Western food products after World War II. In 2007, Indonesia replaced Malaysia as the world's largest producer of palm oil. These two countries represent 90% of palm oil world production. Palm oil prices went down by 33% between January 2011 and July 2013.

Plantations work on 25-year cycles corresponding to the lifetime of the trees. With good management and ideal climatic conditions, modern varieties of oil palms are capable of producing in excess of 20 metric tonnes of bunches per hectare per year, with a palm oil content of 25% per bunch, excluding the palm kernel oil. This is equivalent to a yield of 5 metric tonnes of oil/ha/year. In order to produce palm oil, the fruits must be harvested at the optimum ripeness, i.e., five to six months from pollination; each bunch of fruit weighs 40 to 50 kg at this point. The fresh fruit bunches are then transported to an oil mill, where they are sterilized by steam under pressure. Once cooked, they are transferred to a bunch stripper, which separates the palm fruit from the nut. The pressing process follows.

Given the increase of exports of palm oil in the 20th century, mechanization, meant to increase oil yield and reduce labor requirements, accelerated – The Durschner press, which was initially a wine and cider press, was modified for the palm oil industry. By 1959, the hydraulic press was introduced – finally, the oil discharged from the press is passed through screens, and then to a clarifying centrifuge. The sludge is further treated to recover the residual oil.

Chemically, solid stearin and liquid olein are separated and impurities are removed through the refining process. The oil is filtered and bleached, and smells and coloration are removed. The final product is called 'refined bleached deodorized palm oil,' or RBDPO. Many companies go even further in the refining process and produce palm olein for cooking oil and other products.

The fiber in oil palm branches and leaves left after the harvest can be used as organic fertilizers or to create paper products, such as meal boxes and degradable tableware. This was usually done only by locals, while large plantations would simply burn the branches and leaves after the harvest. Some companies specialize in the creation and distribution of oil palm-based papers and other products.

Palm oil is the most produced of all vegetable oils in the world and can be found in a wide variety of processed foods as an inexpensive substitute for butter. It is also used as cooking oil in many countries. However, although fresh red palm oil has a variety of healthy components such as carotenes, the World Health Organization has recognized that the consumption of palmitic acid increases the risk of heart diseases.

Apart from the food industry, soaps and washing powders, cosmetics, antioxidants, and carotenes from red palm oil are very important industries. Stearin, derived from the refining process of palm oil, is used to manufacture candles and soap. Mixed with sodium hydroxide, it gives glycerin and sodium stearate (a common soap found in many types of solid deodorants, rubbers, inks, some food additives, and flavorings). It is also used in the grinding process of aluminum to produce dark aluminum powder.

Other common uses of palm oil are as a biodiesel and in power generation, where it competes with other vegetable oils.

Bursa Malaysia Berhad, previously known as the Kuala Lumpur Stock Exchange, offers a number of derivative products related to palm oil through its wholly owned subsidiaries. Currently on offer are Crude Palm Oil Futures in Malaysian ringgit and US dollars and Crude Palm Kernel Oil Futures.

For crude palm oil, the contract size is 25 metric tonnes and the contract months are the spot month and the next succeeding five months. Further in the future, contracts are on alternate months up to 24 months ahead. The crude palm oil deliverable for those contracts has to be of good quality, unbleached, and in port tank installations approved by the exchange. The seller can choose among several ports: Kelang or Penang/Butterworth. The physical contract is priced in ringgit while the USD Crude Palm Oil contract is priced in US dollars and it is only cash settled.

Options on Crude Palm Oil Futures are put and call European options, whose underlying is one Crude Palm Oil Futures contract for a specified month.

11.2.2 Markets

The trading flows reflect the fact that the main producers of palm oil are Indonesia, Malaysia, Thailand, and to a lesser extent Colombia and Nigeria. Indonesia and Malaysia are also the main exporters, followed by Papua New Guinea, Thailand, and the United Arab Emirates. The main importers of palm oil are India, China, and the EU-27.

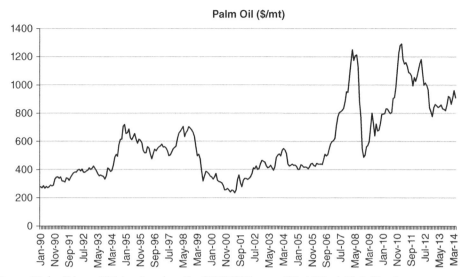

Figure 11.4   Prices of Malaysia palm oil – CIF/NW Europe (World Bank Pink Sheet)

Figure 11.5   First nearby palm oil prices from 1979 to April 2012 – Kuala Lumpur exchange

11.3 ETHANOL, BIOFUELS, AND BIOMASS

Corn does not just compete with sugar as a sweetener for the food industry, it is also connected to sugar in the energy sector, as it is a very important resource for the production of ethanol. Although biofuels have been around for decades, it was not until 2000 or so that they started to play a central role in energy policy and had an increasing impact upon agricultural policy and food security. Due to higher crude oil prices and environmental concern, there have been successive mandates increasing the blending rates in the USA, the EU, and other countries around the world. Those increases have put the public debate regarding the issue of whether to use corn and sugar cane for ethanol or food production on a center stage.

In general, biofuels can be classified as ethanol or biodiesel. Although corn and sugar cane are directly related to ethanol production and constitute the biggest sources for its production, other agricultural products such as rapeseed and palm oil can be used in the production of biofuels.

Ethanol, also known as ethyl alcohol, is produced through the fermentation of carbohydrates. First created synthetically in 1826, ethanol can be produced from molasses, which is a by-product of sugar manufacturing from sugar cane, or directly from the sugar cane juice. It can also be manufactured from cassava, i.e., tapioca, with Thailand being the top world producer. The palm, due to the high content of sugar in its sap, also allows for the efficient production of alcohol.

In recent years, ethanol has been used as a pollution-reducing additive to gasoline but also as a standalone alternative renewable fuel. The USA and Brazil are the dominant producers of ethanol: corn-based ethanol is the main source for blending gasoline in the USA, while in Brazil ethanol is mainly obtained from sugar cane.

Brazil itself leads the world in the use of ethanol as fuel, as it can produce it competitively as long as oil prices stay above $30/bbl. As of 2005, 80% of all new cars in Brazil have had flexible-fuel engines, which can run on any combination of gasoline and ethanol.

Archer Daniels, Green Plains Renewable Energy, and Valero have recently increased corn ethanol output and incomes, in a context of rising demand for sugar cane ethanol from Brazil. As for the USA, ethanol production has grown from 800,000 barrels per day in January 2013 to 900,000 barrels per day in February 2014 (source: CARD, Iowa State University). Ethanol margins increased greatly in 2013.

Biodiesel can be produced from vegetable oils, such as palm oil, and can be blended with diesel from crude oil. Indonesia and Malaysia are the world's largest palm oil producers.

Coconut oil is an edible oil extracted from the kernel of matured coconuts harvested from the coconut palm (Wikipedia). It has various applications in food, medicine, and industry. Because of its high saturated fat content, it is slow to oxidize and can last up to two years without being spoilt. Many health organizations advise against the consumption of high amounts of coconut oil for that reason.

Coconut oil has been tested for use as a feedstock biodiesel to be used in a diesel engine. The Philippines and several other tropical islands are using coconut oil as an alternative fuel in cars, trucks, and buses. Research is conducted on the potential of coconut oil as a fuel for electricity generation.

Coconut oil is an important base ingredient for the manufacture of soap; it is more soluble in salt or poor quality water than other soaps.

The EU used to be the main producer of biodiesel from soy oil, sunflower oil, and rapeseed oil. In October 2012, the European Union shifted its biofuels policy by proposing to limit the share of energy from biofuels made from food crops to no more than 5% by the year 2020. This U-turn in EU policy threatens the hundreds of millions of euros recently invested in biofuel production capacity. Meanwhile, new rules encourage the production of so-called second-generation biofuels, which do not compete with food demand.

Figure 11.6 Ethanol first nearby prices July 2012 to June 2014

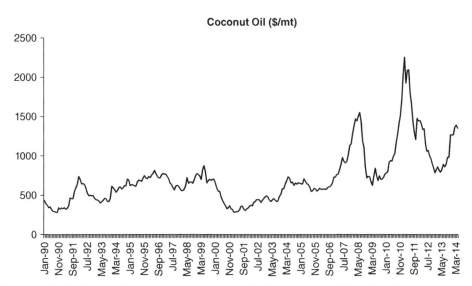

Figure 11.7 Philippines/Indonesia coconut prices – CIF Rotterdam – 1990 to Dec 2013

Table 11.1   Production of major vegetable oils: world supply and distribution

Production in million tonnes 2007 to 2012						
Oil coconut	3.54	3.63	3.83	3.56	3.52	3.59
Cottonseed	4.75	4.6	4.97	5.27	5.28	5.26
Olive oil	2.78	3.08	3.25	3.39	2.87	2.87
Palm oil	44.02	45.87	47.92	51	53.83	54.32
Palm kernel	5.17	5.5	5.55	5.91	6.25	6.25
Peanut oil	5.08	4.74	5.05	5.12	5.29	5.32
Rapeseed	20.59	22.55	23.51	24.29	23.8	23.91
Soy oil	35.89	38.81	41.3	42.35	43.18	43.09
Sunflower seed	11.95	12.13	12.28	15.1	13.75	13.84

Source: USDA.

12

Land, Water, and Fertilizers

'What if soil runs out?'

Professor John Crawford

12.1 LAND TYPES, YIELDS, AND EROSION

It has been suggested several times in this book that soil is a hub for water, food, energy, climate, and health. According to John Crawford, a rough calculation of current rates of soil degradation suggests we have about 60 years of good soil left. Some 40% of soil used for agriculture around the world is viewed as either degraded or seriously degraded, meaning that 70% of the best type of soil is gone. We are in fact *borrowing from the future* in order to get cheap food, cheap water, and cheap energy.

Various farming methods strip the soil of carbon and make it less robust and weaker in nutrients; soil is being lost quickly, even the well-maintained farming land in Europe.

Agriculture accounts for 70% of fresh water use; but this water is wasted if it goes through degraded soil and past the root system.

Several key issues, obviously inter-related, are faced:

- Loss of soil productivity: in the present conditions, soil will produce 30% less food in the next 20 to 40 years. Wheat output in China should face a 40% reduction by 2030.
- Soil is being eroded at a rate that is 10 to 40 times faster than it can be sustainably replaced, in particular because of loss of nutrients.
- Biofuels, fracking, and coal seam gas are threats to land and water.
- Water may be a source of conflict in sensitive parts of the world like the Middle East. It is most serious in China, Africa, India, and parts of South America, as we shall see in Section 12.3.

On the other hand, richer countries will have to deal with more refugees and growing disparities across society. Moreover, efforts have been on breeding high-yield crops that can survive on degraded soil, which explains why 60% of the world's population is deficient in nutrients like iron ore.

In the mid-long term, scientists and farmers should mix their expertise to regenerate the environment while producing harvests as well. Worldwide, a very high number of small farms exist in India and Africa while large ones in Canada and France are regrouped in powerful cooperatives that can afford a risk-management structure.

12.1.1 Yield-at-risk

Yield varies from year to year, mainly as a result of weather but also due to other factors such as disease, the introduction of new technologies, and the expansion of crop production into more marginal land. Global diversification of crop production means that, to some extent, global average yield is insulated from the variations in individual countries. We adapt the concept of 'Value-at-Risk' from finance to estimate 'yield-at-risk,' measuring the likely degree to which yield may depart downwards from trend. This helps to put inventory values in perspective. If we hold 15% of annual production in inventory, but yield-at-risk is 10%, then clearly the inventory situation is less healthy than if the yield-at-risk is only 2%.

Should we measure yield-at-risk or production-at-risk? Since acreage[1] planted figures are unavailable for most countries worldwide, with only acreage harvested data being available, both measures have flaws. Measuring variations in yield, calculated on harvested acres, will not take into account years when conditions are so bad that crops are not even harvested. Measuring production-at-risk also has problems. Production varies because of the acreage planted, a manmade decision, and because of yield, subject to the random effects of weather and other influences. Measuring production at risk does not disentangle these factors, in contrast to the approach of 'precision farming' discussed in Chapter 13.

12.1.2 Land competition

Farmers in many areas enjoy an 'embedded optionality' in their choice of crop. Each year they can choose from several crops, subject to constraints such as soil quality, likely water availability, likely temperature range, available equipment and expertise, etc. Typically, this decision will be based on the respective crop prices, expected yields and possibly different input costs (such as fertilizers) for the crop with the higher expected profit being planted. For example, there is well-documented competition between soybeans and corn in the USA, with farmers keenly following the soybean-to-corn price ratio (*Financial Times*, 2012). Other factors also affect decisions, such as the desire for diversification across several crops.

Land competition is a sign of land scarcity. If 'unused' land is a plentiful resource, then expansion of one crop is independent of other crops. Conversely, if little unused land remains, increased acreage in one crop must be at the expense of another crop.

12.1.3 Farmland in the USA

Based on the USDA 2007 report, the value of US farmland was about $1.9 trillion in 2006.

Farmland is assigned to two broad categories: cropland and grassland/pasture. USDA (2007) estimates suggest that there are about 440 million acres of cropland and 590 million acres of grassland in the USA.

There are over 2 million farms in the USA, with an average size of about 450 acres (USDA, 2007). In 2006, the average value of cropland was $2700 per acre, compared to $1160 for grassland.

The overall value of farmland more than doubled between 1997 and 2006, with most of the gains between 2003 and 2006, according to Waggle and Johnson (2009). Howard (2005) notes that institutional investors typically hire farm management firms to manage their farm properties and farm managers may either lease the land or take on the operation themselves.

---

[1] Although the widely used term 'acreage' meaning the area planted is used here, the metric unit of hectare has been used throughout.

Emerging markets have been a key driver of demand growth for agricultural products since the late 1990s. Changing tastes have increased demand for meat (highly food intensive), corn, soybeans, coffee, and sugar. Note that

Inputs for meat: 1 tonne of meat = 7 tonnes of corn = 7000 gallons of water

A small percentage change in demand per capita can lead to a large absolute increase in demand due to the relatively large size of emerging market populations.

Since 1900, the world population has been multiplied by 4 while water usage has been multiplied by 6 (UN charts from FAOSTAT on water use; map from IWMI on projected water scarcity in 2025).

This has exacerbated shortages in water supplies, crimping production in regions requiring intense irrigation.

12.2 FERTILIZERS

In a world projected to see a dramatic increase in the demand for food, fertilizers are gaining the status of a commodity in their own right. The quantity of land essentially remains unchanged while the world population is increasing and people living in 'developed emerging' countries such as China consume more proteins, in turn using vast amounts of grains (7 kilos of feed grains for 1 kilo of beef, 4 kilos of grain for 1 kilo of pork, and 2 kilos of grain for 1 kilo in the case of poultry). In fact, according to a recent report from the Food and Agriculture Organization (FAO), the amount of arable land per human being should decrease to 0.20 hectares in 2020, a decline from 0.45 in 1960. Along the same lines, a very ominous paper by Hertel (2011) views a 'perfect storm in the making' regarding the issue of adequate supply of agricultural land at the horizon in 2050 and concludes on the likely occurrence of a number of 'regional' storms. Moreover, land erosion is happening in various regions, Africa in particular. One of the few solutions to feeding the planet, which has the merit of being global as well as local, is to increase *yields* in already cultivated land. This, in turn, makes fertilizers an important element of the agricultural commodities picture. According to Stewart *et al.* (2005), fertilizers accounted for 60% of the registered yield increases in the last five years.

China and India have been importing increasing quantities of fertilizers over time to meet their rising food demand. Like the whole mining sector, fertilizers are strongly linked to energy markets as they require vast amounts of energy in the extraction, processing, and shipping phases. Nitrogen, for instance, is available in large volumes in the atmosphere, but its transformation into ammonia is highly demanding in terms of energy, essentially natural gas. Similar to all other storable commodities, fertilizers travel the world, hence the importance of the shipping department in fertilizer companies. Fertilizers go from producing countries to those needing the imports, the latter often being supported by the local government, like in India or Africa. Note that ammonia, as a hazardous material, needs to be transported in special, highly pressurized containers.

In most cases, the three types of fertilizer layers, namely potash, nitrogen, and phosphate, are necessary as nutrients for the soil. With the growth of fertilizers' physical trade, derivative contracts are becoming numerous, swaps in particular; these are related either to one of the three components or a mix embedded in fertilizer indexes proposed by information providers

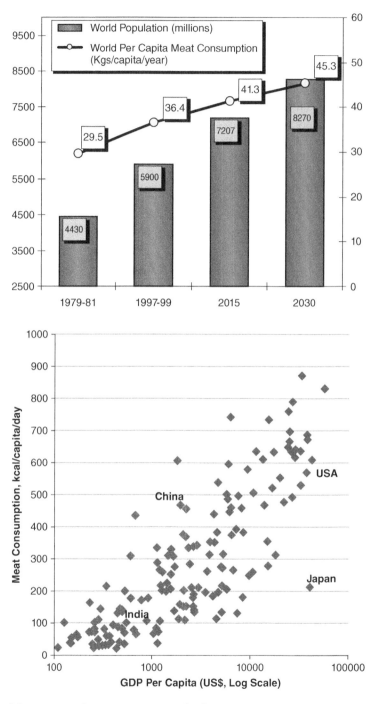

Figure 12.1   Meat consumption: more pressure on land

or brokers. The World Bank publishes the World Fertilizer Index, which is the one analyzed here for its transparency; this index also has the merit of being a weighted basket of the three major fertilizers.

The goal in this section is threefold. First, we analyze the joint behavior of corn, wheat, and fertilizer prices over the last two decades. In particular, we exhibited in Chapter 2 a remarkably quasi-contemporaneous break in the price trajectories of the three commodities in 2006, the year when the first recent food crisis began. Second, we extend to fertilizers the strategy of investing in share prices of oil and mining companies in order to get exposure to the price of the commodity (see Geman and Vergel, 2013). From this perspective, we study the performance of share price returns of firms essentially involved in the production of fertilizers over the period 1990–2011 and listed on an exchange – note, for instance, that the Moroccan Office Chérifien des Phosphates, a major player in the sector of phosphate production, is state owned and hence outside our analysis – lastly, we exhibit the sensitivities of share returns to fertilizer prices over the two subperiods, Jan 2004 to June 2008 and Jan 2009 to Dec 2011. The global period is chosen to include a large number of firms and to start at a time when some market participants, individual and institutional, began investing in agricultural commodities and, in turn, fertilizers. Exposure to the latter was only possible through the purchase of shares of fertilizer companies – which continues to be the case today since Futures on fertilizers do not trade on an exchange yet.

We believe that the issue of 'commodity equities' is an important one and the case of fertilizers as the 'new commodity on the block' is a good prototype.

12.2.1 Fertilizer markets

The use of commercial fertilizers has steadily increased in the last 50 years, rising almost twenty-fold in the case of nitrogen to the current rate of 100 million tonnes per year. The consumption of phosphate has risen from 9 million tonnes per year in 1960 to 40 million tonnes in 2000. The production of potash today exceeds 30 million tonnes per year, mostly for use in fertilizers. According to the FAO, fertilizer consumption over the period 1993 to 2007 has increased at an annual rate of 2.6% for phosphate, 3.6% for potash, and 2.4% for nitrogen. In dollar values, potash prices for instance went from $200 a tonne in 2004 to an expected level of $1500 a tonne by 2020. A maize crop yielding 6 to 9 tonnes of grains per hectare requires 31 to 50 kg of phosphate fertilizer to be applied, soybean requires 20 to 25 kg per hectare. The links of fertilizers with crucial commodities, their importance at a global level in feeding the world population, and the fact that only a few countries and companies control their production have increased the relevance of financial research on the subject, which is fairly thin at the moment.

All three main categories of fertilizers – nitrogen (N), phosphate (P), and potash (K) – are, in general, nutrients that are necessary in improving land yield. Sulfur is sometimes added to help the soil absorb the nitrogen or increase the seed oil content of crops such as soybeans and flax; in this case, sulfur is used in a ratio of 1 to 20 with respect to nitrogen and we will leave it outside our discussion.

Phosphate, the first key fertilizer, contains phosphorus, an important element for the human body to build and repair cell walls. It is found in the form of phosphate rock, which is processed into DAP (di-ammonium phosphate) by the separation of phosphate from the mix of sand, clay, and phosphate. While nearly 30 countries produce phosphate rock, China, the USA, and Morocco are the largest producers, accounting together for two-thirds of phosphate world production.

Morocco alone accounts for more than 30% according to data from the US Geological Survey. Annual global production is around 170 million tonnes while estimated reserves stand at 15 billion tonnes. This means that the reserves that can be developed using current technology would be depleted in 90 years. In 2013, China was the first producer of phosphate rock (97 million metric tonnes), followed by the USA (32) and Morocco (30). World top companies also include Mosaic of the USA, Fos Agro of Russia, and Yuntianhua Group of China. It is important to emphasize that fertilizer firms need large amounts of power, oil, and gas for their mining activities, as well as trucks, pipelines, and shipping facilities for their distribution business.

Potash is the most common name for various mined salts that contain potassium in water-soluble form; it has been used since antiquity as a soil fertilizer. Today, potash is produced worldwide in amounts exceeding 30 million tonnes per year. The largest known potash deposits are spread all over the world, from Canada to Brazil, Belarus, China, Germany, Israel, Jordan, and the world's purest potash deposit in New Mexico, USA. Canada is the world's largest producer, followed by Russia and Belarus. The most significant reserve of Canada's potash – an excellent quality of potash – is located in the province of Saskatchewan, and controlled by the Potash Corporation of Saskatchewan. The world's largest consumers of potash are China, the USA, Brazil, and India. Brazil imports 90% of the potash it needs. Potash is important for agriculture because it improves water retention, nutrient value, taste, disease resistance of food crops, and yield. As established by He *et al.* (2009), rises in fertilizer prices are primarily influenced by rising costs in the production of fertilizers (fuel prices and human labor in particular, like in all mining activities) and increased demand as farmers try to raise their output in a context of higher agricultural commodity prices. Regarding the analysis of fertilizer prices that will follow, we will use the World Bank Fertilizer Index, an index that contains the three types of fertilizers, is transparent, and unlikely to be manipulated. This index is defined by the following weights:

Natural phosphate rock	16.9
DAP	21.7
Potassium	20.1
Nitrogen	41.3

It is interesting to note that phosphate appears twice in the index, both in the form of the extracted phosphate rock and also in the form of DAP, thus showing the importance of this constituent and the property that phosphate is traded both in its raw form (phosphate rock) as well as the transformed one (DAP). The chemical plants that transform the phosphate rock into DAP are quite expensive to build but allow countries, often emerging countries, to benefit from a vertical integration of the supply chain on their own territories. At the same time, the cost of shipping the phosphate rock from the extraction place to very distant destinations around the world becomes obviously lower in the DAP form, where mud and dust around the phosphate have been eliminated. In an analogous manner, potassium is extracted in the form of mined salts and then transformed into nitrate and sulfate of potassium, which are the fertilizer forms.

The flows of fertilizers across the world are quite interesting. In general, potash travels from Canada into the USA and China. It also goes from the former Soviet Union into India. Phosphate rock and DAP go from Morocco and Tunisia into Europe and India, and from Syria into India. DAP goes from the USA into India, nitrogen from China into India. This shows a large array of shipping activities, since no single country produces the three components. In order to feed its population, India is a large importer of the various fertilizers and farmers receive subsidies from the government for this purpose. Note that supporting minimal *yields per acre* has been part of government policies in relation to the agricultural sector all over the world for a long time. Large statistical tables related to yield numbers are built by agri-insurance companies, since these yields are the usual entity to which insurance contracts bought by farmers are related at this moment (some discussions of revenue-related contracts are starting, but involve prices and price volatility, quantities less familiar to agri-insurers so far). This feature of agri-insurance adds to the importance of yields, and in turn fertilizers.

12.2.2   Fertilizer Index, corn, and wheat price trajectories over the period 1991 to 2011

Figure 12.2 displays the individual trajectories of the main fertilizers as of 1991: (a) represents the price of FAS phosphate rock cleared for export in the port of Casablanca (and ready to be lifted to the vessel, as FAS stands for 'free alongside ship'); (b) is the DAP with its remarkable spike in 2008; (c) is urea, FOB Black Sea; and (d) exhibits FOB (FOB stands for free on board: the good is loaded on board the vessel nominated by the buyer; costs of insurance and freight are paid by the buyer) potash, standard grade, available in Vancouver.

As depicted, fertilizer prices have increased steadily since the end of 2002, with a historic peak in 2008 that occurred almost simultaneously for the three types.

Figure 12.3 displays the price trajectory of the World Bank Fertilizer Index, which is a weighted average of the four constituents above. As said before, this index is the right underlying to choose when entering a fertilizer swap as a hedge or a price exposure.

Properties of the Price Trajectories of Wheat, Corn, and Fertilizers
We briefly recall below some elements studied in Chapter 2. For corn and wheat, we will use daily price data transformed into average monthly prices, from which returns are computed. Corn and wheat spot prices are represented by the CBOT first nearby Futures, expressed in cents per bushel. The Fertilizer Index monthly data have been obtained from the World Bank and monthly returns have been calculated in the standard way.

12.2.3   Fertilizer producing companies and share price returns over the period 2004 to 2011

In the coming subsections, we will study 30 fertilizer firms. The sample of listed fertilizer firms studied has been selected from the International Fertilizer Association membership list. The IFA update we will use took place on April 29, 2011; the list includes 618 members in about 85 countries. Members of the IFA include companies with activities related to the production, trade, transport, and distribution of every type of fertilizer, their raw materials, and intermediates. It also includes organizations involved in construction, engineering, consulting, agronomic research, and training.

Only companies mainly dedicated to fertilizer extraction and production have been selected in order to create a comprehensive sample of US and non-US listed firms; this excludes conglomerates whose activities are extended to other industries, as well as auxiliary firms that

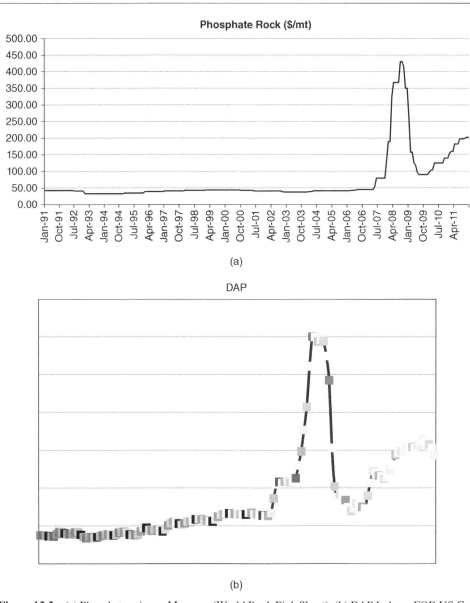

(a)

(b)

Figure 12.2 (a) Phosphate prices – Morocco (World Bank Pink Sheet); (b) DAP Index – FOB US Gulf (World Bank Data); a large spike in 2007; (c) urea prices – FOB Black Sea (World Bank); (d) muriate of potash prices – FOB Vancouver (World Bank)

have no direct involvement in the production of fertilizers. Note that integrated agribusinesses in emerging markets use, as common practice, fertilizers as a way of helping the farmers. In return, the farmers pay back the agribusinesses with part of their harvest, implying a reduction of the credit risk of the latter ones – an interesting example of the raw material use as collateral.

The initial sample of 20 non-US listed fertilizer firms was complemented by eight firms listed on the New York Stock Exchange/Nasdaq. In the sample of non-US listed fertilizer firms, we identify a subsample of five firms connected to the mining of raw materials used

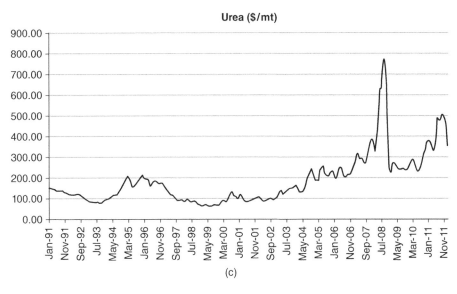

(c)

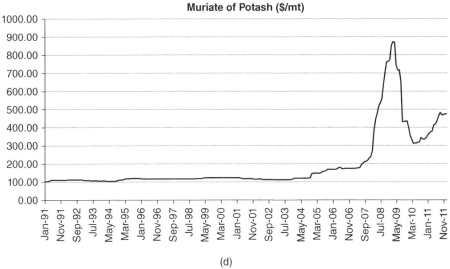

(d)

Figure 12.2 (*continued*)

in the production of fertilizers; by contrast, 15 firms have interests solely in the production and distribution of fertilizers. Among the US listed firms, six firms also have mining interests whereas only two, Andersons and LSB, are exclusively dedicated to the production/processing and distribution of fertilizers.

Due to the availability of more data during the period from 2008 to 2011, two firms have been added to the sample of non-US listed fertilizer firms, namely Yara and Uralkali – note that Yara International is the world's largest producer of nitrogen-based fertilizers. The sample containing the original 20 firms plus these two firms will be referred to as the extended sample throughout this section.

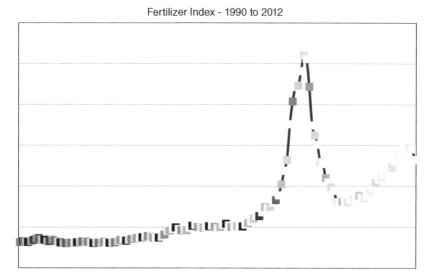

Figure 12.3   World Bank Fertilizer Index, with the same spike in 2008

Investors who wished to get exposure to commodities over the last decade, during which commodity prices were much higher than in the 1990s, first had the choice between buying Futures contracts on individual commodities or passively investing in commodity indexes such as the GSCI Commodity Index or the Dow-Jones UBS, which are baskets of individual commodities weighted according to rules specific to each index. Another way to possibly benefit from a rise in gold or crude oil prices was to buy shares of gold or oil mining companies. In the case of fertilizers, no investment commodity index, as of today, contains phosphate or potash as a component; nor are fertilizers traded on an exchange. Fertilizer swaps do exist, but trading takes place through brokers and these swaps are essentially used by big players in the agribusiness. Hence, the purchase of shares of fertilizer-related companies represent at this point the easiest way of getting exposure to fertilizer prices.

As a first approach to the exchange listed fertilizer-producing firms, we analyze their relative performance with respect to the stock market as a whole and split our analysis between the two periods, Jan 30, 2004 to June 30, 2008 and Jan 30, 2009 to Dec 30, 2011. This choice is motivated by the following reasons: (1) the beginning of the global period of analysis coincides with the moment when new market participants started paying attention to agricultural commodities (and fertilizers), after crude oil and copper; (2) we wish to avoid the second semester of the year 2008, when the disastrous effect of the financial crisis led all investors to liquidate their holdings in equities and commodities to recover cash. Lastly, we separate the analysis of the US and non-US listed firms. For the first ones, we build the Security Market Line using the S&P500 index and the three-month US Treasury rate. (Note that both Agrium and Potash are listed on the Toronto Stock Exchange and the New York Stock Exchange.)

Monthly returns of each individual stock are used to compute the betas (we use the standard beta defined as the covariance between the expected returns on a firm and the market portfolio, divided by the variance of the market portfolio). Over the first period, Jan 2004 to June 2008, the Security Market Line was mildly decreasing – appears as very close to the horizontal axis on the first graph of Figure 12.4; all US listed firms provided much higher returns than those

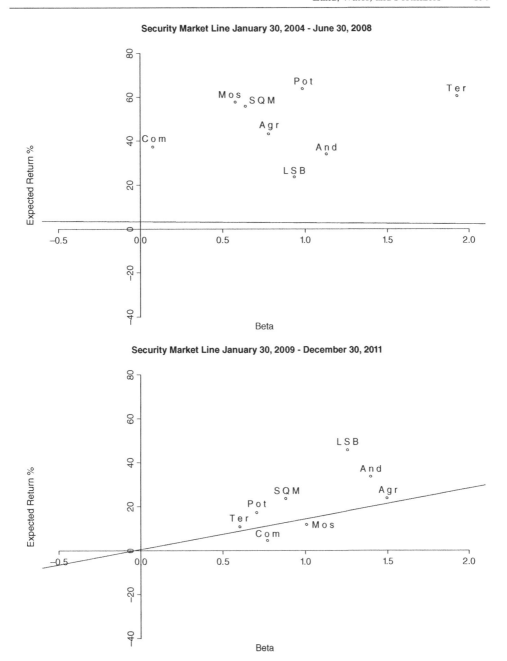

Figure 12.4   Security Market Lines and US listed fertilizer firms

derived from their betas and the Capital Asset Pricing Model (CAPM). Mosaic, SQM, and Potash Corp displayed absolute returns of the order of 60% and 'alphas' (excess performance over the value predicted by the CAPM) higher than 50%, numbers that many hedge funds would have been happy to achieve during that (or any) period. The lowest return, achieved by LSB, has an alpha of 20%. It is also interesting to observe that Mosaic from the USA and

SQM from Chile, both traded on the NYSE, have remarkably similar betas and returns. During the period Jan 2009 to Dec 2011, the stock market recovered from the crash and the SML was strictly upward sloping, with an intercept with the vertical axis close to zero because of the levels of short-term rates in the USA. We see in Figure 12.4 that most fertilizer companies continued to do remarkably well, with an alpha of 30% for LSB and 15% for Andersons; Mosaic and Terra Nitrogen performed in agreement with the Capital Asset Pricing Model and Compass slightly worse.

It is interesting to observe that the excess performance over the SML did not go to the levels reached when fertilizers became known as a valuable asset to the financial world. Note that, in 2010, Potash Inc. was the subject of an all-cash hostile takeover by the Australian mining giant BHP Billiton. As said in the first chapter, the offer was rejected by the Canadian Energy and Resources Ministry. Potash Inc.'s combined capabilities in potash, phosphate, and nitrogen make it the world's largest fertilizer company by capacity; Mosaic is the second largest.

For the non-US listed fertilizer firms (Figure 12.5), the S&P equity index is replaced with the MSCI-Emerging Markets index (the Morgan Stanley Composite Index dedicated to emerging countries) and the appropriate T-bill is used. The results are of the same nature for the first period, with excess performances over the SML reaching 60% for Gub, and more than 50% for the companies K+S, ICL, and EFIC. Together with EFIC, Sinofert also exhibited negative returns over the second period. The company Sinofert Holdings, which is the largest fertilizer importer and distributor in China, supplies about half of the world's fertilizer market. It performed better than the market in the first period but had very poor results over the period Jan 2009 to Dec 2011. Its operating profits became very negative in the first semester of 2009, in particular because the Chinese government imposed price controls on some fertilizers in 2008. The share price of Sinofert has been continuously declining from a peak of eight Hong Kong dollars in 2008 to less than two dollars at the time of writing.

To conclude this subsection, we can observe that investing in shares of Mosaic, Agrium, Potash, and other fertilizer-related companies during the period 2004 to 2011 was a talented way of stock picking in the early days of fertilizers' arrival in the spotlight of the agricultural economic actuality.

12.2.4 A factor model for the share returns of fertilizer firms

Regarding the sensitivities of firms' share values to commodity prices, an abundant literature has existed in the case of oil and gold. Blose and Shieh (1995) consider 23 gold mining companies and present an extension of the work by McDonald and Solnik (1977), who investigated 26 South African and 10 American mining companies. Tufano (1998) extensively studied the sensitivities of 48 North American gold mining firms to gold prices. Our analysis proposes to extend this classical approach to this 'new' commodity called fertilizers. (Note that this section – from Geman and Vergel (2013) – could belong to the last chapter dedicated to investing in commodities and could be repeated in the analysis of companies manufacturing tractors or other equipment as a way to invest in agricultural commodities.)

Globalization and the increase in international trade have brought higher levels of price volatility, which, in turn, have made the need for better risk management more urgent. In this direction, Hess *et al.* (2008) exhibit a triangular relationship involving fertilizer firms, fertilizer prices, and agricultural commodities.

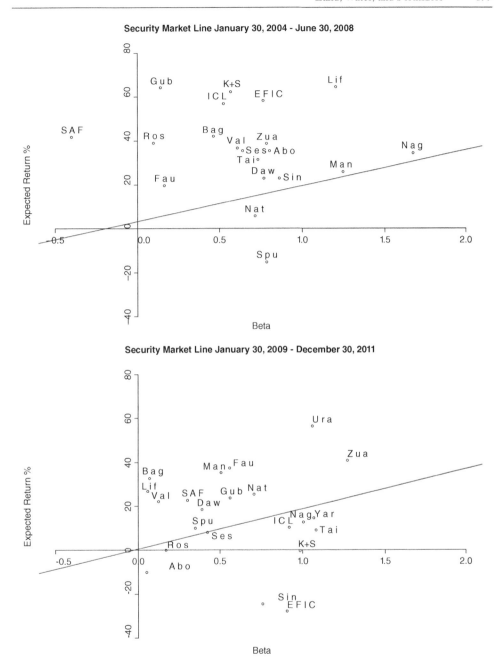

Figure 12.5   Security Market Lines and non-US listed fertilizer firms

For corporate managers of fertilizer firms, a study of the co-movements between agricultural commodities and their share prices is quite useful in their hedging activities. Similarly, the analysis of the exposure of fertilizer firms to agricultural commodities can help investors who wish to get exposure to agricultural commodities. Policymakers, due to their increased interest in the regulation of commodity markets, may benefit from the understanding of the specific relationship between fertilizer firms and agricultural commodities, in particular when subsidies to small farms in countries like India and continents like Africa are essentially granted through fertilizers.

We will examine the sensitivities of fertilizer companies to the global stock market on the one hand and fertilizer/agricultural commodity prices on the other. We categorize our sample in several ways. First, we look separately at the exposures of non-US and US listed firms. As in the previous subsection, we split the period of analysis between the two subperiods, Jan 2004 to Jun 2008 and Jan 2009 to Dec 2011, to avoid the height of the financial crisis and its consequences in terms of investors liquidating all asset classes for cash. In order to study the sensitivities of fertilizer firm share returns to fertilizers, we will use the monthly data series of the World Bank Fertilizer Index. We also analyze their sensitivities to the World Bank Cereals Index, which is composed of wheat (25.3%), corn (40.8%), rice (30.2%), and barley (3.7%). Finally, the IMF food price index has been added to explore the exposure of fertilizer firm returns to a wider basket of goods – this index tracks the spot prices of the 22 most commonly internationally traded agricultural food items, including major grains such as wheat, corn, soybeans, and rice. Monthly prices have been used in all cases.

We introduce a two-factor time series regression to calculate the betas of each company:

$$R_{it} = \alpha_i + \beta_{im} R_{im} + \beta_{ic} R_{ic} + \varepsilon_t \qquad (12.1)$$

where R_{it} is the monthly return on stock i, R_{im} is the monthly return on the market index of the exchange where the stock is listed, and R_{ic} is the monthly return on the commodity index, i.e., World Bank Fertilizer Index, World Bank Cereals Index, and IMF food price index. Thus, the coefficients β_{ic} and β_{im} represent the sensitivity of stock return i to the commodity index, and to the relevant stock market index. For non-US listed fertilizer firms, we use their respective stock market indexes, whereas for US listed firms we use the S&P500 index.

Most companies in the non-US listed category display positive results for the sensitivities to their respective stock markets in both periods (see Table 12.2). The Belgian company Rosier is the exception, presenting a negative sensitivity to the market index in the first period (as visible on the SML), and high sensitivities to fertilizer or agricultural indexes, which allowed it to reach a performance of 40%. In the period 2009 to 2011, these sensitivities as well as the firm return became quite low. In fact, the share price went to a peak of 550 euros in June 2008, then collapsed in the second half of 2008 and has been fluctuating between 200 and 300 euros since then.

In contrast to the non-US listed companies, all US listed firms present positive sensitivities to their respective stock market index during the period from Jan 2004 to June 2008, but exhibit a lower median and larger standard deviation. In the period Jan 2009 to Dec 2011, the standard deviation of US listed firms was significantly reduced; in addition, their general sensitivities to the stock market also increased (results that are in agreement with our previous analysis of the SMLs). One exception was Potash Corp, probably because the news of the hostile takeover by the mining giant BHP Billiton followed by the Chinese bid led by Sinochem

Table 12.1 Listing country, exchange, activities and market capitalization of fertilizer firms

Sample of non-US listed fertilizer firms

Company name	Country	Exchange	Market cap	Currency	Stock index used
Rosier SA	Belgium	EBR	68.88M	Euro	BEL20
Fosfertil (Vale Fertilizantes)	Brazil	SAO	13.77B	Braz real	Bovespa Index
Spur Ventures Inc.	Canada	TSE	16.61M	CAD dollar	S&P/TSX Index
Abu-Qir Fert & Chemical	Egypt	CAI	11.17B	Egypt £	EGYPT EFG Index
EFIC-Egyptian Fin & Ind	Egypt	CAI	793.50M	Egypt £	EGYPT EFG Index
K+S	Germany	ETR	8.32B	Euro	DAX Index
Sinofert Holdings Ltd	China	HKG	17.55B	HK dollar	Hang Seng Index
Mangalore Chem Fert	India	BOM	3.79B	Ind rupee	BSE Sensex
Nagarjuna Fert & Chem	India	BOM	10.11B	Ind rupee	BSE Sensex
National Fertilizers Ltd	India	BOM	33.48B	Ind rupee	BSE Sensex
Zuari Industries Ltd	India	BOM	17.44B	Ind rupee	BSE Sensex
ICL	Israel	TLV	55.93B	Isr shekel	ISRAEL TA 100 Index
AB Lifosa	Lithuania	VSE	305.20M	Lithu litas	OMX Baltic Index
Dawood Hercules Chemical	Pakistan	KAR	18.76B	Paki rupee	KSE All Share Index
Fauji Fertilizer Company	Pakistan	KAR	164B	Paki rupee	KSE All Share Index
SAFCO	Saudi Arabia	SAU	250M	Saudi ryal	TaSI All-Share Index
Sesoda Corp.	Taiwan	TPE	5.19B	Taiwanese $	Taiwan SE Index
Taiwan Fertilizer Co.	Taiwan	TPE	77B	Taiwanese $	Taiwan SE Index
Bagfas Bandirma	Turkey	BSE	504M	Turkish lira	Istanbul Price Index
Gübre TAS	Turkey	IST	1B	Turkish lira	Istanbul Price Index

US listed fertilizer firms

Company name	Country	Exchange	Mark cap in $	Stock index used
Agrium Inc.	Canada	NYSE	12.57B	NYSE Comp Index
Potash Corp./Saskatchewan	Canada	NYSE	39.74B	NYSE Comp index
SQM	Chile	NYSE	8.10B	NYSE Comp Index
Andersons	US	NASDAQ	674.25M	NASDAQ 100
Compass Minerals Intl.	US	NYSE	2.47B	NYSE Comp Index
LSB Ind.	US	NYSE	757.53M	NYSE Comp Index
Terra Nitrogen Company	US	NYSE	3.10B	NYSE Comp Index
Mosaic Company	US	NYSE	25.37B	NYSE Comp Index

Non-US listed fertilizer firms and their activities

Company name	Fertilizer interests
Rosier SA	FP&D
Fosfertil (Vale Fertilizantes)	Supply of raw materials
Spur Ventures Inc.	Development of two large phosphate deposits in China
Abu-Qir Fert & Chemical	FP&D
EFIC-Egyptian Fin & Ind	FP&D
K+S	FP&D and extraction of raw materials
Sinofert Holdings Ltd	FP&D
Mangalore Chem Fert	FP&D
Nagarjuna Fert & Chem	FP&D
National Fertilizers Ltd	FP&D
Zuari Industries Ltd	FP&D

ICL	Mining interests across the world
AB Lifosa	FP&D with mining interests
Dawood Hercules Chemicals Ltd	FP&D
Fauji Fertilizer Company Ltd	FP&D
SAFCO – Saudi Arabian Fertilizer Co.	FP&D
Sesoda Corp.	FP&D
Taiwan Fertilizer Co.	FP&D
Bagfas Bandirma Fabrikalari	FP&D
Gübre TAS	FP&D

US listed fertilizer firms and their activities

Company name	Fertilizer interests
Agrium Inc.	FP&D. Owner of phosphate and potash mines
Potash Corp./Saskatchewan Inc.	FP&D. Owner of phosphate and potash mines
SQM	FP&D with extensive mining operations
Andersons	FP&D
Compass Minerals Intl.	Operates mines and produces fertilizers
LSB Ind.	Wholesale and retail trade of fertilizers
Terra Nitrogen Company	FP&D. Owned by CF Industries
Mosaic Company	FP&D. Owner of phosphate and potash mines

Table 12.2 Summary statistics of sensitivities for 30 US and non-US listed fertilizer firms

	Jan 2004–June 2008						Jan 2009–Dec 2011					
	Stock Index	Fertilizer Index	Stock Index	WB Cereals	Stock Index	IMF Food	Stock Index	Fertilizer Index	Stock Index	WB Cereals	Stock Index	IMF Food
US listed												
Positive sign	8	7	8	7	8	8	8	3	8	8	8	8
Negative sign	0	1	0	1	0	0	0	5	0	0	0	0
Mean:	0.92	0.09	0.92	0.41	1.14	0.76	1.01	0.08	0.96	0.43	0.84	0.84
Median:	0.8	0.15	0.88	0.38	1.18	0.64	0.95	-0.02	0.88	0.37	0.75	0.79
St. dev.:	0.53	0.22	0.52	0.37	0.5	0.57	0.34	0.24	0.35	0.24	0.34	0.56
Non-US listed												
Positive sign	19	15	19	16	19	14	20	15	20	15	20	17
Negative sign	1	5	1	4	1	6	0	5	0	5	0	3
Mean	0.91	0.22	0.87	0.3	0.91	0.39	0.9	0.16	0.88	0.19	0.83	0.36
Median	0.93	0.22	0.9	0.41	0.94	0.5	0.91	0.19	0.94	0.2	0.84	0.35
St. dev	0.46	0.45	0.48	0.41	0.46	0.63	0.37	0.29	0.37	0.25	0.36	0.38
Non-US listed												
Positive sign							22	17	22	17	22	19
Negative sign							0	5	0	5	0	3
Mean							0.93	0.18	0.91	0.21	0.86	0.37
Median							0.94	0.23	0.97	0.24	0.89	0.4
St. dev.:							0.37	0.29	0.37	0.25	0.35	0.37

and the return to normal conditions were the main drivers of the share prices. It is interesting to note that the interest of BHP in Potash Corp brought the importance of fertilizers to the attention of the world.

These generally higher betas to the stock market observed throughout the whole sample during the second period may be explained as follows. Fertilizer companies, while exhibiting overall higher returns than the stock market, in general displayed a higher correlation with the market index for two sets of reasons: first, they became more standard firms, including their managerial and risk management rules; second, after the financial crisis, arrival of news on macroeconomic events was driving investors to implement 'risk-on risk-off' strategies across the whole spectrum of equity markets. To these general features were added regional differences. For instance, LSB, Uralkali or Zuari Industries vastly outperformed the market. On the other hand, the Egyptian revolution disrupted the normal functioning of companies such as EFIC, the biggest publicly traded phosphate producer in the country, and Abu-Qir Fertilizers, which produces about 50% of the country's nitrogen fertilizers.

Turning to the sensitivities to the Fertilizer Index, we see a wide range of numbers for the period Jan 2004 to June 2008 and a general reduction in the period from Jan 2009 to Dec 2011 for both US and non-US listed firms. Generally, we observe lower sensitivities to the Fertilizer Index for US listed firms than those of their non-US listed counterparts, with even a negative median value of −0.02 in the second period. Non-US listed firms present average sensitivities of 0.22 and 0.16 and median values of 0.22 and 0.19 for each time period.

We notice 15 firms with positive sensitivities to the Fertilizer Index in the first period among the non-US listed firms sample, and five firms with negative sensitivities to the Fertilizer Index. Our sample includes four Indian companies: Mangalore Chemicals and Fertilizers, Nagarjuna Fertilizers and Chemicals, National Fertilizers, and Zuari Industries, all of which present negative sensitivities to the Fertilizer Index during the first period. This is representative of the Indian case where fertilizers have been heavily subsidized and retail prices were controlled by the state until recently. Subsidies have mostly been directed towards water-intensive crops, with rice and wheat being the recipients of the larger amounts. For the past three decades, India has pursued a very aggressive program in the subsidization of fertilizers. As a percentage of total government subsidies, fertilizer subsidies accounted for 47% and food subsidies 35.1% during the 1990s. These two types of subsidies have continued over the last decade, which explains the attractiveness of the Indian market for fertilizer companies.

In general, across both samples (non-US and US listed firms) and time periods, we observe that the mean sensitivity to the Fertilizer Index is consistently lower than the mean sensitivity to the WB Cereals Index, itself in turn lower than the mean sensitivity to the IMF food price index (see Table 12.2). This could possibly stem from the fact that farmers adjust the amount of fertilizers they consume and the planting acreage for each crop depending on the expected market prices and their total input costs. Because of its 22 components, the IMF Food Index may be viewed as the best indicator among the three indexes for corporate managers of fertilizer firms.

Also, it is interesting to observe that US listed fertilizer firms present much higher sensitivities to the IMF Food Index than their non-US listed counterparts. The exposure of US listed firms to the IMF food price index has increased, on average, in the second period while it has decreased for non-US listed fertilizer firms.

In order to investigate the changes in sensitivities of fertilizer firms, we divide the sample among US and non-US firms without mining interests and global firms with interests in mining, production, and distribution of fertilizers. During the first period, vertically integrated firms, i.e., firms owning mining, production, and distribution interests, could take full advantage of favorable market conditions, such as the increase in prices of mined raw materials as well as final agricultural commodities. Global firms like ICL, K+S, Potash Corp, Agrium, and Mosaic, typically involved in the production and mining of fertilizers, exhibited positive sensitivities to the WB Cereals and IMF Food indexes. Many of the firms involved only in the processing of fertilizers with no mining interests and thus dependent on the cost of the raw material showed much lower sensitivities or even negative ones to the WB Cereals and IMF Food indexes.

During the second period of the study, we observe fewer companies showing positive sensitivities to the Fertilizer Index. Global firms experience increased sensitivities to the IMF food price index and reduced ones to the Fertilizer Index. This is in clear contrast to the case of firms with no mining interests, which maintain their average sensitivities to the Fertilizer Index while the ones to the WB Cereal Index and to the IMF Food Index are clearly lower.

Indeed, vertically integrated companies, US and non-US listed alike, had a higher exposure to the agricultural commodity indexes. As an exception, the Brazilian company Fosfertil exhibited a positive sensitivity solely to the IMF Food Index and only in the period Jan 2004 to June 2008. In the second period, its sensitivities to all indexes sharply declined, as in the case of many companies. Fosfertil (currently Vale Fertilizantes) was acquired by Vale in 2010, which also acquired Bunge's nutrient assets in Brazil (Vale Fosfatados) – Brazil still imports 50% of the fertilizers it consumes; with these acquisitions, Vale is aiming to become less dependent on imports.

This average increase in sensitivities to the IMF Food Index is visible throughout the sample of global firms, with companies such as Potash Corp showing high sensitivities to WB Cereals and IMF Food indexes. The German company K+S, which extracts potash and magnesium salts in Germany, and ICL from Israel, which exploits various products based on phosphate rock, are also among the largest potash producers. Both continued to do well after the financial crisis but had different responses to the agricultural indexes; the two presented high sensitivities to the WB Cereals and IMF Food Indexes, with ICL presenting a much lower sensitivity than K+S to the Fertilizer Index.

Moreover, the sensitivities of fertilizer firms to the chosen factors varied widely depending on their specific circumstances, geographical location, range of activities, and agreements throughout the supply chain such as in the case of Lithuanian company AB Lifosa. AB Lifosa became fully owned in 2010 by Eurochem, a non-listed company and the private property of a Russian billionaire. Due to the specific situation during the second period of AB Lifosa, with Eurochem becoming an exclusive distributor and its vertical integration inside that firm, it has exhibited high levels of returns that are only mildly related to the Fertilizer Index (and negatively to the World Bank Cereals Index).

Finally, it is interesting to observe that after 2008, a number of companies located in different regions shared the feature of not having been able to maintain the very strong profits they made during 2006 and 2007. The sensitivities of the firms to the different indexes have changed from the first to the second period, but the average sensitivities are highest to the IMF Food Price Index for all firms in both periods. We have thus shown that it was possible to create a portfolio of fertilizer firms exhibiting a positive exposure to a wide basket of agricultural food products.

Conclusion on fertilizer companies

We have argued here that increasing crop yields is a crucial source of additional food supply necessary to satisfy future generation needs in a world of *arable land scarcity*. We chose to adopt both an agricultural and finance approach to this fascinating commodity class of fertilizers. In order to do this, we described the main features of fertilizer markets and the co-movements of fertilizer prices with corn and wheat over the last decade and in particular during the first recent food crisis. We also showed that early movers in the purchase of fertilizer-related companies in the first moment where fertilizers became known to the investment community achieved returns as high as 60% over the period 2004 to mid-2008. This was also the time of large price increases in fertilizers, with the corresponding leverage effect on fertilizer-producing companies' shares. Among other virtues, this new asset class has the quality of *tangibility* compared to some opaque financial instruments.

At the time of writing, the major shareholders of the Russian potash producer Uralkali are ready to end the conflict with Belarusian Belaruskali, which made the price of potash dive.

12.3 WATER AND ITS CRUCIAL ROLE IN THE WORLD ECONOMY

Oil used to symbolize the 'black gold'; water is now referred to as the 'blue gold.'

As droughts and floods have become more frequent and extreme around the world, a large variety of companies, from food and beverage producers to energy and mining firms, have started paying great attention to water costs and the sensitivities of their revenues to disruption in water supply (*International NYT*, June 2, 2014). The concept of *water risk* (see Geman and Kanyinda (2006)) is finally emerging – a risk that includes shortages, pollution, and increases in prices of water and water-dependent raw materials.

Water supply stresses are becoming more severe everywhere, from California to China, from Australia to South Africa. They are generated by climate change, large increases in the world population, and growing numbers of people moving to cities all over the world and adopting resource-intense lifestyles and diets. The 2014 annual report of the World Economic Forum ranked water crises as the third biggest risk in the coming decade after financial crises and unemployment. Without changes in business practices, the demand for fresh water could be 40% higher than supply by 2030.

Water is essential to the survival of all living creatures but the gap between demand and investment requirements is immense, at least in some regions of the world. Estimates suggest that more than 1 billion people have no access to safe water. Hence, the World Bank is in favor of outsourcing and privatization in the water sector until developing countries can handle the problem themselves.

Only 2.5% of the earth's water is fresh water and barely 0.3% is suitable for human use. Out of this, agriculture consumes 70 to 75% – a huge number; industry and commerce use around 20% and 5 to 10% is used for domestic and drinking water purposes.

The supply chain of water starts with the collection and storage of water in wells and groundwater; it is then transported via pipelines to treatment plants where it is treated to the point of desired quality before being distributed to households, agriculture, industry or mining.

12.3.1 The case of Australia, China, and Saudi Arabia

In one of the biggest infrastructure projects in the country's history, Australia's five biggest cities are spending $13.2 billion on desalination plants capable of removing salt from millions of gallons of sea water and yielding potable water. The country needed to find an answer to the decade-long drought worsened by climate change.

A desalination plant covering 6 acres of land provides water to Brisbane, the capital of Queensland, the nation's fastest-growing region.

SEQ Water Grid Management is the utility that oversees this region's water supply. The state spent nearly $8 billion building dams and a web of pipelines to connect 18 independent water utilities in a single grid. Other cities are following suit. Perth, which opened the first desalination plant in 2006, is now building a second one. Sydney's started operating in 2012 and plants near Melbourne and Adelaide are under construction.

The Water Services Association said that desalination in Australia costs between $1.75 and $2 per cubic meter of water, including the costs of construction, clean energy, and production. Even though Australia relies on coal for most of its electricity, desalination plants are using power from new wind farms, which should nearly double household water bills since the power needed to remove the salt from sea water accounts for 50% of the cost of desalination.

With water shortages looming across the globe, other countries, including China and the USA, are also looking to the sea. So far, large-scale desalination plants have been operating in the Middle East, particularly Saudi Arabia. China, which recently opened its biggest desalination plant in Tianjin, could eventually overtake Saudi Arabia as the world leader, according to the International Desalination Association.

It is forecast that by 2030, actual demand for water will outstrip supply by 40% under a 'normal' scenario. In 2010, the UN Principles had cited water scarcity as a critical challenge to be addressed, amid a growing consensus that the availability of fresh water will be vulnerable to climate change. In the predicted 40% supply/demand gap, there will not be enough water to grow the food needed to sustain population growth or to provide raw materials such as cotton or timber: the world could face annual losses of grain production equivalent to the entire grain crops of India and the USA combined by 2025.

Water is also crucial to energy production. In 2003, France was forced to shut down 58 nuclear power stations responsible for 75% of the nation's electricity because of severe cool water shortages. One needs to remember that any type of power plant, and even more so a nuclear plant, needs to be cooled at all times. This explains the location of power plants alongside rivers or by the ocean, like the plant in Japan at Fukushima that was unfortunately hit by a tsunami. In the UK, the power plants serving London, hence the spot price of electricity, depend so much on the Thames river temperature to continue to function during the warm season that option contracts related to this temperature are traded among the big utilities (a situation where both parties have a good and similar view of the value of the weather derivative; see Chapter 12 for a whole discussion of the subject of weather derivatives).

12.3.2 The case of Brazil

In the first quarter of 2014, a severe drought – the worst in 50 years – reduced water and electricity supplies in the wealthy southeastern region, home to Sao Paulo and Rio de Janeiro. The drought severely depleted the reservoirs in a country where 67.8% of electricity comes from hydroelectricity.

Since the start of 2014, only 40% of the normal amount of rain has fallen in Sao Paulo, Rio, and Minas Gerais states, which represent about half of the country's economic output.

The dry spell affected the production of sugar cane, coffee, and oranges largely produced in Sao Paulo and Minas Gerais states. At the same time, water is crucial for the large General Motors operations in the Sao Paulo state.

In May 2014, with the persisting drought, Alcoa – the US aluminum maker – cut its production of the metal in Brazil and instead sold the electricity produced by its power plants to benefit from soaring prices.

Conversely, in the water-abundant USA, energy independence coming from cheap shale gas and oil has led several companies like Dow Chemical, General Electric, Ford, the Germany-based BASF, and Caterpillar to announce in 2014 hundreds of millions of dollars of investment either in new plants or in reopening shutdown facilities. In fact, between 2010 and the end of March 2013, almost 100 chemical industry projects valued at around $72 billion were announced, according to the American Chemistry Council.

12.3.3 Competition for electricity, water, and land

- Urbanization competes with land available for agriculture.
- The mining industry competes with agriculture for land, fresh water, and energy.
- Salt water can be turned into fresh water dedicated to livestock and people as long as one can afford the electricity, such as energy-rich countries.

Conversely:

- Agricultural commodities may be produced or imported; the latter choice is called *virtual water* in countries that are water scarce, like Saudi Arabia.

Hence, all these fundamental components of human life are remarkably intricate. A world equilibrium model involving all these elements would be quite hard to build and solve, with or without the inclusion of emission constraints.

12.4 PROJECTIONS FOR THE FUTURE OF AGRICULTURE

Studying agricultural scarcity in the long term requires long-term projections of supply and demand. The UN FAO's 'Looking Ahead in World Food and Agriculture: Perspectives to 2050' (FAO, 2011) is the conclusion of an extended series of expert consultations started a decade earlier (FAO, 2002).

Population projections, at least in the medium term, can be considered as relatively precise. For example, world population projections for the year 2000 made in the early 1970s by the UN Population Division were only 2.3% higher than the actual value observed 30 years after the prediction. The world population is expected to increase from 6.9 billion in 2010 to 9.3 billion in 2050 (UN 2010), an annual growth rate of 0.75%.

Income is somewhat harder to estimate, but most projections suggest moderate growth will continue, apart from a few outlying predictions of 'world collapse' (Meadows, 2004). The projections for 2000 were only slightly higher than the outturn values (projection: 3.9% p.a.

growth, outturn: 3.3%). World Bank projections of future GDP growth point to growth rates gradually falling from 5% to 4% p.a. (developing countries) and from 2 to 1% p.a. (developed countries), reported in FAO (2011). Rather than treat the world as a homogeneous consumer, more accurate forecasts of food consumption can be obtained by modeling different countries and different income groups within countries separately.

12.4.1 Farm insurance

Farmers in the USA have the benefit of federally subsidized, cheap crop-insurance programs to insure them against natural disasters, low yields, and low prices. The insurance is written through private companies; premiums are the same regardless of the provider (see National Crop Insurance Services (NCIS)).

A whole farm insurance contract insures farmers against both crop and price failure that results in declining incomes. It covers the whole farm rather than a specific commodity.

The Canadian Grain Growers Association differs from other revenue programs in an interesting manner; instead of an average of historical prices, it uses spot and forward prices for the price coverage.

This subject is crucial and very interesting and will be developed in another book. Farm insurers have more experience at this point on yield risk than commodity price risk.

12.4.2 Estimating long-term agricultural supply

Detailed supply predictions need detailed agricultural data, such as the frequently updated Global Agro-Ecological Zones database, which identifies suitable locations for increased crop production through a high-resolution global database of soil, water, terrain, and agro-climatic properties. Based on this, FAO (2011) predicts that total acreage of arable land will only grow 9% from 2005 to 2050 (it grew 14% from 1961 to 2005, a similar duration). In contrast, yields will have to rise by 70–80% over a similar period if the FAO's own projections of agricultural demand are to be met.

However, some studies report greatly higher predictions for acreage expansion, with global acreage more than doubling. The pool of unused suitable cropland is very unevenly distributed. By the end of the 20th century, sub-Saharan Africa and Latin America were still farming only around a fifth of their potentially suitable cropland. More than half the remaining global land balance was in just seven countries in these two regions: Angola, Argentina, Bolivia, Brazil, Colombia, Democratic Republic of Congo, and Sudan. At the other extreme, in the Middle East and North Africa, 87% of suitable land was already being farmed, while in South Asia the figure was no less than 94%. In a few countries of the Middle East and North Africa, the land balance is negative – that is, more land is being cropped than is suitable for rain-fed cropping. This is possible where, for example, land that is too sloping or too dry for rain-fed crops has been brought into production by terracing or irrigation.

While both Latin America and sub-Saharan Africa have significant land available for new crop production, infrastructure and political stability issues may present major obstacles to the development of certain regions. As a result, investors may be somewhat limited in farmland investment opportunities, unless they are willing to take the benefits of local populations at heart.

12.4.3 Market concentration

High market concentration poses two risks to agricultural commodities' consumers.

First, political reasons may cause the sudden withdrawal of exports from a country either to maintain domestic supply (Russian wheat, 2010) or as retaliation against foreign countries (China/Japan rare earths conflict). Second, if production is concentrated in a few countries, unfavorable weather – a severe frost in Brazil in 2011 and a drought in 2014 sending Arabica coffee prices to a spike – or a natural disaster in a single producing country will greatly affect global supply.

When production is lower than expected, and despite potentially high international prices, countries typically first feed their own citizens, only exporting the remainder. A classic case is Russian wheat during its extreme drought of 2010, when production fell from 61 million tonnes in 2009 to 41Mt in 2010. Exports were banned for most of the year, allowing domestic consumption to continue almost unchanged, falling from 39Mt to 38Mt, while exports fell dramatically.

12.4.4 Spare capacity

Once the planting season is complete, the current year's crops are sown and little more can be done to increase total production apart from nurturing crops to maintain their yield. Yield has steadily risen globally over many years due to increases in technology, crop improvement, irrigation, etc. It is nonetheless exposed to unpredictable weather, and thus varies widely at the national level. For a given crop year, there exists therefore no spare capacity in the system to grow more crops once the planting season is complete.[2]

For the following crop year, technology may allow a slight growth in the yield, but this may not happen. The only way to ensure additional production is to plant additional acreage. This can come (1) at the expense of acreage currently devoted to other crops ('substitution'), or perhaps used in the past but currently fallow, or (2) by using land never previously allocated to crops, whether currently uncultivated grasslands, forest or allocated to livestock. For a given crop in a given country, we consider the *highest ever acreage* of that crop to be a good proxy for the maximum acreage *currently* attainable (i.e., able to be planted in the next crop). The extent to which this exceeds the currently planted acreage can be called the *spare capacity*.

12.5 SUBSIDIES AND EXPORT BANS

Our view is that government subsidies are a major source of price distortion, which is ultimately detrimental to all, and particularly to poorer countries. Despite the continuing support of some agricultural markets, the European Union has cut the most (in relative terms only). The USA and Europe have essentially eliminated any direct intervention on prices. China,

---

[2] This assumes all countries follow the same yearly planting cycle, clearly not the case due to multiple crops per year in some fertile regions, and also due to production in both northern and southern hemispheres. Nevertheless, as a first approximation we can say that acreage is fixed after planting.

on the contrary, is now practicing direct intervention in the form of very large subsidies' programs ($180 billion in 2012, more than any country or region).

In Europe, the combination of higher land prices and subsidies has resulted in steady yields over the last two decades because of farmers' disincentives to invest in new equipment and infrastructure.

12.5.1 Subsidies

As a percentage of gross farm receipts, different nations' subsidies are as follows:

2.1% in Australia

4.8% in Brazil

7% in the USA

17% in China

18% in OECD – total

19% in EU27.

The move of some developed countries in the direction of *reducing subsidies* to their own farmers to give some breath to poorer countries is certainly welcome and should be strongly encouraged.

Some examples

In Thailand, a developed country by many standards, rice subsidies have been costly and in fact harmful as they cost the country its status as the world's number one rice exporter.

In Europe, which is certainly a developed continent, the Common Agricultural Policy (CAP) is aiming at reducing subsidies; these should in fact be limited to very small farmers.

In India, the world's second largest sugar producer after Brazil, a rule allows states to fix cane rates to help about 50 million farmers (a large voting group) earn more. As a result, in November 2013, sugar mills in Uttar Pradesh, the biggest growing region, decided to extend a shutdown to curb losses after the government retained cane prices at a record high, and to limit output.

12.5.2 Export bans

In the same way, cross-border trades should be preserved at all costs. The Russian export ban on wheat in 2010 was certainly an element that exacerbated the food crisis, including psychologically – as is presently the ban on nickel exports on and off decided by Indonesia, for instance.

12.6 MARKET-ORIENTED FARMING

The global changes of population growth, urbanization, and market liberalization directly impact farming, making it more market oriented and competitive. In fact, 'market-oriented farming' is recommended by the Food and Agriculture Organization of the United Nations. The main sources of risk can be categorized under the labels of production risk, financial risk, human resources risk, and operational risk. These categories include climate change and extreme weather events, price volatility, regulation changes, and availability of hired labor and machinery breakdown. Even small-scale farmers, who used to be essentially producing food for their families, need to become more entrepreneurial and run their farms as businesses. Choosing the type of crops to grow, buying the inputs, and transforming the raw materials into agricultural products are part of a value chain where one important goal is to increase the farmer's profits.

Over the last three decades, agriculture has undergone rapid changes in most developing countries as a result of changing policies, urbanization, climate change, and reduced role of government in the economy. Globalization and increase of trade between nations have also given some farmers opportunities to enter regional and international export markets, but at the cost of higher risks for the farm – household structure. Another global change is demography, with rural populations decreasing and more people migrating to towns and cities, resulting in a larger population being fed by a smaller number of farmers. At the same time, the emergence of an urban wealthier middle class in many countries has created demand for high quality food and raw materials. But the limited natural resources are creating long-term problems of environmental sustainability. As said before, the expansion of arable land has considerably decreased. Soil depletion is occurring in many tropical countries and land degradation continues to accelerate in fragile regions. Water scarcity threatens farmers in arid areas where it may be beneficial to have recourse to drip irrigation. All these global and local changes in the environment make market-oriented farming a necessity.

12.6.1 Open wheat market takes root in Canada

- In January 2012, a Canadian farmer signed a forward contract with Viterra, a multinational grain trader based in Calgary, promising to deliver 1000 tonnes of durum wheat in October to a silo in Saskatchewan. It was the first time in 70 years that a western Canadian farmer had sold wheat or barley to anyone other than the Canadian Wheat Board (CWB).
- Many farmers are already selling canola, lentils, and other crops on the open market.
- The CWB has been up to now the world's biggest single wheat exporter; it is due to lose its monopoly on wheat and barley exports. The new system will open new opportunities for traders and processors; at present, the traders act only as agents for the CWB.
- The CWB unveiled in January 2012 a series of new sales tools including Futures contracts to manage risk.
- Three companies, Viterra, Cargill, and Winnipeg-based Richardson International, will have a quick start as they already own networks of silos and export terminals, which they rent to the CWB.

12.6.2 Kansas City wheat Futures trading coming to an end after 157 years

- CME Group announced on January 2013 that it will move wheat Futures pits from Kansas City to Chicago, ending 157 years of floor trading in a city that was a center of agricultural markets over the decades.
- The move follows the exchange acquisition of the Kansas City Board of Trade (KCBOT), the historical home of Futures and options on hard red winter wheat. Open-outcry trading of the bread ingredient shifted to CME's Chicago trading floor in July 2013.

- Merchants founded the KCBT in 1856, in the heart of the Great Plains wheat region.
- CME is the latest Futures exchange to close or consolidate pits once thronged by brokers and market makers yelling orders in colorful jackets, as technology changes the face of trading.
- In 2011 ICE closed the floor of its New York soft commodities exchange after successfully listing options on its screens.
- CME merged its floor with the Chicago Board of Trade when the latter was acquired in 2007; it bought the Kansas City exchange for $126 million in 2012.
- CME was already listing benchmark Futures on lower-protein soft red winter wheat and will make easy the trading of both types of wheat and the spread between them.
- The very liquid wheat/corn spread has been fluctuating between 2003 and January 2013 in the range [0, 500] cents, with a peak around 500 cents in Q3–Q4 2007, and an average value of 150 cents in Q2 2011.

In parallel, ICE recently launched Futures in milling wheat, durum, and barley; these should bring greater transparency on market prices.

12.6.3 China food needs

Under Beijing's policy of 'self-sufficiency,' corn imports, along with rice and wheat, were first kept to a minimum since China lowered its import barriers in 2001. By contrast, the soybean market was opened to imports to release land for the key staples and China has become the world's largest importer of oilseed. In the view of commodity trading houses, China will in the long term become a major importer of corn while representing now over 75% of global seaborne trade in soybeans. According to the State Council's Development and Research Centre, 'importing 20 million tonnes of corn would not be a big matter since it would only be about 10% of the total Chinese consumption.' The corn imported by China is mostly for livestock feed, whose demand is growing with higher meat consumption. By 2020, the country is forecast to be the leading corn importer, buying up to 20 to 30 million tonnes from world markets. After being caught by the US 2012 drought, China does not want to depend only on the USA and is also importing corn from Argentina and Ukraine to diversify its sources.

Rising income and richer diets mean a shortage of arable land and clean water, forcing the country to look abroad for feed grains.

- To feed roughly one-fourth of the world population, China may also have to import as much as 7 million tonnes of wheat in 2013–2014, compared to 5 million in 2012–2013 and 100,000 tonnes in 2007–2008. The import forecast goes to 20 million tonnes for the year 2020.
- Barley to China comes from Australia, cocoa from West Africa.
- Demand from Chinese dairy farms has driven up North American alfalfa hay prices.
- Rice imports should also surpass the record number of the year 2012–2013. It is interesting to note that the total cost of rice imported from Vietnam is 10% lower than the cheapest Chinese varieties. Rice to China also comes from Thailand.

Rice production in China, the world's largest rice consumer and producer, is coming under pressure as people continue to leave the countryside for cities.

According to Rabobank's analysts, a shift is taking place in land use toward industrial and residential use by farmers in the humid southern regions where rice grows best. Production has increasingly moved to more arid northern regions where big yields are harder to get.

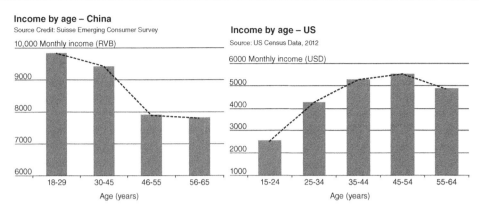

Figure 12.6

Also, logistical bottlenecks make it cheaper to buy foreign rice than ship it from north to south China.

Affordable technological innovations to increase yields have reached their limits. In fact, rice yields have started sliding: in 2013, they went down 1.7% to 6.7 tonnes per hectare, according to the China National Grain and Oils Information Center, a state grain policy think-tank.

For decades, China has poured billions into agricultural R&D and partnered with industry experts to reach a goal of 95% self-sufficiency for its 1.3 billion citizens.

The massive movements of workers to the cities in the last two decades as well as rapid urbanization and climate change have combined to shrink the amount of Chinese land available for agriculture.

China has 19% of the world population, but just 7% of its farmland, i.e., 0.23 acres per person versus 3 acres in the USA. And the predictions are that by 2050, there could be another 200 million more citizens to feed.

But China has made remarkable progress. In 2011, it spent $164 billion on agriculture (up from $71 billion in 2008), in the direction of crop and income support for farmers; construction of irrigation equipment and income support for farmers; subsidies for seeds, fertilizers, and farm equipment; and R&D in agriculture sciences and technologies.

China is now the world's largest agricultural producer, having increased production of grains by 114% since 1983, meat by 395%, and milk by more than 1100%.

It plans to greatly reduce the number of people living in poverty by 2015.

In February 2014, 10 years after China became a net food importer and in a major ideological shift, Beijing abandoned the grain self-reliance, which was a central goal of the Communist Party for years. The state council issued a new policy stance, according to which it placed a greater emphasis on food safety and quality. For the first time, it set a grains output target well below domestic consumption. The guidelines state that grain production will stabilize at the level of 550 million tonnes by 2020, below the harvest of 602 million tonnes reached in 2013, up from 300 million tonnes in 1978. Under the new rules, the country will prioritize the supply and quality of meat, vegetables, and fruit, all of which require less land and create more agricultural jobs. This will lead to increased imports from countries such as the USA, Australia, Canada, and Ukraine – the last country receiving loans from China in exchange for its cereals.

At the same time, Chinese imports of soybean oilseeds have risen from nearly none in 1990 to 70 million tonnes in 2013. Rising Chinese meat consumption necessitates a vast amount of corn and soybeans to feed the livestock. The soybeans come from Argentina and Brazil; China is also investing in Eastern European agriculture.

China has spent billions of dollars in the past decade acquiring commodity assets in metals and energy, but it has recently stepped up investing in food assets outside China, for example buying farmland in Latin America and Africa.

Trust in the safety of Chinese food took a hit in 2008 when a number of children died from baby formula containing a chemical product, which prompted France, a large milk producer, to raise its exports of dairy products of various types – baby food, yoghurts – to China.

13

Infrastructure and Farming Management in the Digital Age

'I had always imagined paradise as a kind of library.'

Jose Louis Borges

13.1 INTRODUCTION

Risk is an important aspect of the farming business. The uncertainties of weather, yields, prices, government policies, global markets, and other factors can cause wide swings in farm income. Risk management involves choosing among alternatives that reduce the financial effects of such uncertainties.

Seven types of risk may be identified:

- Production risk derives from the uncertain natural growth processes of crops and livestock. Weather, disease, pests, and other elements affect both the quantity and quality of commodities produced.
- Price (or market) risk refers to uncertainty about the prices producers will receive for commodities or costs of the inputs such as seeds and fertilizers. The nature of price risk varies significantly from commodity to commodity.
- Changes in the macroeconomic environment.
- Financial risk occurs when the farm borrows money and needs to repay its debt. Rising interest rates, the prospect of loans being called by lenders, and restricted credit availability are some other facets of financial risk.
- Institutional risk refers to government actions: tax laws, regulations for pesticide use, rules for animal waste disposal or income support payments are examples of government decisions that may impact the farm business, together with political risks and trade restrictions.
- Operational risk refers to accidents, illnesses or human problems that can threaten a farm business.
- Country risk.

When a very bad drought hit Russia in 2010, Moscow banned grain exports, making the situation of foreign investors difficult with respect to their promises of cereals sales and letting them resort to high world market prices to honor them. When in 2012 the USA suffered its worst drought in 80 years, the US government let grain exports go freely.

Obviously, the right of countries to protect their citizens first in the case of a food crisis is quite legitimate, but has to be announced ahead of time.

13.2 AGRICULTURAL INFRASTRUCTURE

Agricultural infrastructure can be categorized by its role across several dimensions: location, time/storage, grades and quality, inputs and yields.

- Location

    Transportation and logistics improve spatial efficiencies and allow demand in a specific region to be satisfied.
- Time

    Silos and warehousing facilities allow grains to be stored up to the moment of delivery.
- Quality

    Blending and crushing facilities allow for efficient matching of the commodity type with end users, e.g., soy oil.
- Yields per acre

    Irrigation, fertilizers, and better seeds improve productivity, reduce volatility, and may be scheduled and monitored.
- Distribution networks

    Delivery of perishable products (fruit, vegetables) requires dedicated transportation means (e.g., containers) and distribution lines.

Returns to agriculture infrastructure are typically related to a greater efficiency in the value chain and not to rents.

The main objectives of agriculture infrastructure are to:

1. Develop land and water resources for the purposes of increasing farmers' incomes and protecting the environment through land terracing and collecting runoff water in small hill ponds.
2. Increase access to and from rural areas through the construction of agriculture roads and paths.
3. Strengthen the institutional support through the establishment of large cooperatives, exchanging data and elaborating mid-term strategies compatible with sustainability and farmers' income.

Such examples of cooperatives are provided by CHS in the USA, Invivo in France, and many others around the world.

CHS is in fact a very large group of cooperatives in the USA. It exports 2 billion bushels of grains to 65 countries through a network of 20 offices around the world.

CHS owns port terminals in Louisiana, Oregon, and Washington State, as well as terminals on the Mississippi, Ohio, and Illinois rivers.

At the other end of the spectrum, small farmers in Africa need to be organized in cooperatives to share their equipment while consolidating their bargaining power in the purchase of seeds, fertilizers and new machinery.

13.2.1 Total factor productivity

An indicator denominated 'total factor productivity' (TFP, see Martin (2013)) is defined as the ratio of aggregate output to aggregate inputs. Increases in TFP benefit producers through better yields and consumers through lower prices.

Unsurprisingly, North American productivity is the highest in the world, as measured by dollar output per agricultural worker or per unit of land.

Rates of increase in productivity are among the highest in Latin America and Oceania. Unfortunately, developing countries lag decades behind developed countries.

- Low TFP-growth states and countries are more likely to benefit from infrastructure investments that increase input productivity like irrigation.
- High TFP-growth states are more likely to benefit from post-production infrastructure like transport and storage.

13.2.2 Climate change

Climate change is expressed by heat waves, extreme temperatures, drought, extreme cold or floods and has a negative impact on agriculture.

Increased weather variability may affect the predictability of snow falls, hence the amount of water collected in rivers and basins.

More frequent droughts induce producing countries to keep grains in inventory instead of selling it to the outside world, disrupting the free flows of agricultural commodities. However, increased average temperatures open up very cold regions for feasible crop production; in turn, the transportation and processing infrastructure must efficiently adjust to the evolving spatial production and distribution.

13.2.3 Irrigation and increased productivity

- Irrigated acres make up about 40% of the value of agricultural production while amounting to only 7.5% of the land.
- Nebraska and California are the states in the USA with the greatest surface under irrigation. For instance, almond production in California needs irrigation throughout the year, while water is very scarce in this state often struck by droughts and depleting aquifers.
- In US production, irrigation is most beneficial for corn and selected horticulture.
- Crop stress should primarily be built upon water deficits/droughts and secondarily on heat stress.

13.2.4 Trends in irrigation

- There is a move towards better efficiency in water delivery through pressurized irrigation: pressurized systems, like linear or center pivot systems (typically found on the West Coast of the USA), generally increase uniformity of water distribution, hence minimize evaporation and runoff, but are more capital intensive than gravity-fed systems.
- 'Efficient' pressurized systems, like drip/trickle systems, reduce the amount of water needed for a given crop yield and lower the amount of *energy* required in pumping the water to the destination site. However, these systems are even more capital intensive than regular pressurized systems.
- Central pivot systems are the primary method of irrigation for corn in the US Midwest, but have the drawback of not irrigating all the land in a given space as they rotate.
- Subsurface drip systems are capable of irrigating the land uniformly; hence, they have a productivity benefit proportional to the corn price times the yield differential between irrigated land and dry land (see Martin (2013)).

    Subsurface drip systems use approximately 25% less water than central pivot systems through direct application of water to the roots. According to numbers produced by the state of Kansas, subsurface dripping has a net advantage compared to central pivot for yields higher than 170 bushels per acre and expected corn prices greater than $5.20 per bushel. However, such an advantage must be financed by an upfront investment of roughly $1307 per irrigated acre for a subsurface dripping system versus $575 for a central pivot system.

13.2.5 Storage

Up to the events in Ukraine in March 2014, the US 2013–2014 corn crop was perceived as very large – of the order of 13.9 billion bushels – and US farmers were trying to keep their harvest in storage to avoid a selling price of $4.5 to $5 per bushel which prevailed in the second half of 2013, down from $7 in January 2013. US on-farm storage capacity totals 13 billion bushels, 2 billion more than 10 years ago.

The biggest US trading houses, including ADM, Bunge Cargill, CHS, and Gavilon (a unit of Japan's Marubeni), have added about one billion bushels of US storage capacity in the past decade, as soaring prices in 2012 after the worst drought since the 1930s had enabled farmers to reinvest part of their income in their own storage facilities.

13.2.6 Grain elevators

In the grain world, a grain elevator is a tower containing a bucket elevator that scoops up grains from a lower level and deposits them in a silo or another storage facility (see Wikipedia).

Prior to the creation of grain elevators, grain was handled in bags rather than in bulk. Elevators were invented in Buffalo, NY, in 1842, upon the specifications of a merchant named Joseph Dart and realized by the engineer Dunbar as a device able to scoop loose grain out of the hulls of ships and elevate it to the top of a marine tower.

Grain elevator bins, tanks, and silos are today usually constructed of steel or reinforced concrete.

When needed, silos and bins are emptied by gravity flow. Grain is then loaded into trucks, railroad or barges and shipped to grain wholesalers, exporters, and end users such as flour mills, breweries, and ethanol distilleries.

Today, grain elevators are a common picture in the grain growing areas of the world, and in the USA in places like Toledo or Buffalo. Large terminal elevators are found in distribution centers such as Chicago or Thunder Bay, Ontario, where trucks, railways, and shipping facilities are present.

13.2.7 Soybean crushers

The primary goal of a soybean crusher is to maximize the pounds of oil and meal processed from every bushel of soybeans.

An average soybean bushel of 60 pounds contains 35% proteins, 18.5% oil, and 5% fiber, and yields 11 pounds of oil and 48 pounds of 44% protein meal. The crush margin, which is the difference between the value of soybean meal plus oil and the purchase price of raw soybeans, is generally based on this average yield. However, there is considerable variability in the protein and oil content of soybeans across regions and countries, and across varieties.

The actual yield of oil and meal per bushel of raw soybeans is determined by the soybean protein and oil content. Higher soybean protein content allows the processor to include more hulls in the meal while still meeting protein specifications. This results in a greater meal yield and improves the *crush margin*.

13.2.8 The Brave New World of Monsanto

It was in the 1990s that biologists took over Monsanto to make it the number one in the seed market. Twenty-nine countries in North and South America and Asia adopted genetically modified organism (GMO) technology. In the USA, 90% of soybeans and 80% of corn are transgenic, meant to resist pesticides, and solely directed to animals. Others disagree, like the Center for Food Safety, which complains that GMO planting was never specifically regulated in the USA, but instead the result of a fierce lobbying by Monsanto in Washington. Still, anti-GMO feelings are growing in the USA, even though bioculture covers only 5% of the land at this point. A number of households wish to see, like in Europe, the products labeled GMO/non-GMO at the supermarket.

For the time being, Monsanto has given up on GMO planting in Europe and instead focused on selling its traditional seeds. At the time of negotiations between the USA and the European Union around a free trade agreement, the explosive subject of food norms won't be avoided. The USA will repeat that no serious study has exhibited health risks generated by GMO plants, and argue that only a scientific and transgenic agriculture will satisfy the food needs of an expanding world population. In fact, The European Food Safety Agency has approved the studies on GMO viability and some believe that the opposition is in fact political, in France in particular where the MON810 corn, accepted by European and some French authorities, was opposed by the French government.

13.2.9 Infrastructure in sub-Saharan Africa

The number of infrastructure projects in sub-Saharan Africa is on the rise, together with the interest of investors to achieve exposure to one of the world's most buoyant economic regions. In 2014, sub-Saharan Africa is predicted to grow 5.4%, according to the International Monetary Fund, making it the second fastest growing region in the world behind developing Asia, including China and India.

Energy projects are particularly important for agricultural development. A shortage of power in many countries is seen as one of the main barriers towards improving agriculture productivity and developing a manufacturing base. A visible transaction that took place in April 2014 secured a $200 million six-year lending facility by a group of international banks in favor of Saur Energie Côte d'Ivoire. The deal was greatly oversubscribed and will deliver 60% of the natural gas, of which the country has large deposits, necessary to fire power stations in and around Abidjan – the commercial capital and a major export harbor for cocoa exports in particular.

13.2.10 Gabon: after black gold, green gold?

Gabon has repeatedly announced its strategy of diversifying away from crude oil into many agricultural projects. One hundred kilometers away from Libreville, the Avala plantation created by Olam will, according to the Singaporean group, produce palm oil while dedicating 65% of its 20,000 hectares to the preservation of the equatorial forest. Western Africa imports today 1.9 million tonnes of palm oil. Olam intends to cover Gabon's needs and exports as well, creating jobs for the local population.

Closer to Libreville, in the 'economic zone' of Knok, Olam has rendered viable 1126 hectares, together with the necessary infrastructure in electricity, water, and roads, in order to produce wood, furniture, and wood-derived products, which represented in 2013 only 4% of the Gabon GDP, according to the African Bank of Development. In 2010, many small firms had suffered from an export ban on tree trunks.

Yeap group, a fund from Luxemburg, is investing together with the Gabonese sovereign fund $100 million in a unit producing poultry and vegetables.

The New York African Forum, which took place in May 2014, concluded on the necessity of infrastructure to manage natural resources in Gabon.

13.2.11 Agricultural Transformation Agenda (ATA) in Nigeria

The ATA was launched in 2011 in order to bring Nigeria back on track for the production of agricultural products. According to Javier Blas (*Financial Times*, May 5, 2014), Nigeria was growing enough rice 50 years ago to feed itself and export to other African countries. Today, it is one of the world's top three importers of rice, buying the cereal as far away as Thailand.

Supporters of ATA say that transforming agriculture, which represents more than half of the work force in Nigeria, is critical to creating more food in a country where the majority of the population lives on only $1.25 per day.

The oil boom of 1973–1974 in Nigeria was unfortunately a remarkable example of the 'resource curse' mentioned before – also called 'Dutch disease' because of the recession that took place in the Netherlands after the discovery of the massive natural gas field of Groningen. Besides rice, Nigeria was in the 1960s and early 1970s the largest cocoa producer in Africa and cocoa exports represented a large piece of foreign currency flow. After the oil bonanza came along, the production of cocoa did not keep pace and Nigeria today is behind Ivory Coast and Ghana in African cocoa production.

Lack of infrastructure – roads, storage facilities, and electricity supply – as well as insecurity in the grain producing northern states created by extremist groups are acting as impediments to the boost of agricultural output. The IMF, in its 2014 annual report on Nigeria, cited the example of Brazil for its remarkably successful transformation of its farming sector over the last two decades.

The expected impact of the ATA is to contribute to the private-sector led agricultural growth for food security, job creation, and shared wealth. Its specific objective is to increase on a sustainable basis the income of 43,500 small farmers and rural entrepreneurs engaged in the production, storage, and marketing of priority commodity value chains.

Some elements of progress are visible today: agricultural production and exports have increased for cocoa, cashews, and cotton. Before ATA, 0.7% of bank lending was directed to farming; today, it is 5%, and expected to grow, hopefully reducing the crude oil curse.

13.2.12 Digital age on the farm: prescriptive planting

Prescriptive planting is essentially a system that tells farmers with great precision which seeds to plant and how to cultivate them in each piece of land. According to *The Economist* (May 24, 2014), this could be the biggest change in agriculture for rich countries since genetically modified (GM) crops. Another controversy is brewing, this time on the ownership of the data on which the recommendation is based. Monsanto's prescriptive planting system, FieldScripts, had its first trials in 2013 and was already for sale in four American states in 2014.

The Climate Corporation, a Silicon Valley startup, was founded in 2006 by two former Google employees with the goal of selling data-based crop insurance. It used remote sensing and sophisticated cartographic techniques to map every single field in the USA (roughly 25 million) and add to them all possible climate information.

By 2010, the Climate Corporation had 150 billion soil observations in its database and 10 trillion weather simulation points. Before it went ahead with selling crop insurance, it was snapped up in October 2013 by Monsanto for about $1 billion, one of the highest amounts paid at that point for a data firm.

Monsanto, as the world's largest hybrid seed producer, has a library of hundreds of thousands of seeds and very large data on their yields. By consolidating them with the Climate Corporation's soil and weather database, it produced a map of the USA that says which seeds grow best where and under which weather conditions.

FieldScripts uses these data to run machines made by Precision Planting, a company bought by Monsanto in 2012, which makes seed drills and other mechanical devices pulled along by tractors, in contrast to the old boxes used by farmers, which were pushing seeds into the soil at fixed intervals. In the new system, different types of seeds are planted at different depths and spacing, all varying with the weather.

By doing this, the largest seed company in the world is trying to diversify away from its gigantic business in GM seeds and, accordingly, improve its image by stepping up its efforts into proposing 'precision agriculture,' GPS applications and remote sensing techniques for farming.

In November 2013, Du Pont Pioneer, another major seed producer, linked up with John Deere, a famous farm-machinery maker, in order to advise farmers on seeds and fertilizers in specific fields. A farm cooperative, Land O'Lakes, bought in December 2013 a satellite-imaging company to boost its farm data.

Farmers who have tried Monsanto's system said it had increased yields by 5% over two years, a gigantic number. The seed companies think that providing farmers with more data could increase the US corn yield from 10 tonnes per hectare (160 bushels per acre) to 200 bushels, and boost growers' margins.

At the same time, farmers may have mixed feelings about the reduction of the role of their competence and skills in farming. More importantly, they fear that their commercial secrets may be passed to rival farmers or underperforming farms; or that big companies could use data on harvests to trade in the commodity markets to the detriment of farmers who sell their grains to these markets.

The American Farm Bureau, the country's largest organization of farmers and ranchers, is defining a code of conduct establishing that farmers own their data and companies must not sell the information to third parties or use it for any other purpose than the one for which the information was passed along. Again, another issue arises about the ownership of these data once they have been anonymized. For this reason, some Texan farmers have grouped together to form the Grower Services Cooperative in order to negotiate with data providers.

On the other side of the Atlantic Ocean, Green Spin is a Germany-based startup that is also proposing a data-driven approach to modern farming. Satellite imagery collects data on weather, soil, and other input factors that are aggregated in plant growth models, leading to better information on crop acreage, potential yields, and optimal planting decisions.

It seems clear that, in a first stage, big companies will dominate the space of prescriptive planting and make the best use of collecting data. But this technique could boost yields everywhere, just as mass (and anonymized) patient records could improve healthcare in the world (cf. the Brain Project at the Swiss Technology Institute in Lausanne or the Big Data medical company Med Nexus Inc.). But its success depends on service providers convincing users (farmers or patients/hospitals) to trust them. A clear chart of benefits should obviously be established in both cases.

13.2.13 Sugar biofactory for ethanol in Brazil

In the village of Monte Alegre in the heart of Brazil's southern sugar growing region, Centro de Tecnologia Canavieira (CTC) – the world's biggest sugar cane biofactory – monitors the growth of cane from computer-generated DNA that could increase the industry's productivity by up to 50% (*Financial Times*, May 5, 2013). CTC is also experimenting with genetically engineered varieties.

CTC was founded by a group of local sugar mills in 1989 and went public in 2010. It hopes to win approval for its first generation of engineered cane within three years, as conventional cross-breeding cannot increase the sugar content by more than 10 to 15%. By taking this number to 30% or even 50%, CTC expects to greatly reduce ethanol prices – Brazil already accounts for half of global sugar exports, and 90% of cars are built to run on ethanol.

CTC has partnerships with the firms BASF and Bayer and contracts with 200 mills.

Since 2004, CTC has created 21 varieties of sugar cane with up to 15% higher sugar content and greater resistance to disease and bad weather conditions. In order to double sugar and ethanol production per hectare by 2020, CTC also develops second generation ethanol made from *bagasse and leaves* and wants to bring GM sugar cane to the market. Genetically engineered soybeans and corn for animal feed are common today, but transgenic cane is not commercially available.

13.2.14 After ethanol, railway, and natural gas

Following the wise acquisition of railways by Warren Buffet in the USA, Brazil's ethanol billionaire Rubens Ometto launched in 2014 a $3 billion acquisition of the country's biggest railway operator America Latina Logistica (ALL) in order to manage the freight of about 60 to 65% of Brazilian agribusiness.

In the last 30 years, the entrepreneur has turned a sugar mill in the state of Sao Paulo into the world's largest sugar and ethanol processor (*Financial Times*, May 28, 2014); his compatriots, the Batista brothers, had built during the same period the world's largest meat processor, JBS.

As mentioned earlier in the book, sugar and ethanol are Brazil's third-largest agricultural export group, after soybeans and meat, with sales close to $14 billion last year.

During the period 2007–2013, the ethanol boom was damaged by a major drought in 2010 and by government-made fuel prices that were lower by 20 to 30% than international levels, in order to control inflation. This in turn led to the closure of 58 mills and left only 15 companies profitable out of 200 in the south-central region of Brazil. One of them is Cosan, Mr. Ometto's company.

In 2010 Cosan had built a joint venture with Shell to set up Raizen Energia, Brazil's major biofuel company, and acquired from British Gas in 2012 the largest gas distribution company in Brazil.

On the front of ethanol, the entrepreneur plans to open a mill that will produce a highly productive form of ethanol known as cellulose ethanol, which has the added merit of being produced from the inedible parts of the plant.

13.2.15 From iron ore mining to cattle farming in Australia

In the early days of July 2014, the iron ore magnate Gina Rinehart bought a 50% stake in two Western Australian cattle stations in order to be part of the booming food exports from Australia to Asia. Her company, Hancock Prospecting – which is building the mammoth Roy Hill iron ore project in the Pilbara – has purchased half of the sprawling Liveringa and Nerrima cattle stations in the West Kimberly region, in a joint venture called Liveringa Station Beef (LSB), covering 700,000 hectares. The joint venture partner is Dowford Investments, which is owned by the agribusiness group Milne Agrigroup.

The move comes just months after another Australian iron ore billionaire Andrew Forrest bought the Harvey Beef Group and added two large cattle stations to the one he bought in 2009. The two mining magnates were already shipping Australian primary products to offshore markets (*Australian Financial Review*, July 3, 2014).

As for LSB itself, it is moving away from live cattle exports and towards boxed beef, with the purchase of Waroona Abattoirs (formerly Clover Meats).

13.2.16 Robots for cow milking

Automatic milking systems were developed in the 1990s and allow complete automation of the milking process through the use of computers and specific software.

Today, in a situation of lack of skilled workers, dairy operations in upstate New York are experiencing robotic milkers that feed and milk cows one after another without human intervention (*New York Times*, April 24, 2014).

Robots allow cows to set their own hours, lining up for automated milking.

Lasers scan and map the cows' underbellies and a computer charts each animal's 'milking speed.' The robots also monitor the amount and quality of milk produced, the frequency of visits to the machine, how much each cow has eaten per day, and the number of steps it took – the way some of us try to keep track of the distance we cover every day...

Thirty farms have installed more than 100 robotic milkers in the state of New York where workers are difficult to find for long-day dairy operations. The state of New York is the third-largest milk producer in the USA.

The same robots are established in the Netherlands and other places in the world; because of the elective milking schedule, the process is supposed to be more comfortable for the animals (a great piece of news for vegetarians!). However, the automation removes the animal from social contact with the farmer, which is not optimal.

The system is more difficult to use within pasture schemes, which is why it is used particularly in countries like the Netherlands where land is so scarce that the farmer brings the feed from the field to the barn. In pasture schemes, cows graze in the fields and may not wish to walk to the milking facility.

The machines cost up to $250,000 a unit, which includes a mechanical arm, cleaning equipment, computerized displays, and sensors to detect the position of the animal.

Manufacturers of robots include Lely from the Netherlands, GEA Farm Technologies from Germany, Boumatic from the USA, and Fullwood from the UK.

13.2.17 Containers for agricultural commodities

In the very interesting paper by J.P. Rodrigue (2012, Van Horne Institute, University of Calgary), the author emphasizes the benefits for Canada of containerization of a specific range of commodities such as lumber and specialty grains such as canola, alfalfa, and lentils.

He argues that the availability of empty containers in backhaul movements together with the rising long-term price of commodities can be cost effective and bring the commodity to a variety of foreign markets. In general, the higher the price, the more suitable it is for containerization.

For resource-rich Western Canada, containers are a good solution to send agricultural commodities to Asian Pacific markets, particularly those that need to be kept refrigerated such as meat, fruits, and vegetables, all of them being of high value.

In the 2000s, inland ports had been developed in Western Canada around railway terminals. In general, inland ports need to have:

* A connection to a port terminal by rail or barge.
* An array of logistical activities that organize the freight/transit, such as temporary warehousing facilities, customs clearance, distribution centers, with a clear definition of the interdependence between vessel charterers, railway inland ports, and trucking companies.

13.2.18 Singapore as a hub for refrigeration containers

Carrier Transicold, the world's largest manufacturer of refrigerated containers, builds its refrigeration units in Singapore.

The company, which is part of the US conglomerate United Technologies Corp, delivers $6 billion worth of cargo each day in its containers.

The containers, known as reefers (see Kara Quek, *Business Times*, May 5, 2014), comprise a refrigeration part and an isolated shipping container, and cost around $200,000 each. They are employed in the transport of temperature-sensitive perishable or frozen cargoes, an industry worth $150 billion in 2014.

The reefers can be used to convey wine or medical vaccines, but they primarily carry food today, including seasonal fruit like bananas. For reefer builders, the biggest demand will come from Asia, citing the growth of the economy in the region and the fast developing middle class mentioned before.

13.2.19 The trip of the banana

A banana, part of a bunch, is picked, processed, and packaged for shipping at a banana plantation in the Philippines. It is loaded into a refrigerated container unit and transported to Manila, where it is loaded onto a large container ship that can hold 5000 containers. It arrives in Singapore where it is taken to the ripening room of a cold storage facility (see *Business Times*, May 5, 2014).

When the banana has reached a half-ripened stage, it is transferred to a fruit wholesale market. It is then delivered to retail in a refrigerated van at a constant temperature of 12 to 14°C (fresh for that hot region) and a humidity level of 90–95%; any deviation can damage the entire load of bananas. After a 16-day journey from the point of production (plus the ripening time), the banana ends its trip as a smoothie in a Singaporean bar.

13.2.20 Energy, water, and infrastructure for DAP and agriculture in Saudi Arabia

Like Morocco, Saudi Arabia is an exemplary situation; it uses energy, water, and phosphate to produce di-ammonium phosphate, the key fertilizer discussed in a previous chapter, to boost the productivity of its agriculture.

At the end of a stretch that goes along the southern Mediterranean (Morocco, Tunisia) and into the Middle East is located one of the world's largest reserves of phosphates, in northern Saudi Arabia. This fertilizer production is obviously a diversification from crude oil in Saudi export earnings. And in Florida, a key region for the production of phosphate rock, output has declined by one-third over the 2000s.

In 2011 the Saudi Arabia Mining Company (MAADEN) started commercial production of di-ammonium phosphate at the Ma'aden Phosphate Company (MPC) complex of Ras Al Khair. MPC is a $5.5 billion joint venture between Ma'aden (70%) and the Riyadh-headquartered SABIC.

The phosphate deposits (phosphorite containing 25% of penta-oxide of phosphorus) are exploited by drilling and blasting the rock; they are then cleaned into concentrates and transported to the crushing station via railway or trucks. Finally, they are used in the production of DAP, which has a large development agenda in the coming years.

Chemical plants that are currently under extension convert 4.5 million tonnes per year of concentrates into 2.9 million tonnes of granular DAP, by dissolution of the phosphate concentrate in sulfuric acid in order to produce phosphoric acid. We can note that Saudi Arabia produces sulfur as a by-product during its extensive process of oil extraction. Ammonia is then added to obtain the di-ammonium phosphate in a soft solid form that can be dried and granulated to a size of 3 millimeters, which is easy to handle.

Obviously, a large amount of *energy* is consumed in the above process and will be provided by fuel-oil generators, with an installed capacity of 28 megawatts. But *water* is also a key ingredient when drilling and blasting the deposits. In this desert environment, water is obviously a concern. Extensive drilling has indicated that water acceptable for processing is available from nearby aquifers through boreholes, which is then purified through an energy-intensive reverse osmosis process (mentioned in a previous chapter). Hydrological modeling of the Tawil aquifer has revealed a sustainable flow rate of 13 million m^3 per year, which is quite sufficient for the processing units that exist or are being built.

New units are being built by Ma'aden, after which its total production will be around 16 million tonnes per year and include phosphate concentrate, dicalcium and monocalcium phosphate used in animal feed, and purified phosphoric acid used in food industries.

On the other hand, Morocco saw in 2013 the completion of two DAP plants with a production capacity of 850,000 tonnes per year each. The industrial complex is located on Jorf Lasfar, on the Atlantic coast of Morocco, at 120 km from Casablanca. It is a major export center for phosphates and DAP. The site belongs to the company Maroc Phosphore SA. It also includes four phosphoric acid tanks of 2,000 m^3 each and new extensions are coming into production.

13.3 COUNTRY RISK: THE EXAMPLE OF UKRAINE IN 2014

The annexation of Crimea by Russia in March 2014, together with anticipations of drought in major producing countries, pushed wheat prices up by 25% within a period of two weeks.

Crimea's grain production is relatively small – it produced 44,000 tonnes of corn and 361,000 tonnes of wheat in 2012–2013. In fact, Crimea accounted for roughly 7% of total grain and oilseed production in Ukraine.

But, more importantly, the annexation of Crimea could also cost Ukraine 11% of its total port capacity in seaborne agriculture, which is 3.5 million tonnes. The main loading facilities in the Odessa and Mycelia regions should ensure the continuity of grain shipments from Ukraine since Crimea's ports are mostly used for storage; still, this storage was quite useful to Ukraine, and easily accessible from the Black Sea.

Another noticeable impact of the crisis for Ukrainian farmers will be higher production costs for seeds in the coming season because of the currency devaluation. At the same time, short-term loans in the national currency went up to 23% in March 2014.

Lastly, Ukraine will face larger energy costs due to the cancellation of the 30% discount granted by Russia on natural gas supplies. Nitrogen fertilizer producers will be hit by the impact of higher energy prices.

13.4 ANALYZING THE RISKS INVOLVED IN AN INTERNATIONAL WHEAT TENDER OFFER

On August 25, 2012 the Egyptian state-run General Authority for Supply Commodities (GASC) issued a tender offer to buy, for shipment in December 2012, 180,000 tonnes of soft or milling wheat from one of the following origins: USA, Canada, France, Australia, Germany, Britain, Russia, Kazakhstan, Romania, Ukraine or Poland.

It was GASC's third international wheat purchase since July 1, the start of the 2012–2013 fiscal year in the Arab Republic of Egypt. The world's top wheat importing nation moved to secure supplies amid rising concerns about weather-reduced crops in key exporting countries.

During the 2011–2012 fiscal year, GASC had purchased 5.33 million tonnes of wheat, which included 3.24 million tonnes of Russian wheat, 530,000 tonnes of US wheat, 360,000 tonnes of Ukrainian wheat, 300,000 tonnes of Argentinian wheat, 300,000 tonnes of French wheat, 240,000 tonnes of Kazakhstan wheat, and 60,000 tonnes of Canadian wheat (see anyfoodanyfeed.com).

Returning to the August 2012 tender offer, the bids ranged from $319 to $361.65 dollars per tonne on an FOB basis. Finally, GASC bought:

- 60,000 tonnes of Russian wheat from Olam at the price of $319 FOB per tonne, and freight costs of $11.70 per tonne.
- 60,000 tonnes of Russian wheat from Aston at the price of $320.94 FOB per tonne, with freight costs of $10.10 per tonne.
- 60,000 tonnes of Romanian wheat from Ameropa at $323.38 FOB per tonne, with freight costs of $10.10 per tonne.

One year later, in a tender offer made on December 3, 2013 for shipment in the last 10 days of 2013, GASCA bought 60,000 tonnes of Romanian wheat.

The offer came from Ithad El Arabi, at a price of $304.89 per tonne on a *CIF basis*, hence a significantly lower price than those obtained the previous year. In fact, in December 2013, world grain inventories were quite high; in Ukraine, for instance, they were 43% higher than the previous year.

After that purchase, GASCA had secured for the fiscal year 2.745 million tonnes of wheat, more than two-thirds of the 3.375 million tonnes of wheat it had bought in the fiscal year 2012–2013, which included 1.14 million tonnes from Russia, 720,000 tonnes from France, 635,000 from the USA, 480,000 from Romania, 280,000 tonnes from Ukraine, and 60,000 tonnes from Argentina.

The 2.745 million tonnes of wheat prudently booked by the end of 2013 were 1.08 million tonnes from Romania, 720,000 tonnes from Russia, 705,000 tonnes from Ukraine, and 240,000 tonnes from France.

If we consider one international merchant that answered one of the coming 'invites for tender' from GASCA and signed an agreement to deliver 60,000 tonnes of wheat in Cairo in December 2014, we can identify the following list of risks this merchant will face, depending on the moment when the offer was signed, the location of the country where wheat will originate from, the merchant's operating currency, and so forth:

- Futures price changes.
- *Premium* above the Futures price paid to the warehouse if delays occur in the physical delivery – a quantity very hard to hedge up to now.
- Pick-up logistics, including truck and barge to the Mississippi river if the wheat comes from Minnesota.
- Export elevation in the Louisiana port.
- Changes in shipping rates and fuel costs.
- Port congestion at departure.
- Weather on the way.
- Port congestion in Cairo.
- Discharge elevation.
- Political risk in the country of departure or arrival.
- FX risk.
- Changes in the world debt rates applicable to the working capital over the period.

13.5 WEATHER RISK AND WEATHER DERIVATIVES

Weather plays a key role in commodity markets, with the exception of metals. It has been consistently the first factor in explaining the yield and quality of agricultural commodities.[1] We have seen that in electricity markets, a long heat wave can send power prices to hundreds of dollars; a dry winter in the northern countries of Europe where most of the electricity is hydro can be easily identified in a database of power prices.

Turning now to agricultural markets, prices follow seasonal patterns where periods of extreme volatility coincide with the time when the harvest is most exposed to extreme weather. Late frosts can decimate the Brazilian coffee crop and this translates into the high volatility observed on coffee Futures prices during summer in the northern hemisphere. Frosts can also damage orange juice production in Florida: in the subtle paper 'Orange juice and weather,' Roll (1984) examines whether the prices of orange juice Futures contracts could be identified

---

[1] Film lovers may remember from the movie *Trading Places* the crucial role early information on weather played in building and destroying fortunes in orange juice (OJ) Futures contracts.

as the best predictors of the weather in Florida. In a multi-year database of soybean Futures prices, Geman and Nguyen (2005) exhibit that volatility is highest at pre-harvest times and goes down when the crop is known. The seasonal nature of agriculture implies that the supply side is inelastic or 'sticky' and any shock in production has a high impact on prices.

Besides temperature, rain is another major element in agricultural commodity markets. Too little rain can cripple the crop during the growth phase; too much rain can cause crop failure or damage crop quality at harvesting. An example of an extreme weather event is drought, which is regularly a severe concern for many arid parts of the world such as India or Ethiopia. Even in a highly sophisticated production environment such as Australia, the drought of 2002 caused wheat production to plummet from 20 million tonnes in 2001 to 9 million tonnes. In India, low rainfall is the most dangerous factor in monsoon-season crop production. During the 2002–2003 season, India received the lowest ever recorded amount of rain in July, the crucial month for crops; the drought caused a drop of 19% in food grain production and a 3.1% decline in GDP. The 2002 report by the Wisconsin Agricultural Statistical Services notes that corn and soybean farmers reduce their planting volume if they anticipate lower than normal rainfall; high rainfall, however, implies a higher probability that crops will incur disease.

In the case of Australian wine, Gladstone (1965) argues that temperature, sunshine, humidity, and rainfall are the dominant weather risks that affect the wine industry. Given the rapid growth of Australian wine production between 1998 and 2003, with export volumes increasing by 170% to AU\$2.4 billion in value, there is an increasing demand for financial instruments that allow wine grape producers to hedge against weather risks. The 1998 report into the Australian wine and grape industry established that weather risks account for 42% of the loss in Australian Chardonnay grape production.

Prior to the introduction of weather derivatives, agricultural companies had essentially two ways of hedging the volatility of their revenues: get crop insurance from the state or a private insurance company, or take positions in Futures markets.

In the case of France, over the last 15 years champagne growers have built up reserves of wine from those years when the vintage was excellent both in quality and quantity. The reserves are made up of grapes that are transformed into wine, but do not go through the second fermentation procedure that leads to champagne. These reserves can be kept for 10 years. In April 2003, a frost destroyed many young buds, resulting in a yield of 8250 kg/ha in October 2003 compared with the average yield of 10,400 kg/ha and leading to the use of the reserves. In 2004 the vintage was excellent and the reserves were replenished (see Declerck (2004)).

Weather derivatives trading
Most of the weather derivatives traded on exchanges or contracted in OTC transactions as of today have been tied to temperature and appeared in the course of deregulation of the electricity and gas industry worldwide as a valuable hedging instrument. For a long time, utilities have been facing *volume risk* in the form of a lower demand in the case of a warm winter or cool summer but gas and electricity prices used to be regulated. Utilities now facing demand risk and *price risk* have in most cases chosen to buy hedging instruments against variability of demand, a risk they have learnt to quantify in terms of missing dollar revenues.

Since the underlying source of risk – the temperature – is not traded, defining the price of the weather derivative as the cost of hedging collapses, together with the Black–Scholes formula or anyone attached to *dynamic hedging*. We still need today an alternative paradigm to price these instruments, whose market is *incomplete because of the physical nature* of the underlying (see Geman (1998)). Alternatively, we may want to define a criterion under which a transaction becomes *admissible* (see Carr, Geman and Maden (1999) for the notion of acceptable risk in a situation of imperfect hedging). The recent literature has proposed a number of criteria to address the problem of market incompleteness since the no-arbitrage argument is insufficient to deliver a unique answer in terms of pricing and hedging. A possible approach is to have a *business pricing* approach to the valuation of weather derivatives (see, e.g., Geman and Leonardi (2005) for a general discussion of this valuation).

Weather derivatives are traded on the Chicago Mercantile Exchange for monthly and seasonal contracts on 21 locations: fifteen in the USA, five in Europe, and one in Japan. In Japan, the monthly or seasonal index defining the payoff at maturity is formed as the average temperature across the period of the contract. In the case of the USA and Europe, the index is expressed in terms of *degree days*. In meteorological terms, a degree day is the difference between a reference temperature, typically 65°F or 18°C, and the mean temperature on a given day defined as the arithmetic average of the daily maximal and minimal temperatures. During winter, meteorologists calculate heating degree days by subtracting the mean daily temperature from the reference 65°F; if this difference is negative, it means that neither heating fuel nor electricity is consumed, and the number of heating degree days set to zero. In other terms:

$$(HDD)_{day\ j} = Max(0, 65°F - Aver\ Temp_j)$$

Cooling degree days (CDD), typically attached to summer, are symmetrically defined on day j as:

$$(CDD)_{day\ j} = Max(0, Aver\ Temp_j - 65°F)$$

Consequently, a utility wishing to hedge its revenues against a warm winter will buy a *put option* written on *cumulative heating degree days*. If we define winter as the period covering the months of December, January, and February, the cumulative degree days attached to that season will be defined as

$$Cum\ HDD = \sum_{i=1}^{90} (HDD)_j$$

where $(HDD)_j$ denotes HDD on day j.

For example, a Brazilian coffee producer will identify the number k of total HDD over the month of August above which its revenues will be severely damaged and hedge its revenues by buying a call option whose payoff at maturity T = August 31 is defined as

$$PC(T) = Nominal\ Amount.\ Max(0, Cum\ HDD(T) - k)$$

where the nominal amount A represents the loss in revenues per missing heating degree day.

Symmetrically, a wine producer who may lose his crops in the case of a very hot month of August in the south of France will buy a call option written on cumulative coding degree days providing at maturity:

$$C(T) = A\ Max(0, Cum\ CDD(T) - k)$$

To conclude this section, we will recognize weather derivatives as an instrument very useful to protect small farmers from extreme weather events; more valuation models for the derivatives are necessary to bring to this market the liquidity it deserves.

14
Investing in Agricultural Commodities, Land, and Physical Assets

'Stock brokers will become taxi drivers. Farmers will be driving Lamborghinis.'
Jim Rogers, Commodities Investor

During and after the global financial crisis, commodities moved in lock-step with equities and bonds as the financial markets were in the mode of 'risk-on, risk-off' trading.

For investors, commodities are a difficult asset class, however, as they pay neither coupons nor dividends.

Retail and institutional commodity assets under management had fallen from $525 billion in April 2011 to about $350 billion three years later. In 2013 alone, there was a record $50 billion of net redemptions in passive index tracking and commodity ETFs. During the first four months of 2014, the Dow Jones-UBS commodity index outperformed the S&P500 by more than 8% and the 90-day rolling correlation between the two indexes has been consistently negative. During that time period, the inflows into commodities amounted to $6 billion, with declining correlations to other asset classes and significant volatility in coffee, cocoa, and nickel, in all cases because of weather or political events. Overall, commodity indexes have been a less popular investment vehicle as of 2013 and are again now the space of natural players such as mining companies and commodity trading houses, but with large investments from equity funds into physical assets.

14.1 PURCHASE OF COMMODITY FUTURES

Traditionally, commodities have been viewed as a hedge against inflation and continue to be so. For instance, life insurance companies that have sold variable annuities tied to a price index like the CRB (Commodity Research Bureau) index can hedge their exposure by buying credit derivatives from a bank at a possibly high cost. They can also get long in commodities as part of their asset management strategy. As of 2001, commodities emerged as a very desirable asset class in its own right, offering remarkable returns because of the strong increase in demand coming from India and China in particular, as well as a very low correlation with stocks and bonds. Since 2008, each commodity has behaved according to its own market conditions.

We can identify the following avenues to get exposure to commodities:

Purchase of physical commodities (and face storage and insurance costs)

Futures

Options on Futures

Commodity index investing (with the choice of many indexes)

Commodity-linked bonds

Structured products

Exchange-traded products (ETFs, ETNs)

Shares of mining or oil companies

Purchase of physical assets (generating the sure transformation spread)

Purchase of land.

An investor or a hedge fund can, in principle, buy any commodity in the spot market, either by a direct transaction with the producer or through an intermediary. Let us suppose the transaction is conducted by a Dutch fund with a coffee grower in Vietnam and involves 1 million coffee bags. Even if the shipping is organized by an intermediary, the fund manager will have to deal with the storage issues related to these coffee bags: space, humidity level, and perishability. With a commodity such as natural gas, the situation gets worse since a salt cavern or the like is necessary to store the gas; with electricity, storage is in general not feasible. An exception to the great difficulties attached to the purchase of the physical commodity is provided by precious metals, which do not require much space or care; they cannot, however, constitute the bulk of the diversified commodity portfolio an investor wishes to hold.

Both private and institutional investors, if they are not commodity producers, trade Futures contracts in order to gain exposure to commodity prices while avoiding the hurdles of inventories, shipping, warehousing, and so forth. Commodity Futures have been the typical financial instrument used by CTAs (Commodity Trading Advisors) who have been active in commodities for more than a century. They have also become the standard tool for all the new entrants in the commodity space. The learning curve starts with the first nearby Future as the natural instrument to purchase as a proxy for the spot price. Then, the choice of the maturity of the forward/Future becomes a more subtle exercise.

An obvious and direct way to build a targeted exposure to a given commodity is to take a long or short position in Futures written on that commodity. We recall here some properties collected in the previous chapters:

• Futures contracts are traded on an exchange that provides the transparency and integrity of the clearing house. Hence, the investor only needs to build an account with a broker holding a seat on the exchange. Note that Futures accounts may be opened with licensed Futures commission merchants (FCMs) who are registered with the Commodity Futures Trading Commission (CFTC).
• Only a fraction of the Futures contract face value – the margin deposit or *initial margin* – needs to be paid upfront. It represents, in general, a small percentage of the contract dollar amount and may often be paid under the form of Treasury bills or other type of collateral.
• As mentioned before, the Futures contract may be financially settled by design or the position closed prior to maturity by a symmetric position in Futures with the same maturity. In both cases, the investor does not need to worry about physical delivery and related concerns.

- Hence, the only real issue is a proper roll of the Futures position if the investment horizon of the investor is further away than the most deferred liquidity maturity. This part of the strategy deserves a lot of care and attention, as discussed in Section 14.3, which is dedicated to commodity Futures indexes.

14.2 PURCHASE OF COMMODITY OPTIONS AND STRUCTURED PRODUCTS

In Chapter 4, we observed the leverage effect created by an investment in options, namely the fact that investing in a long call, for instance, when anticipating a rise in the underlying price S, provides the buyer with a higher return (negative if he is wrong, and of a greater magnitude) than putting his wealth in S directly. Hence, a market participant wishing to be positively exposed to a commodity price will buy a call on a Future contract, choosing the maturity of the option and the maturity of the Future on considerations of liquidity (and market price). In the case of a wrong view on the direction of the commodity market, he will lose his *total* wealth invested in the purchase of the call as the calls expire worthless.

On the other hand, the investor may decide to choose a protected position in the commodity or the commodity index by buying a so-called 'principal protected' structured product represented by a number of units of $S(t) + P(t)$, which is extremely popular in all types of equity markets.

The fund manager will invest a fraction of the wealth in zero coupon government bonds maturing at the investment horizon T and playing the role of the riskless asset, and the rest in calls written on the commodity. Such a position can be represented at date t by the value

$$C(t) + kB(t, T)$$

which, as shown in the put call parity of Chapter 4, is equal to

$$S(t) + P(t)$$

i.e., an *insured portfolio*, where the stock price is replaced by the commodity price or commodity index.

In principle, the option may be written on the commodity spot price. For liquidity considerations, the investor will buy an option written on the Futures price. In both cases, the strategy provides at maturity of the option the wealth:

$$V(T) = \text{Max}(S(T), k)$$

where k is the strike chosen for the option, hence the minimal value (floor) of the wealth at the horizon T.

When the bank has issued such a product to a client, it will dynamically replicate the option involved in the product; hence it will need a *model*, for instance the Black–Scholes model.

Since one of the assumptions of the model may be contradicted by the market over the lifetime of the product – typically three years – such as the *continuity* of the trajectory of S, the bank faces *model risk*, which cannot be hedged but only protected against by a reserve fund created from management fees in particular.

Structured notes

The following example is prototypical:

Issuer:	Bank XYZ
Type:	Euro Medium Term Note (EMTN)
Currency:	USD
Nominal:	$1,000,000
Trade date:	February 15, 2005
Strike date:	February 15, 2005
Final fixing date:	February 15, 2008
Payment date:	March 3, 2008
Underlying:	Goldman Sachs Agriculture Index Return (GSAER)

At maturity, the investor receives the maximum between

$$\text{Nominal} \times 95\%$$

and

$$\text{Nominal} \times 95\% \ (1 + \text{return on the GSCI Ag over the 3-year period})$$

We recognize a portfolio-insurance type product, where $k = 95\% \times 1$ million, and the underlying source of risk S is the agriculture index.

In this instance, the note turned out to be an excellent choice for the investor because of the gigantic rise in agricultural prices between February 2005 and February 2008. For the issuing bank, the spike in corn and wheat was a difficult moment in the option replication.

14.3 COMMODITY INDEX INVESTING

Index investing has long been popular in the securities markets. Now it is bringing a new source of liquidity to commodity Futures contracts and allows pension funds and other institutional investors to add commodity exposure to their portfolio.

14.3.1 Some prominent commodity indexes

We can recognize essentially two families of indexes:

1. The first one where the main choices in the definition of the index were:
   - the number of commodities in the index (small versus large)
   - the choice of these commodities
   - the weights of these commodities. In the case of equity indexes, the weights are straightforward and chosen to be the relative market capitalization of the specific stock

in the index. For commodities, the choices vary between constant weights (CRB) to weights related to production, or consumption, or volume traded in the Futures where the money related to a commodity in the index will be invested

– the frequency and choice of the rebalancing rule, decided in general by the Board of the index.

2. In the so-called second generation of commodity indexes that appeared in 2006 and later, a deserved emphasis was placed on the way Futures carrying the investments in the various commodities were rolled. It was the time when contango shapes lost their status of 'abnormality' and prevailed as often as backwardated shapes, hence consuming part or the entirety of the performance.

We can recognize, in a non-exhaustive way, the following indexes (which sometimes change names after acquisitions):

Goldman Sachs Commodity Index

Dow Jones-AIG Commodity Index, now DJ-UBS Commodity Index

Deutsche Bank Liquid Commodity Index

Rogers International Commodity Index

S&P Commodity Index

Reuters CRB Commodity Index

- The Reuters-CRB Commodity Futures Index

    It is the oldest and most published index
    CRBI Futures contracts have been trading on the New York Futures Exchange (NYFE) since 1986
    It involves 17 components
    All 17 components have equal weightings (roughly 5.88%)
    Orange juice, a popular product in the USA, has the same weight as crude oil
- Dow Jones-UBS Commodity Index (previously DJ-AIG)
    The index is rebalanced annually
    It is US centered – only 12% of the Futures it uses are traded outside the USA
    It involves 19 components
    Futures on the index were launched on the Chicago Board of Trade (CBOT) in 2001
- Goldman Sachs Commodity Index
    It involves 24 components
    Only includes Futures denominated in dollars
    It is world production weighted; hence the weights fluctuate over time
    GSCI Futures contracts have been trading on the Chicago Mercantile Exchange since 1992
- The RICI Index
    It contains 35 single components
    Agriculturals are quite important (34.9% of the index) and include soybean meal, canola, and azuki beans
    Crude oil represents 35% of the index; wheat is the second constituent with 7% of the index.
    Metals as a whole represent 21.1% of the index
    TRAKERS on the index have been traded on the CME since November 2005.

14.3.2 How commodity indices are constructed

The 'normal backwardation' theory relied on the view that prices tend to mean revert and high prices in the near future will generate new production, hence lower forward prices for more distant maturities. However, many contango curves have been observed over the last few years; during the year 2009 for instance, most forward curves were in contango since the market view was that prices were poised to become higher after the collapse of the second half of 2008. In all cases, a safe statement is to observe that the shape of the forward curve, like the yield curve of interest rates, evolves randomly over time.

Hence, the particular time to maturity of a Future contract chosen as the investment vehicle became particularly important in the last few years during which billions of dollars were poured into the commodity markets. The Deutsche Bank Optimal Yield Commodity Index focuses on the optimal timing to roll over the Futures contracts in which the index funds are invested: choosing those time periods where the forward curve is in backwardation – the most frequently observed one prior to the price collapse of summer 2008 – in order to generate a positive *roll yield* that will obviously be a key component of the overall return on the index. Among other merits, avoiding the first nearby allows one to avoid the hurdles of frequent and unavoidable rolls. The UBS-Bloomberg Commodity Index launched in January 2007 gives the investors the choice, for a given commodity and exchange, among various maturities (selected by criteria of liquidity such as trading volume and open interest), of the Future contract where their money is going to be positioned; the time to maturity of this contract is not changed over time, hence the name of Constant Maturity Commodity Index (CMCI) given to this index family. Obviously, different index strategies give changing performances over different time periods.

Typically, index managers today ignore the front month contract in order to avoid the issues associated with expiration and delivery, as said before. Instead, they build the index based on one or more of the deferred contract months, then 'roll' to the subsequent month as the front month reaches expiry.

As said before, the *roll return* is quite important: when forward curves are in backwardation, deferred months are cheaper, and the roll return is positive. Otherwise, part of the investment is lost when rolling the position. Although the returns on commodity indices are broadly similar, there are significant differences in the way they are constructed. Some indices, once constructed, never change the weightings. Others engage in an annual reweighting process to take into account changes in the level of global commodity production or consumption.

There are also significant differences in the number of commodities tracked by the indices. At one extreme, the Rogers International Commodity Index tracks 35 commodities. At the other end, the family of Deutsche Bank Liquid Commodity Indexes tracks just six commodities – crude oil, heating oil, aluminum, gold, wheat, and corn.

Another difference is the frequency of rebalancing. Some indices rebalance on a monthly basis, reducing their exposure to commodities that have appreciated and increasing it towards depreciated ones. Such an example is the Deutsche Bank Liquid Commodity Index – Mean Reversion.

In May 2006, the DBLCI-Optimum Yield was launched to address the random shapes of commodity forward curves: instead of rolling Futures contracts on a predefined schedule, these are rolled in a way that maximizes the positive roll yield in the case of backwardation or minimizes the negative roll yield in contango.

The two DB indices contain the same components: sweet light crude oil (WTI), heating oil, gold, aluminum, corn, and wheat but follow different strategies.

Our view is that, together with 'financialization,' the most successful time for commodity indexes is behind us, and that, today, commodities deserve to be traded individually because of idiosyncrasies related to weather, countries' regulations and royalty policies, and other factors. The above discussion is mainly useful for the economic quantities to focus on when building new products related to commodities.

14.3.3 Commodity-linked bonds

These allow sharing the appreciation (depreciation) of the underlying commodity market price with the bondholders by the commodity-producing country issuing the bonds.

There are two types of commodity-indexed bonds:

1. Coupon and principal payment to the bearer of the bond are linearly related to the price of a reference commodity (prevailing at the payment date).
2. Coupon payments are similar to those of a conventional bond but at maturity the bearer receives the face value plus an option to buy a predetermined quantity of the commodity at a specified price (an interesting feature for commodity-producing countries).

In 1863, the Confederate States of America, not yet the United States, had already issued bonds payable in bales of cotton.

14.4 INVESTING IN COMMODITY-RELATED EQUITIES

Buying shares of oil or gold-mining companies had been for a long time the way a number of investors chose to get exposed to crude oil or gold prices, as recalled earlier in the book and as investigated by a number of empirical finance papers.

Moreover, when Futures contracts do not exist for a given commodity, structured notes or ETFs typically do not exist either (by absence of hedging opportunities for the issuer); hence, buying stocks of companies producing this commodity becomes one of the few possibilities to gain a positive exposure to the commodity price. Since Futures contracts are not yet traded on an exchange, the case of fertilizers in Chapter 12 has been chosen to examine in detail the returns on fertilizer-producing companies' shares.

Lastly, we mentioned in Chapter 1 the vibrant activity that has taken place during 2012–2014 in mergers and acquisitions across the food industry.

Hence, we can recap the discussion as follows:

1. Buying the shares of natural resource companies has been for investors a traditional way of benefiting from an anticipated rise in the price of a commodity. The author's view, tested on data related to raw materials and the companies producing them, is that buying 'commodity equities' is in fact a *leveraged* way of being invested in the commodity. Chapter 12 exhibited the very large returns and alphas generated by investments in listed fertilizer-mining companies at the time of the first spike in corn and wheat prices, and fertilizers' prices shortly after. Conversely, in the last two years of declining gold prices, a large decrease in the shares of gold-mining companies has been observed.

Obviously, the role of corporate governance and the existence of risk management activities also have an impact on the company's earnings and may introduce a noise in the share price behavior.

2. Chapter 1 also mentioned the gigantic M&A activity that is currently taking place in the world of commodity trading houses and coffee and food companies, and in particular the desire of US companies to compete with giants like Nestlé and the decision of China to secure food for its citizens outside China as well as within the country. In the case of listed companies, this provides investors with the usual profits related to 'merger arbitrage' strategies.
3. An investor may also want to buy the shares of companies manufacturing tractors, caterpillars, and other equipment leading to the improvement or construction of the infrastructure being put in place in the agricultural world.

14.5 INVESTING IN LAND

Some argue that agricultural land is the best place to make money in the coming decade: in June 2009, then in August 2011, George Soros stated that 'Farmland is going to be one of the best investments of our time' and his view is shared by many others.

Capital is being attracted to this asset class by a combination of drivers including:

- Population growth
    By 2050, there will be an estimated 9.2 billion people in the world, a dramatic increase from the number of today, with the highest growth in developing countries.
    To meet current targets set by the USA, EU, Canada, Japan, Brazil, India, and China, the estimate is that 240 million acres will have to be committed to biofuel production worldwide.
- Loss of arable land worldwide
    The US National Academy of Sciences estimates we are losing arable soil 10 times faster than it is being replaced and the UN says that, on a global basis, the rate of loss is 10–100 times faster than that of replacement, with urbanization being one of the key reasons.
    As stated before, in 1950, there were 0.5 hectares of arable land per person in the world, but it has already fallen to just 0.2 hectares. Analysts estimate that global food production needs to rise in the year 2050 by more than 70% above the 2005–2007 levels to cope with rising food demand.
- Water supplies in decline
    In the USA, 13% of all farmland requires irrigation and 42% of America's fresh water is used for this purpose. In contrast, in China, 40% of all farmland must be irrigated, consuming 90% of the nation's fresh water supplies.
- Slowing improvement of crop yields
    Over the past 40 years, yield per acre increased 2.1% per year, but since 2000, the increase in yield per acre has averaged less than 1% per year and seems to have plateaued in many parts of the world.
    There are opportunities for companies in everything from fertilizers to irrigation equipment.
    Moreover, investors are increasingly looking for tangible assets; conversely, more investment is needed to boost agricultural productivity.

It seems that private investors share Mark Twain's view on land: farmland values in the UK have increased by 134% in the last 10 years – the fourth fastest decade of growth since 1800, according to the latest agricultural land survey by Savills Private Finance.

While the average value of UK farmland hit £5000 an acre in 2008, analysts forecast that prices could rise another 40% by 2015. As exhibited by the US example provided below, farmland prices continue to rise.

According to the UK Royal Institution of Chartered Surveyors, the number of individuals viewing investment in pasture or arable land as an attractive investment has heavily increased in the last few years.

Note that new owners often go to shared-profit farming arrangements with farmers. Farm managers may either lease the property or take on the operation themselves.

Global private investment in farmland by financial investors was estimated to be between $10 and $20 billion in 2010. As said before, the rationale for such investment has typically centered around three themes:

- Farmland as an inflation hedge since it is a real asset that is linked to food and energy production.
- Farmland as a diversifying source of return: it is a private market investment subject to its own physical and economic dynamics.
- Farmland as asset positioning for a food and energy scarcity world, leading to the search for new farmland and price appreciation in existing farmland assets.

14.5.1 The US case

- The US corn-belt farmland values have increased by 212% between 2002 and 2012.
- The farm rent-to-value ratio has gone down by 22%.
- The farm debt-to-asset ratio has gone down by 25% during the same decade.

From 1900 to 1919, US farmland gained 70%: interest rates were low, grain prices were high, and US agriculture exports were booming. After World War I, the US farming economy was hit by a rise in interest rates and a slowdown of agricultural exports. Land prices collapsed in 1940 to their levels of 1900.

Over the decade 2000–2012, US farmland prices more than doubled – with a rapid increase as of 2008 – in presence of interest rates held by the Fed at historically low levels and a strong demand for grains. Big investors poured billions of dollars into farmland as it was viewed, for good reasons, as a *real asset*. Timber land was the first investment, with a maintenance perceived as minimal, then acreage planted with corn, soybeans or cotton (see Geman and Martin (2011)). Recently, sorghum deservedly regained a new interest in the USA for animal feed, but its consumption may be extended to human beings in this part of the world.

14.5.2 The world case

In order to make the comparison currency-independent, we look at the world land prices per tonne of corn output measured in dollars. The average numbers over the period 2009–2011 have been:

- $1162 in central Illinois (USA)
- $1065 in Santa Fe (Argentina)

- $680 in Matto Grosso (Brazil)
- $221 in Central Black Earth (Russia)
- $113 in Poltava (Ukraine).

It appears that land in Russia's Central Black Earth region costs one-fifth of land in central Illinois and twice the value in Ukraine. These disparities explain why investors may decide to buy farmland in foreign countries – when feasible, however, as some countries like Canada or Brazil wisely limit this right to citizens.

Another interesting quantity is the *price-to-rent multiple*, an agricultural indicator that is the equivalent of the price earnings ratio in the stock market. This number has increased in the USA in the last decade and is the highest in the world in the case of US farmland; conversely, the ratio of rents paid to land value fell by about 1 to 3.5% in the last decade.

The argument for the non-collapse of farmland prices is obviously the fact that the world population is set to hit 9 billion by 2050. Over 2013, an investment in farmland returned 2.5%, compared to 9% for timber land, and minus 5% for the S&P GSCI commodity index. However, in the USA, the investors in farmland coming from financial institutions represent less than 1%; cash-rich farmers the rest. Pension funds and university endowment funds constitute the bulk of institutional investors; for instance, TIAA-CREF, the university professors' pension fund, manages more than $3.5 billion in its unit 'Natural Resources and Infrastructure.'

As far as infrastructure is concerned, the USA has a remarkable transportation system (roads, railways, rivers, harbor equipment) compared to the rest of the world. Asia has made enormous progress, and a good and modern infrastructure should be available soon in a number of countries in sub-Saharan Africa, from Ethiopia to Gabon and Ghana.

14.6 ACQUISITION OF INFRASTRUCTURE AND PHYSICAL ASSETS

We can take the situation of a soybean crusher where soybean is crushed into soy oil; or an ethanol plant where sugar is transformed into ethanol; or that of a chemical plant where phosphate rock is transformed into the directly usable fertilizer di-ammonium phosphate.

14.6.1 Valuation of a transformation plant using a real options approach

In the following subsections we will start with some general considerations on the use of real options in the world of commodities.

Validity of the real options approach
There are a few necessary conditions that need to be satisfied for the real options approach to be legitimate:

1. The option must have a clear starting date and maturity T.
2. The underlying sources of risk S_1, S_2 or more must be clearly identified (or more).
3. One should be able to exhibit appropriate stochastic processes for the evolution over time of $S_1(t)$ and $S_2(t)$, in particular because data series of past values are available.

4. The type of option must be recognized: European, versus American, versus exchange or compound[1] option, since it will obviously impact the price obtained for the physical asset. In practice, this choice is rarely unique and one will make a compromise between the tractability and accuracy of the representation.
5. The processes identified for S_1 and S_2 should not be too complicated, leading to a situation where the hedging strategy for the physical asset is easy to understand and implement.

Valuation of a transformation plant as a portfolio of spread options

Splitting the estimated lifetime of the transformation plant into N subperiods (years, semesters or quarters), we can state by replication arguments that the value of the plant at time 0 is

$$V(0)=\sum_{j=1}^{N}C^j(0)$$

Each spread option j has a payoff:

$$C^j(j) = \text{Max}(0, Q_1 S_1(j) - Q_2 S_2(j) - O\&M_j)$$

If the operation and maintenance costs are perceived as very small compared to the costs/selling prices of the input and output, the spread reduces to an exchange option. We have seen in Chapter 6 that the price at date 0 (or any t prior to maturity) of a commodity exchange option does *not* (cf. Margrabe's formula, 1978) include any interest rate, risk-free or risky or weighted average cost of capital (WACC), which is a beautiful property compared to the discounted cash flow (DCF) approach discussed below. The value of the option – and the transformation plant – resides in the *relative* price of soy oil versus soybean. Interest rates, which are usually present everywhere in finance since they convey the time value of money, play no role here since there is a kind of *barter* process between the input and the output, except that a plant is necessary for the process to take place. Mathematically, the right *numéraire* at any time (see Geman *et al.* (1995)) is the price of the input.

In practice, the valuation of the transformation plant will involve a mixture of positions in forward contracts to secure future revenues while keeping a fraction of the capacity available as options to benefit from periods of high prices.

14.6.2 DCF approach to the valuation of a transformation plant

The other way to proceed is to return to the fundamental lessons of corporate finance and use the discounted cash flow (DCF) approach, leading to write the plant value V at the date 0 of analysis as:

$$V(0) = \frac{E(\tilde{\phi}_1)}{1+r^a} + \cdots\cdots + \frac{E(\tilde{\phi}_n)}{(1+r^a)^n}$$

---

[1] A compound option is an option written on an option.

where:

> n is the number of years the plant is supposed to be operating in the future before being obsolete;

> $E(\tilde{\phi}_j)$ denotes the estimated profits to be made from operating the plant in year j: leaving aside the taxes and amortization schemes, the benefits will be the revenues from selling the output minus the cost of raw material (and energy) and the payment of operation and maintenance (O&M) costs;

> r^a is a crucial quantity, namely the proper *discount rate* to apply to the project. Obviously, the use of a discount rate of 4% versus 8% will drastically shift the estimated value.

The value of the discount factor will be the WACC if the buyer of the transformation plant is a corporation financed with debt and equity.

The discount factor will be the *opportunity cost of capital* for a private equity that can employ its capital in other projects; or for the government of a developing country that has alternative projects on its agenda.

Lastly, it may be estimated as the expected return in the corresponding industry through the Capital Asset Pricing Model (CAPM):

$$r^a = r_f + \beta(E(\tilde{r}_m) - r_f)$$

where r_f is the risk-free rate; β is the one of the industry sector (its definition was recalled in Chapter 12) and it multiplies the expected market return over the 'risk-free rate' (represented as the return on money-market instruments).

We now turn to the identification of the numerators. The expectation

$$E(\tilde{\phi}_j) \quad \text{for} \quad j = 1, \dots, n$$

of the profits generated in the future

$$\tilde{\phi}_1, \dots \tilde{\phi}_n$$

where:

$$\tilde{\phi}_j = Q_j \tilde{S}_1(j) - Q'_j \tilde{S}_2(j) - (O \& M \text{ costs})_j$$

> Q_j is the production of output in year j (in tonnes, for instance);

> Q'_j is the quantity of raw material consumed for that output;

> $\tilde{S}_1(j)$ is the average selling price of the output in year j;

> $\tilde{S}_2(j)$ is the average purchase price/extraction cost of the raw material;

> $(O \& M \text{ costs})_j$ denotes the operation and maintenance costs in year j.

A great solution is offered for the computation of the expectation if there exist liquid forward markets both for the output and the input as they are providing the expectations of the prices under the 'pricing measure.' Since O&M costs do not vary too much over time and can be adjusted in a deterministic manner, in particular to adjust to inflation, we can write the expected revenues in year j as:

$$E(\tilde{\phi}_j) = Q_1 F_1^j(0) - Q_2 F_2^j(0) - (0 \& M \text{ costs})_j$$

where the two forward prices $F_1^j(0)$ and $F_2^j(0)$ can be currently *locked in* the forward markets (if the expectation of profits is positive). Now, the cash flows attached to the transformation plant are not random any more – as long as there is no counterparty risk – and the discount factor r^a can be reasonably approximated by the cost of capital of the acquiring company.

Comments

1. Obviously, the value of the transformation plant obtained with the second method will be lower since the owner won't be able any longer to benefit from spikes in the output, or periods of low prices of the input, as both sales and purchases are locked in at date 0 in the forward market; in the real options approach, all market optionalities/opportunities are available as time goes by.

   In practice, the acquiring party will sell (buy) part of his output (input) in the forward market, let's say 80% and will keep the rest available to benefit from higher prices of the output due to some weather events in corn markets and larger demand in fertilizers, for instance. Since the 'hedging' strategy must reflect the pricing of the plant, he will bid a number equal to the weighted average of the values above, with the weights 0.8 and 0.2.

2. The beauty of the commodities space is that both approaches are quite valid and *accurate*. In the case of the valuation of a startup, for instance, we do not have a liquid forward market where we can lock in the values of expected cash flows.

3. It is also quite interesting to observe how, in our analysis, the two subclasses of derivatives – forwards and options – can be used to obtain two different but deeply *complementary* results.

14.6.3 Valuation of a silo (or an aquifer, or any storage facility)

We discussed in Chapter 3 the benefits of inventory as a buffer against unexpected changes in supply and demand. In a more precise manner, we can recognize that the ownership of a vast silo allows one to store the grains after a very good harvest, when grains are abundant and purchase prices low, and extract the grains to send them to the markets at moments when prices are higher. Note that these calendar spread options may be complemented by options to substitute corn with wheat in the silo (exchange options), illuminating the fact that there is not a unique price obtained for a physical asset with the method of real options – a result in agreement with the trading strategy that will be adopted by the specific buyer of the storage facility.

The same representation prevails for an aquifer located in a region where mining activities compete for water with farming activities and droughts may be severe (Brazil being a good example).

Such a storage facility may be quite useful to take advantage of the spread winter/summer if there is seasonality in the prices of the relevant commodity; or the possible price differences between two consecutive agriculture years.

Considering the commodity to be stored in the facility under analysis, we see that the storage facility may be viewed as a portfolio of options on a seasonal spread that we know how to price using the results of Chapter 5, leading to a first valuation of the storage facility (which may be acquired or leased, obviously). Other optionalities may also exist in the form of several location deliveries.

Besides the 'real options' approach, we can proceed with the DCF approach discussed above, and again propose in practice both methods when quoting a purchase/leasing price and implementing the subsequent trading strategy.

Lastly, in a world where water will be traded and priced, which should be soon, the aquifer will be represented as the ownership of a swing option, where on any day one has to decide how much to deliver – under a volumetric constraint over the period between injection and withdrawal. The (complex) valuation of this swing option has been vastly studied over the last 15 years in the context of a gas storage facility.

In the case of a silo where we identify successive seasons or agriculture years across which prices will be different, we can propose as a valuation the sum of discounted expected revenues under an optimal strategy over all possible future trajectories of the gas price process:

$$V(0) = \underset{C}{\text{Max}} \ E \left[\sum_{t=1}^{T} (L_t - L_{t+1}) S(t) e^{-rt} \right]$$

where:

L_t denotes the inventory level;

$L_t - L_{t+1}$ represents the change in inventory between dates t and $t + 1$;

$S(t)$ is the market price of corn at date t;

C denotes the constraints related to the storage capacity, its volume at the beginning and at the end of the operating period, such as a non-negative volume at any time and a half-full (or empty) storage at the end.

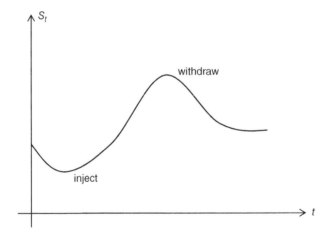

The most elementary strategy consists in using the current forward curve, in particular if we have several years of liquid maturities, to find the optimal portfolio of long and short forward contracts attached to injections and withdrawals of corn. The corresponding value is the *intrinsic value* of the storage facility, i.e., the one that can be locked in ahead of time in a non-dynamic way. Like in the case of the transformation plant, one should not destroy all optionalities attached to the physical asset by committing all volumes in and out in the forward market and keep part of them to benefit from swift changes in the spot market. As time goes by, this intrinsic value can be dynamically adjusted over the remaining period using again the forward market. Or a pure option strategy – in the form of a fully dynamic swing option – can be implemented for part of the volume starting at the acquisition of the physical asset.

14.7 CONCLUSION

The International Monetary Fund and the World Bank produced in November 2014 a study suggesting the possible end of the so-called period of hyperglobalization during which international trade grew twice faster than the world economy. According to the authors, this effect is not a momentary consequence of the 2008 financial crisis, but rather a new norm due to a tepid growth in western economies and the multiplication of factories and production lines within China.

These interesting points do not conflict with our view that, in parallel, the established actors (and some new ones, Chinese in particular) in the space of agricultural commodities are embracing all new technologies in the logistics of their activities in order to benefit from all possible 'locational arbitrage' opportunities around the world; and competing for the acquisition of additional physical assets to extend their profits to the entirety of the supply chain.

Glossary

Acre 0.4046 hectare

American option An option that can be exercised any day prior to or at maturity. Most exchange-traded options are American. A standard corn Futures option on the CME for instance is written on a Future contract of a specific maturity. The option exercise results in a Future market position

Asian option This option can only be exercised at maturity but the underlying is an average of the spot (or specific Future) over the lifetime (or a subinterval of it) of the option

Ask The level at which sellers are willing to sell

At-the-money An option whose strike is the current market price of the underlying

Backwardation A forward curve is backwardated when forward prices decrease with the maturity of the contract

Barge A small vessel used to carry commodities along a river or a canal; barges vary in capacity, usually from 1000 to 5000 tonnes

Basis risk The risk that a Future contract used as a hedge will not move in line with the underlying exposure. Basis risk may be related to a location, quality, type or calendar gap

Bill of lading (B/L) A legal document issued by a carrier or its agent to the shipper as a contract of carriage of goods. It is also a receipt for cargo accepted for transportation

Book The set of spot and derivative positions held by a trader or a desk

Bunker fuel A crude oil distillate used in vessels

Bushel There are 60 pounds in a bushel. CBOT corn and wheat Futures involve 5000 bushels of the cereal

Calendar spreads These are options on the price differential between two Futures contracts of different maturities; examples are corn, wheat, and soybeans

Carry arbitrage A strategy whereby a trader takes advantage of a steep contango of the forward curve by selling a Future contract, buying and storing the physical commodity, and making a riskless profit at maturity of the Future when delivering the commodity

CAT coverage Purchase of an insurance contract against catastrophic events

Chicago Mercantile Exchange (CME) Established in 1898 as the Chicago Butter and Egg Board, it became the CME in 1919

CIF Index The cost of insurance and freight to a named destination is included in the index, meaning that the seller takes responsibility for shipping and freight insurance. The buyer, however, must assume the charges of getting the commodity into his warehouse

Clearing House An entity, in general part of the exchange, that settles transactions executed on the floor, collects the margin deposits and margin calls, and oversees the delivery procedures for positions not liquidated prior to maturity

Convenience yield The yield accruing to the owner of a physical commodity, but not the holder of a contract for future delivery. It represents the benefit of having the physical good immediately available

Corn Futures Main exchange = CBOT; Futures maturities: March, May, July, September, December; 5000 bushels per contract

Crop revenue insurance Purchase of insurance against the event of realized revenues going below a predefined level

Crop yield insurance Purchase of insurance against the event of realized yield going below a predefined level

Cross-commodity options Options on the spread between commodities; for instance, CME wheat/corn spreads, or soybean to corn price ratio options

Delivery month The month in which a Futures contract matures and settles by physical delivery (if no further specification); also known as the contract month

Delta Sensitivity of an option to changes in the underlying, or partial derivative of the option price with respect to the underlying

Dynamic hedging Hedging an option position by buying or selling the underlying in an amount equal to the option delta (or in a more sophisticated way) and monitoring the hedge over time

Elevator A large facility allowing the farmer(s) to store and dry grains, with compartmented interior and different levels; also the device for loading grains into the facility

European option An option that may only be exercised at maturity, in contrast to an American option

Exchange for physical (EFP) A private transaction between two parties in which a Futures contract on a commodity is exchanged for the actual physical good

Feedstock The food for animals, or the raw material used in a processing unit (sugar cane is a feedstock for ethanol production in Brazil)

Forward contract An over the counter agreement between two parties on the purchase/ sale of a commodity for a specified future delivery at a price defined at inception of the contract

Forward freight agreement A forward contract in the shipping market related to an index and a route or a time period and financially settled at maturity. It is used to hedge risk in the shipping sector, like FRAs are used in the domain of interest rates

Forward pricing Agreeing on a price or pricing formula for later delivery

Free on board (FOB) index The index does not include the cost of insurance and freight, which will be paid by the buyer of the good whose vessel needs to lift the good on board

Futures contract A forward contract, standardized in terms of size and maturity, where the exchange is the counterparty for the buyer and a seller

Hedging The act of eliminating randomness in the revenues of a harvest or the costs of purchase of agricultural commodities for an agrifood company

Historical volatility The annualized standard deviation of historical returns over a specific period; an indication of past market volatility

Implied volatility The volatility value derived from market prices of options on Futures by inversion of the Black formula (definition applicable to agrimarkets). An indication of future market volatility and risk aversion of options' sellers

Index A reference number that represents the commodity price in a given region. It may be an estimate quoted by an independent information provider or an average of prices (freight rates). In all cases, a reliable and transparent index is necessary for the existence of derivative transactions. Alternatively, an index may represent a basket of commodities and is proposed by banks or financial institutions as an investment vehicle

Inventory Amount of commodity in storage available for immediate consumption or transportation

Leverage Use of borrowed funds to increase a farm's revenues

Live cattle Futures Main exchanges = CME and BM&F Bovespa; CME maturities: every other month starting in February; BM&F Bovespa available maturities as of June 2014: July, August, September, October, November, and May 2015

Margin call Payment to be made to the exchange on a daily basis to adjust for a loss in a derivative position and keep one's account value above the maintenance margin

Margin deposit A deposit of money or Treasury bills to be made to the exchange prior to taking a long or short position in a Future, swap or option traded on the exchange

Market risk Commodity price risk and volatility of price; fertilizer and seeds price volatility; interest rates volatility; exchange rates – against the dollar in particular – volatility; counterparty risk affecting the farm income

Mark-to-market To mark-to-market is to compute the value of an instrument or a portfolio of spot and derivative positions from currently observed market prices of spot and forward prices of the underlying(s)

Monte-Carlo simulations for derivatives valuation A method that provides the price of a derivative by simulating a large number of trajectories of the underlying variable (or vector of variables), according to a model that has been specified under the pricing probability measure. Averaging (and discounting) the payoffs gives an approximation of the derivative price

Multi-factor model A model in which a number of state variables (or factors) are driving the dynamics of the spot price or the forward curve evolution

Production risk Weather events (droughts, floods, frost, heat waves); disease outbreaks; bush fires are major risks that lead to price volatility

Real option An optionality related to the ownership of a physical asset; hence, the terminology 'real options' approach to the valuation of physical assets

Risk transfer Passing risk to a third party through a financial contract or an insurance premium; hedging and commercial insurance are the usual forms of risk transfer in agricultural markets

Speculation The activity of taking risk exposure in order to make profits

Speculator In commodity markets, this refers to any actor who does not deal with the physical commodity but takes financial positions that he expects to profit from

Spot The term spot (or cash) refers to a good that is available for immediate delivery, at a price called the spot price

Spot market The market for immediate delivery

Standard deviation The most popular measure of the dispersion of a random variable around its expected value, defined as the square root of the mean-centered second moment

Theta Partial derivative of the option price with respect to time; measures the speed of the time decay of the option price

USDA US Department of Agriculture

Vanilla option A standard European call or put

Vega Partial derivative of the option price with respect to volatility

Wheat Futures Main exchanges = CBOT, KCBT; Maturities: March, May, July, September, December

References

Ané, T. and H. Geman (2000) Order flow, transaction clock and normality of asset returns, *Journal of Finance* 55, 2259–2285

Bachelier, L. (1900) Théorie de la spéculation, *Annales Scientifiques de l'Ecole Normale Supérieure* 17, 21–85

Bai, J. (1997) Estimation of a change point in multiple regression models, *Review of Economics and Statistics* 79, 551–563

Bessembinder, H., J.F. Coughenour, P.J. Seguin, and S.M. Smoller (1995) Mean reversion in equilibrium asset prices: evidence from the Futures term structure, *Journal of Finance* 50(1), 361–375

Black, F. (1976) The pricing of commodity contracts, *Journal of Financial Economics* 3, 167–180

Black, F. and M. Scholes (1973) The pricing of options and corporate liabilities, *Journal of Political Economy* 81, 637–659

Borovkova, S. and H. Geman (2006) Seasonal and stochastic effects in energy commodity forward curves, *Review of Derivatives Research* 9, 167–186

Box, G. (2010) *An Accidental Statitician: The Life and Memories of George E.P. Box*, John Wiley & Sons

Brennan, M.J. (1958) The supply of storage, *American Economic Review* 48, 50–72

Brennan, M.J. (1959) A model of seasonal inventories, *Econometrica* 27, 228–244

Brennan, M.J. and E.S. Schwartz (1985) Evaluating natural resource investments, *The Journal of Business* 58, 2

Carr, P., H. Geman and D. Madan (1999) Pricing and hedging in incomplete markets, *Journal of Financial Economics* 62, 131–169

Chambers, M.J. and R.E. Bailey (1996) A theory of commodity price fluctuations, *Journal of Political Economy* 104(5), 924–957

Clemmons, L., V. Kaminski, and J. Hergovcic (1999) Weather derivatives: hedging Mother Nature. In H. Geman, ed. *Insurance and Weather Derivatives*, RISK Books

Cootner, P. (1960) Returns to speculators: Telser versus Keynes, *Journal of Political Economy* 68, 396–404

Cox, J.C., J.E. Ingersoll, and S.A. Ross (1981) The relation between forward prices and Futures prices, *Journal of Financial Economics* 9, 321–346

Dana, J. and C. Gilbert (2008) Risk management in agricultural commodities. In Geman, H., ed. *Risk Management in Commodity Markets*, Wiley Finance

Deaton, A. and G. Laroque (1992) On the behaviour of commodity prices, *Review of Economic Studies* 59, 1–23

Declerck, F. (2004) *Où va le Cycle du Champagne?*, Ed. Ceressec

Derman, E. and I. Kani (1994) Riding on a smile, *RISK*, January

Dishel, R. (1999) A weather risk management choice: hedging with degree-day derivatives. In *Insurance and Weather Derivatives*, RISK Books

Dupire, B. (1994) Pricing with a smile, *RISK*, January

Edwards, F. and C. Ma (1992) *Futures and Options*, McGraw-Hill

Eydeland, A. and H. Geman (1995) Asian options revisited: inverting the Laplace transform, *RISK*, March

Fama, E.F. and K.R. French (1987) Commodity Futures prices: some evidence on forecast power, premiums and the theory of storage, *Journal of Business* 60, 55–74

FAO Report (2002) Food and Agriculture Organization of the United Nations

FAO Report (2010) Food and Agriculture Organization of the United Nations

FAO Report (2011) Food and Agriculture Organization of the United Nations

Gay, G. and S. Manaster (1986) Implicit delivery options and optimal delivery strategies for financial Futures contracts, *Journal of Financial Economics* 16, 41–73

Geman, H. (1989) The importance of the forward neutral probability measure for the valuation of derivatives under stochastic interest rates, ESSEC Working Paper

Geman, H. (1999) *Insurance and Weather Derivatives*, RISK Books

Geman, H. (2000) Scarcity and the shape of the forward curve, *Bachelier World Congress Proceedings – Collège de France*

Geman, H. (2002) Pure Jump Lévy Processes for asset price modelling, *Journal of Banking and Finance* 1297–1316

Geman, H. (2005) Commodity prices: is mean-reversion dead? *Journal of Alternative Investments* 8, 31–45

Geman, H. (2005) *Commodities and Commodity Derivatives: Energy, Metals and Agriculturals*. Wiley Finance

Geman, H. (2011) Volatility in agricultural markets: speculation or scarcity? *Swiss Derivatives Review*

Geman, H. and G. Martin (2011) Understanding farmland investment as part of a diversified portfolio: an analysis of farmland in the United States and Brazil, *Bunge Technical Report*

Geman, H. and A. Kanyinda (2006) Water as the next commodity, *Journal of Alternative Investments* 10(2), 22–30

Geman, H, N. El Karoui, and J.-C. Rochet (1995) Changes of numéraire, changes of probability measure and option pricing, *Journal of Applied Probability* 32, 443–458

Geman, H. and M.P. Leonardi (2005) Alternative approaches to weather derivatives valuation, *Managerial Finance* 31(6), 46–72

Geman, H. and B. Liu (2013) Are natural gas markets moving toward integration: evidence from the HH, NBP and JKM indexes, forthcoming in the *Journal of Energy Markets*

Geman, H. and V.N. Nguyen (2005) Soybean inventory and forward curves dynamics, *Management Science* 51(7), 1076–1091

Geman, H. and S. Ohana (2009) Spread of the forward curve and inventories in the US crude oil and natural gas markets, *Energy Economics*

Geman, H. and A. Roncoroni (2006) Understanding the fine structure of electricity prices, *The Journal of Business* 79(3), 1225–1261

Geman, H. and S. Sarfo (2012) Seasonality in cocoa spot and forward markets: empirical evidence, *Journal of Agricultural Extension and Rural Development* 4(8), 164–180

Geman, H. and W. Smith (2012) Theory of storage and inventories in base metals, *Resources Policy*

Geman, H. and O. Vasicek (2001) Forwards and Futures on non-storable commodities: the case of electricity, *RISK*, August

Geman, H. and P. Vergel (2013) Investing in fertilizer companies in times of food scarcity, *Resources Policy* 38(4), 470–480

Geman, H. and M. Yor (1992) Processus de Bessel, options asiatiques et fonctions confluentes hypergéométriques, *Note aux Comptes Rendus de l'Académie des Sciences*

Geman, H. and M. Yor (1993) Bessel processes, Asian options and perpetuities, *Mathematical Finance* 4(3), 349–375

Gibson, R. and E.S. Schwartz (1990) Stochastic convenience yield and the pricing of oil contingent claims, *Journal of Finance* 45, 959–976

Gladstone, J. (1965) The climates and soils of South-Western Australia in relation to grape growing, *Journal of Australian Institutional Agricultural Science* 31

Glasserman, P. (2000) *Monte Carlo Methods in Financial Engineering*, Springer

Grandmill, W. (1991) *Investing in Wheat, Corn and Soybeans*, Probus Financial Publishing

Grossman, S.J. (1977) The existence of Futures markets, noisy rational expectations and informational externalities, *Review of Economic Studies* 44, 431–449

Halvorsen, R. and T.R. Smith (1991) A test of the theory of exhaustible resources, *The Quarterly Journal of Economics* 106, 123–140

Hertel, T.W. (2011) The global supply and demand for land in 2050: a perfect storm? *American Journal of Agricultural Economics* 93(2), 259–275

Hess, D., H. Huang and A. Niessen-Ruenzi (2008) How do commodity Futures respond to macroeconomic news? *Financial Markets and Portfolio Management* 22, 2

Heston, S.L. (1993) A closed-form solution for options with stochastic volatility with applications to bond and currency options, *Review of Financial Studies* 6(2), 327–343

Hotelling, H. (1931) The economics of exhaustible resources, *Journal of Political Economy* 39, 137–212

Jacks, D.S (2007) Populists versus theorists: Futures markets and the volatility of prices, *Explorations in Economic History* 44, 342–362

Jarrow, R. (1987) The pricing of commodity options with stochastic interest rates, *Advances in Options and Futures Research* 2

Kaldor, N. (1939) Speculation and economic stability, *The Review of Economic Studies* 7, 1–27

Kavussanos, M. and N. Nomikos (2003) Price discovery, causality and forecasting in the freight Futures market, *Review of Derivatives Research* 6(3), 203–230

Kemna, A. and T. Vorst (1990) A pricing method for options based on average asset values, *Journal of Banking and Finance* 14, 113–130

Keynes, J.M (1930) *The Applied Theory of Money*, Macmillan & Co., London

Khan, H. (2013) Estimating elasticities of demand and willingness to pay for clean drinking water: evidence from a household survey in northern Pakistan, *Water and Environment Journal*

Kirk, E. (1995) Correlation in the energy markets. In *Managing Energy Price Risk*, Risk Publications, London

Kleinman, G. (2001) *Commodity Futures and Options: A Step-by-Step Guide to Successful Trading*, Prentice Hall

Lowry, M., J. Glauber, M. Miranda, and P. Helmberger (1987) Pricing and storage of field crops: a quarterly model applied to soybeans, *Journal of Agricultural Economics* 69, 740–774

Malthus, T. (1798) *An Essay on the Principle of Population*, J. Johnson Publisher, London

Margrabe, W. (1978) The value of an option to exchange one asset for another, *Journal of Finance* 33, 177–187

Martin, G. (2013) Opportunities in agriculture infrastructure, Wood Creek Capital Management Report

Mazieres, D., H. Geman, and S. Hubbert (2014) A tensor of radial basis functions for swing contracts valuation and hedging in high dimension, Birkbeck Working Paper

McKean, H. (1965) Appendix: a free boundary problem for the heat equation arising from a problem in mathematical economics, *Industrial Management Review* 6 (Spring), 32–39

Meadows, M.E. (2004) Land degradation and development: geographical perspectives, *Land Degradation and Development*, 15

Merton, R. (1973) The theory of rational option pricing, *Bell Journal of Economics and Management Science* 4, 141–183

Metropolis, N., A. Rosenbluth, M. Rosenbluth, A. Teller, and E. Teller (1953) Equation of state calculations by fast computing machines, *Journal of Chemical Physics* 21, 1087–1092

Pindyck, R. (1994) Inventories and the short-run dynamics of commodity prices, *Rand Journal of Economics* 25(1), 141–159

Pindyck, R. (2001) The dynamics of commodity spot and Futures markets: a primer, *Energy Journal* 22(3), 1–29

Reagan, P.B. (1982) Inventory and price behavior, *Review of Economic Studies* 49, 137–142

Roll, R. (1984) Orange juice and weather, *The American Economic Review* 74, 5

Samuelson, P. (1965a) Proof that properly anticipated prices fluctuate randomly, *Industrial Management Review* 6, 41–49

Samuelson, P. (1965b) Rational theory of warrant pricing, *Industrial Management Review* 6 (Spring), 13–31

Scheinkman, J. and J. Schechtman (1983) A simple competitive model with production and storage, *Review of Economics Studies* 50, 427–441

Schneeweis, T. and R. Spurgin (1997) Comparisons of commodity and managed Futures benchmark indexes, *Journal of Derivatives* 4(4), 33–50

Schwartz, E.S. (1997) The stochastic behavior of commodity prices: implications for valuation and hedging, *Journal of Finance* 52(3), 923–973

Shah, J. and B. Rath (2009) *Roots of Commodity Trade in India*, Takshashila Academia of Economic Research

Slade, M.E. (1982) Trends in natural-resource commodity prices: an analysis in the time domain, *Journal of Environmental Economics and Management* 9, 122–159

Sorensen, C. (2002) Modeling Seasonality in Agricultural Commodity Futures, *Journal of Futures Markets,* 22(5), 393-426

Stewart, W.M., D.W. Dibb, A.E. Johnston, and T.J. Smyth (2005) The contribution of commercial fertilizer nutrients to food production, *Agronomy Journal* 97, 1–6

Stopford, M. (2008) *Maritime Economics*, 3rd edition, Routledge

Taleb, N. (1998) *Dynamic Hedging*, Wiley Finance

Telser, L.G. (1958) Futures trading and the storage of cotton and wheat, *Journal of Political Economy* 66, 233–255

Till, H. (2006) Separating the wheat from the chaff: backwardation as the long-term driver of commodity Futures performance. In *Advanced Topics in Performance Measurement*, RISK Books

Till, H. (2008) Case studies and risk management in commodity derivatives trading. In Geman, H., ed. *Risk Management in Commodity Markets*, Wiley Finance

Tufano, P. (2002) The determinants of stock price exposure: financial engineering and the gold mining industry, *The Journal of Finance* 53, 3

Waggle, D. and D.T. Johnson (2009) An analysis of the impact of timberland, farmland and commercial real estate in the asset allocation decisions of institutional investors, *Review of Financial Economics* 18

Williams, J.C. (1986) *The Economic Function of Futures Markets*, Cambridge University Press

Williams, J.C. and B.D. Wright (1991) *Storage and Commodity Markets*, Cambridge University Press

Working, H. (1948) Theory of the inverse carrying charge in Futures markets, *Journal Farm Economics* 30, 1–28

Working, H. (1949) The theory of the price of storage, *American Economic Review* 39, 1254–1262

Working, H. (1953) Futures trading and hedging, *American Economic Review* 43, 314–343

Index

accumulators 89, 92–93
acidity, orange juice 166
acquisitions *see* mergers and acquisitions
acreage 25, 26
ADM *see* Archer Daniels Midland
Africa
    fertilizers 189
    financial agricultural markets 2–3
    infrastructure 221–222
    sorghum 129–131
Agricultural Transformation Agenda (ATA)
        222
American Farm Bureau 223
ammonia 189
aquifer valuations 245–246
Arabica coffee 146, 147,
        148
arable land 240
arbitrage 12, 49
Archer Daniels Midland (ADM) 3, 5, 124,
        146, 184
Argentina 124, 167
Arla Foods 172
Asia 18–21
    see also China
Asian options 89, 95–102
    cocoa 144

    floating-strike 102
    valuation 95–102
assets 59, 197–198, 233, 242–246
ATA *see* Agricultural Transformation
        Agenda
Australia
    cattle farming 171, 225
    iron ore mining 225
    sugar 139
    timber and wood 156
    water 208
    weather 230
    wool 162–163
average annualized volatilities 29
AWEX-Eastern Market Indicator 162

Bachelier models 54
Bachelier–Black–Scholes formula 59,
        66–75
backwardation 48–49, 101, 117, 238
Baltic indices 18–23
bananas 226
Bangkok 128, 178
bank notes 161–162
bans on exports 211, 212
barter schemes 11–12, 103
Batista brothers 224

Bayes Information Criterion (BIC) 29
BCI *see* Capesize Index
BDI *see* Dry Index
bear calendar spreads 53–54
beets, sugar 133–134
benchmark-based pricing mechanisms 16
BFI *see* Freight Index
BHKP indices 159, 160, 161
BIC *see* Bayes Information Criterion
biofuels/biomass 177, 183–186
Black formula 59, 78–79
Blackstone 4
Black–Scholes formula 66–75, 94–95,
    96–97, 110, 230–231
Black–Scholes–Merton models 54, 103
bonds, commodity-linked 239
boneless beef 171
bovine spongiform encephalopathy (BSE)
    170
BPI *see* Panamax Index
Brazil
    Arabica coffee 147, 148
    ethanol 184, 224–225
    financial agricultural markets 2
    futures exchanges 53
    natural gas 224–225
    orange juice 165, 166
    railways 224–225
    soybeans 123–125
    sugar 135, 137
    sugar biofactories 224
    water 208–209
    weather 2229
Brennan, M.J. 47–48
Bright Food 3
'brix', orange juice 166
brokerage houses 13
Bruges, Belgium 1

BSE *see* bovine spongiform
    encephalopathy
BSI *see* Supramax Index
Bunge 6–7
Bursa Malaysia Berhad 182
business pricing 231
butterfly spread 64

Cailler, Louis-François 140–141
calendar spread options 89, 93–95
call spread 63
calls and puts 62–64, 66–75
calves 167
Canada 157, 213
cane, sugar 133–134, 140, 184
CAP *see* Common Agricultural Policy
Capesize Index (BCI) 18, 21
capital 197–198, 243, 244
Capital Asset Pricing Model (CAPM)
    197–198, 244
Cargill 3, 5, 146
Caribbean 133, 134, 135, 137
Caribou Coffee 4
carry-over 26
cash and carry arbitrage 49
cash flow (DCF) 243–245
cashmere 163–164
cattle 88, 168–169, 225
CBOT *see* Chicago Board of Trade
CDD *see* cooling degree days
cement 179
Centro de Tecnologia Canavieira (CTC)
    224
Cereal International Council 128
Cereals Council 27
cheapest to deliver options 44
Chicago Board of Trade (CBOT) 14–16
    corn 116

futures exchanges 40, 46, 47, 53
   rice 127
   soybeans 123, 126
   wheat 118, 119, 121
Chicago Mercantile Exchange (CME)
   futures trading 213–214
   livestock 88, 167
   rice 127
   soybeans 126
   timber and wood 158
   weather derivatives 231
chickens 174–175
China
   barter schemes 11–12
   commodities markets 3
   dairy 172–173
   fertilizers 189
   food needs 214–216
   income by age 215
   livestock 171
   meat consumption 190
   plastic bank notes 161–162
   pulp and paper 160–161
   rice 126–128
   shipping and freight 19–22
   sugar 135–136, 138
   timber and wood 156
   water 208
China National Cereals, Oil and Foodstuffs
   Corp. (Cofco) 3, 8
China on the Zhengzhou Commodity
   Exchange (CZCE) 135
Cholesky decomposition 108
clear-cutting 158
climate change 219
Climate Corporation 223
CMCI *see* Constant Maturity Commodity
   Index

CME *see* Chicago Mercantile Exchange
Coca-Cola 2
cocoa 133, 140–146
coconut oil 184–186
coefficients of variation 33–36
coffee 3–4, 133, 146–149, 150
Coffee America 3
cold storage reports on cattle 168
Colombo tea auctions 150
commodities
   actors 13
   containers 226
   equity investments 239–240
   exchanges 13, 39–40, 48
   exposure 233–235
   futures 12–17, 49, 78–79, 86–88
   global flows 10–11
   mergers and acquisitions 3–4
   numéraire 17
   outlook 3–12
   purchase of 233–236
   spot markets/prices 16, 25–38, 59–88
   structured product purchases 235–236
   sugar 134
   swaps 89–92
Common Agricultural Policy (CAP) 136,
   212
competition for resources 188, 209
conservation tillage 154
Constant Maturity Commodity Index
   (CMCI) 238
consumers 13
containers for agricultural commodities
   226
contango 49, 50, 116, 122, 147
contracts
   cotton 153
   definitions 41–44

contracts (*continued*)
  fish markets 173
  futures exchanges 41–45, 54
  linear instruments 42
  live cattle 170
  maturity 53–54
  OTC 41
  risk premiums 43
  speculators 42
  sugar 135–136
convenience yields 52
cooling degree days (CDD) 231
copper price trajectory decoupling 23
corn 113–118
  backwardation 50
  coefficients of variation 33–36
  ethanol 183–184
  export shares 37
  fertilizers 193
  price deviations 33–36
  quasi-contemporaneous effects 34
  spot markets 28–34
  stocks-to-use ratios 37, 38
  volatility smile 87
Corn Index (NCI) 114
Cosan 224
cotton 153–156
country risk 217
coupons 239
cow milking 225
Crinipellis perniciosa 143
crush spread 47
CTC *see* Centro de Tecnologia Canavieira
Cuba 139
CZCE *see* China on the Zhengzhou Com-
    modity Exchange

dairy 165, 172–173, 225
Dana report 13
DAP *see* di-ammonium phosphate

Data Transmission Network (DTN) 115
DCF *see* discounted cash flow
Degas, Edgar 154
delta options 71–72
demand in price formation 25, 26
Denmark 174
Deutsche Bank commodity indices 238
di-ammonium phosphate (DAP) 192–193,
    194, 227
diesel 184
digital technology 217, 222–224
disaccharides 133
discounted cash flow (DCF) 243–245, 246
dividend-paying stocks, Merton formula
    75–76
Dow-Jones UBS Commodity Index 196,
    237
Drax power station 157–158
Dry Index (BDI) 19–23
dry tape irrigation 154
DTN *see* Data Transmission Network
Dutch disease 222
dynamic hedging 230

EFP *see* exchange of futures for physicals
eggs 175
Elaeis guineensis 180–183
electronic trading 114–115
energy 208, 209, 227
equity 83–86, 239–240
erosion 187–189
ETCs *see* Exchange Traded Certificates
ETFs *see* Exchange Traded Funds
ethanol 183–186, 224–225
ETNs *see* Exchange Traded Notes
EU *see* European Union
Euronext 39–40
Europe
  calls and puts 62–64, 66–75
  ports sugar prices 137

subsidies 212
timber and wood 156–158
weather derivatives 231
European Union (EU) 136, 184
exchange of futures for physicals (EFP)
    44–45
exchange options 103–105
Exchange Traded Certificates (ETCs) 136
Exchange Traded Funds (ETFs) 40, 136,
    157
Exchange Traded Notes (ETNs) 136
export bans 211, 212
export crop shares 37

factor models 198–207
FAO *see* Food and Agriculture
        Organization
FCOJ *see* frozen concentrate orange juice
feeder cattle market 169
fertilizers 29–34, 187, 189–207
FFAs *see* forward freight agreements
fiber diameter, wool 163
financial risk 217
first nearby prices 44, 46, 47
    Arabica coffee 147
    cocoa 141
    corn 115
    cotton 156
    ethanol 185
    palm oil 183
    rice 127
    rubber 179
    soybeans 124, 126
    sugar 135
    timber and wood 158
fish markets 165, 173–174
fleece weight, wool 163
floating-strike Asian options
        102
Florida 165–166, 229–230

Food and Agriculture Organization (FAO)
        11
    fertilizers 189
    fish markets 174
    future of agriculture 209,
        210
    sugar 136
Food Price Index 9, 10
forward contracts 41–43, 54,
        173
forward curves 39, 43, 46, 47
    Asian options 97–98, 101
    benefits 52–54
    cocoa 142, 145
    corn 116, 117
    floating-strike Asian options 101–102
    ICE coffee 147
    spread options 106
    stochastic modeling 55–57
    sugar 140
    theory of storage 47–48
    wheat 122
forward freight agreements (FFAs) 21–22
forward prices 39, 59–88
forward volatility 107
forward-start options 89, 93–95,
        106
Fourier transform 100
France 172, 173, 230
freight *see* shipping and freight
Freight Index (BFI) 18
frozen concentrate orange juice (FCOJ)
        165–166
fruit 165–166, 226, 229
fuel 183–186
furrow irrigation 154
futures 12–17, 39–57
    commodity purchases 233–235
    cotton 153
    grain cereals, corn 114–118

futures (*continued*)
    growth 14–15
    implied volatility 86–88
    Kansas City 213
    options 78–79
    price volatility 15–16
    zero strike calendars spreads 105–106
FX commodity markets 95

Gabon 221–222
gamma options 72–74
gas 224–225
General Authority for Supply Commodities
    (GASC) 228–229
genetically modified (GM) crops 114, 221,
    223
Ghana 2
Globex CBOT 121
GM *see* genetically modified crops
Goldman Sachs Commodity Index 237
governance rules 14
grain cereals 113–131
    see also corn; soybean; wheat
Grain Corp. 3
grain elevators 220
The Greeks 66, 71–75, 100
Green Plains Renewable Energy 184
Green Spin 223
GSCI Commodity Index 196
GSCI Sugar Index 136
Guatemala 139
guilds 1
Gulf ports 130

Handysize Index 18
Hanseatic League 1
hard red winter wheat 119, 120
hedge funds 16
hedging 12, 42, 230–231
Hevea brasiliensis 177

Hillshire Brands 3, 4
hogs 169

ICCO *see* International Cocoa and Coffee
    Association
ICE *see* Intercontinental Exchange
IMAREX *see* International Maritime
    Exchange
IMF *see* International Monetary Fund
implied volatility, smile, and skew 83–86
inception date definition 59
income 209–210, 215
India 127–128, 135, 138–139, 189–191
indices
    Baltic 17–24
    commodity investments 236–239
    commodity spot markets 16
    fertilizers 196
    National Corn Index 114
    National Soybean Index 114
    pulp and paper 158–162
    S&P GSCI Sugar Index 136
Indonesia 185
information 12
infrastructure 14, 217, 218–227, 242–246
initial public offerings (IPOs) 4
institutional investors 13
institutional risk 217
insurance 210
Intercontinental Exchange (ICE) 14–15
    cocoa prices 141, 145
    coffee 147
    cotton 153, 156
    futures 39, 40, 214
    orange juice 166
    sugar 135, 140
International Cereals Council 27
International Cocoa and Coffee Associa-
    tion (ICCO) 142, 143

International Maritime Exchange (IMA-REX) 23
International Monetary Fund (IMF) 136, 205–206
International Rubber Consortium 178
International Rubber Council 178
inventories 47–52, 148
investing 13, 236–242
IPOs *see* initial public offerings
iron ore mining 225
irrigation 154, 219–220

JAB Holdings 4
Japan 135, 190
JP Morgan 3, 16
jump–diffusion processes 86
jump-reversion models 20

Kaldor, 47, 52
Kaldor–Working hypothesis 48
Kansai Commodities Exchange (KEX) 135
Kansas City Board of Trade (KCBOT) 119, 213
KEX *see* Kansai Commodities Exchange
Keynes, J.M. 48
Kraft process 158–159
Kuala Lumpur 39, 182, 183

land 187–189, 209, 233, 240–242
Laplace transform 100
law of large numbers 79–80
LDC *see* Louis Dreyfus Commodities
LIFFE *see* London International Financial Futures and Options Exchange
linear instruments in forward contracts 42
liquidity 40, 86, 117
Liveringa Station Beef (LSB) 225
livestock 88, 165, 166–171, 225
loading-out rates 14
log prices 29, 30, 32

log-normal distributions 97–98
London International Financial Futures and Options Exchange (LIFFE) 40, 135, 142, 145
London Metal Exchange 14
Louis Dreyfus Commodities (LDC) 6
LSB *see* Liveringa Station Beef
lumber and wood 153, 156–158, 162

Ma'aden Phosphate Company (MPC) 227
macro-factors driving volatility 37–38
mad cow disease 170
Maison Cailler 140–141
major commodity exchanges 39–40
Malaysia, palm oil 183
managed funds 13
margining systems security 15
markets 1–3, 9–10, 25–38
    actors 12–13
    Africa 2–3
    Asian options 95–102
    concentration 211
    exchange options 103–105
    fertilizers 191–193
    fish 165, 173–174
    growth 14–15
    implied volatility, smile, and skew 83–86
    indices 16
    liquidity 86
    livestock 167–168
    makers 13
    market-oriented farming 212–216
    mergers and acquisitions 3–4
    numbers 2
    outlook 3–12
    palm oil 183
    price formation 18–24, 25–27
    price volatility 15–16
    quanto options 109–112

markets (*continued*)
  risk 217
  spread options 105–109
  volatility 15–16, 27–38, 86–88
Mars (cocoa) 146
Marseille Robusta coffee prices 146
maturity date definition 59
Mauritius 140
MCX *see* Multi Commodity Exchange
mechanical pulping 158, 159
Mercantile Exchange Limited 135
Mercantile and Futures Exchange, Brazil
    135
Mercuria 16
mergers and acquisitions 3–4, 14–15, 40
Merton formula 59, 75–76
MGEX *see* Minneapolis Grain Exchange
micro-factors driving volatility 36–37
milk 172–173, 225
mining 225
Minneapolis Grain Exchange (MGEX)
    114, 119
Mombasa, tea 149
Mondelez International 4
monosaccharides 133
Monsanto 221
Monte-Carlo simulations 79–83, 98–99,
    107
MPC *see* Ma'aden Phosphate Company
Multi Commodity Exchange (MCX) 135
Mumbai Exchange 39
muriate of potash 194, 195

NAFTA *see* North American Free Trade
    Agreement
NASDAQ OMX Group 40
National Commodities and Derivatives
    Exchange (NCDEX) 135
National Corn Index (NCI) 114, 115
National Oil Processor Association
    (NOPA) 126
National Soybean Index (NSI) 114, 115

natural gas 224–225
NBSK indices 159–160, 161
NCDEX *see* National Commodities and
    Derivatives Exchange
NCI *see* National Corn Index
Nestlé 2, 4, 140–141, 146
New York Board of Trade (NYBOT) 165
    first nearby Arabica coffee prices 147
New York Stock Exchange (NYSE) 39–40
    cocoa forward curves 142
    sugar 135
New Zealand 162, 169, 171, 172
Nidera 8–9
Nigeria 222
nitrogen-based fertilizers 189, 191–192,
    195
Noble Group 7
non-deterministic volatility 85
non-dividend paying stocks 64–66, 80–82
NOPA *see* National Oil Processor
    Association
Nord Pool Clearing (NPC) 173
normal backwardation 238
North American Free Trade Agreement
    (NAFTA) 137
North Sea ports 162
Norway 173, 174
notes, structured 236
NPC *see* Nord Pool Clearing
NSI *see* National Soybean Index
numéraire and commodities
    17
NYBOT *see* New York Board of Trade
NYSE *see* New York Stock Exchange

O&M *see* operation and maintenance
off-exchange (ex pit) transactions 44–45
oil 47, 125–126, 177, 180–183
OJ (orange juice) 165–166, 229
Ometto, Rubens 224
open interest 44
operating exchanges 39

see also Intercontinental Exchange
operation and maintenance (O&M)
    244–245
operational risk 217
options
    cocoa 144
    commodity futures 78–79
    commodity spot prices 77–78
    definition 59
    exchange options 103–105
    The Greeks 66, 71–75
    implied volatility, smile, and skew 83–88
    liquidity 86
    Monte-Carlo simulations 80–83
    purchase of 235–236
    quanto options 109–112
    spread options 103, 105–109, 243
    transformation plant valuations 242–243
orange juice (OJ) 165–166, 229
ore mining 225
out of the money (OTM) options 84
over the counter (OTC) forward contracts
    41

Pakistan 127–128, 135
palm oil 177, 180–183
Panamax Index (BPI) 18
paper *see* pulp and paper
pellets, wood 157–158
Philippines 184, 185
phosphate-based fertilizers 191–192, 193,
    194
Pilgrim's 174
Pinnacle Foods 4
plain vanilla options 59, 80–83
plastic bank notes 161–162
polyols 133
population 209, 240
pork bellies 169–170
position type definition 59
potash 191, 192, 193, 194, 195
poultry 174–175

premiums 14, 43
price discovery 14
price formation 18–21, 25–27
price risk 217
price transparency 44
price volatility 15–16
price-to-rent multiples 242
processors 13
producers 13
production risk 217
Profit & Loss (P&L) 46, 60–61
prompt months 46
pulp and paper 153, 158–162
pure jump processes 86
put-call parity 64–66

Qatar 39
quanto options 103, 109–112

railways 224–225
rational expectations hypothesis 43
raw sugar 134
RBDPO *see* refined bleached deodorized
    palm oil
real options approaches 242–243
refined bleached deodorized palm oil
    (RBDPO) 182
refrigeration containers 226
renewable obligation certificates (ROC)
    157
resource curse 2, 222
returns 32–36, 193–207, 238
Reuters-CRB Commodity Futures Index
    237
rice 113, 126–128
RICI Index 237
risk 42–43, 187–188, 217, 227–231
robots, cattle milking 225
Robusta coffee prices 146
ROC *see* renewable obligation certificates

roll return/yield 238

roll rules 53

rubber 177–180

S&P GSCI Sugar Index 136

Samuelson effect 49

Sao Paulo 165

Saudi Arabia 227

  water 208

scarcity

  financial agricultural markets 2

  futures exchanges 48

seasonality-based futures spreads 53–54

securities, margining systems 15

security market lines, fertilizers 196–198, 199

sedentarization 1–3

SGX *see* Singapore Exchange

share price returns, fertilizers 193–198

share returns, fertilizers 198–207

shipping and freight 17–24

  Asian options 95

  forward freight agreements 21–22

  international trade 18

  price formation 18–24

  trading activity 22–24

silo valuations 245–246

Singapore, refrigeration containers 226

Singapore Exchange (SGX) 15

Singapore exchange (SICOM) 178, 179

skew, equity option markets 83–86

smile

  agricultural commodity markets 86–88

  equity option markets 83–86

Sodiaal 172

soft red wheat 119, 120

sorghum 113, 129–131

South America, soybeans 124, 126

soy meal (SM) 47, 125–126

Soybean Index (NSI) 114, 115

soybean oil (SO) 47, 125–126, 186

soybeans 113, 123–126

  coefficients of variation 33–34

  crushers 220–221

  futures exchanges 47

  intra-year coefficients of variation 35

  volatility smile 87, 88

SPAN *see* Standard Portfolio Analysis

spare capacity 211

speculators 13, 42

spot calendar options 106

spot commodities 82–83

spot markets 14–17, 25–38

spot prices 48, 49–50, 77–78, 93–95

spread options 103, 105–109, 243

sprinkler irrigation 154

Sri Lanka 149, 150, 151

Standard Portfolio Analysis (SPAN) 15

staple length, wool 163

stochastic modeling 55–57

stochastic volatility 85

stocks-to-use ratios 26–27, 37, 38

storage 36, 39, 47–52, 220, 245–246

straddle and strangle strategies 62–63

strike of the option 59

strike price definition 59

structured product purchases 235–236

subsidies 211–212

Sucden (Sucres et Denrées) 3, 9

sugar 133–140, 183–184, 224

sulfite pulping 158–159

supply chains, wheat 120–123

Supply Commodities (GASC) 228–229

supply estimates 210

supply in price formation 25, 26

Supramax Index (BSI) 18

swaps and swaptions 89–92
Synutra 172

tea 133, 149–151
technology 114, 217, 221, 222–224
Tecnologia Canavieira (CTC) 224
Teicholz, Nina 166, 168
TFP *see* total factor productivity
Thailand 127–128, 139, 178
Theobroma cocoa 140–146
theory of storage 39, 47–52
theta options 74
tillage, conservation 154
timber and wood 153, 156–158, 162
Tnuva 3
Toepfer International 10–11
Top Glove Corp 178
total factor productivity (TFP) 218–219
trading
    company actors 13
    forward curves 52–53
    Kansas City 213–214
    shipping and freight 22–24
    sugar 135–136
    volatility 36
    weather derivatives 230–231
    wheat 119
transformation plant valuations 242–243
transparency, price 44

UBS-Bloomberg Commodity Index 238
Ukraine 11, 12, 118, 123, 227–228
underlying assets definition 59
United Kingdom (UK) 157, 164
United Nations (UN) 170
    see also Food and Agriculture
        Organization
United States (US)

agricultural commodity spot markets 27
barter schemes 11
cattle contracts 170
cotton 153
ethanol 184
farmland 188–189
fertilizers 193–198, 202, 203–204
financial agricultural markets 2, 3
global flows of commodities
    11
grain cereals 113, 119, 120, 123,
    124–125, 126, 127–130
income by age 215
insurance 210
land investments 241
livestock 167, 170, 171
meat consumption 190
orange juice 165–166
plastic bank notes 162
poultry 174–175
pulp and paper 160
sugar 136–137
timber and wood 156, 157–158
weather derivatives 231
see also US Department of Agriculture
Uralkali (fertilizer firm) 195
urea 194, 195
US Department of Agriculture (USDA) 11
    cattle 168
    cotton 153
    farmland 188
    hogs 169
    orange juice 166
    pork bellies 169
    poultry 175
    sorghum 130
    sugar 136

Valero 184

vega options 75

vegetable oils 47, 125–126, 177, 180–183, 186

vertical call spread 63

Vietnam 127–128

Vitol 8

volatility
  commodity markets 27–38, 86–88
  equity option markets 83–86
  financial agricultural markets 2
  futures 15–16, 49, 51
  spread options 107
  swaptions 91–92

volume risk 230

WACC *see* weighted average cost of capital

warehousing and delivery rules 44

water 187, 207–209, 227, 240

weather 219, 229–231

weighted average cost of capital (WACC) 243, 244

wheat 113, 118–123
  agricultural commodity spot markets, price volatility 27–38
  contango 50
  export shares 37
  fertilizers 193
  forward curves 53
  international risk 228–229
  intra-year coefficients of variation 34
  market-oriented farming 213
  quasi-contemporaneous effects 34

stocks-to-use ratios 37

Wilmar 7–8

wine 230

witches' broom 143

wood 153, 156–158, 162

wool 153, 162–164

Working, Holbrook 51

World Bank
  commodity exchanges 13
  commodity spot markets 27, 30
  fertilizers 191, 193, 194, 196, 206
  grain cereals 114, 120
  Marseille Robusta coffee prices 146
  orange juice 166
  palm oil 183
  physical markets 10
  poultry 175
  rice 128
  soybeans 125
  sugar 136
  tea 150
  timber and wood 162

World Fertilizer Index 30, 32

World Trade Organization (WTO) 2, 11

Yara (fertilizer firm) 195

yields 52, 187–189, 238, 240–241

Yor, M. 100–102

zero strike futures calendars spreads 105–106

Zhengzhou Commodity Exchange (CZCE) 135

Printed and bound by CPI Group (UK) Ltd, Croydon, CR0 4YY

23/04/2025

14660971-0001